Crime & Possession

Josiah Cornell

CONTENT WARNING

This book discusses real-life crimes, violence, abuse, death, and psychological distress. It includes accounts of murder, fatal exorcisms, self-harm, neglect, religious extremism, and severe mental illness. Some chapters describe traumatic events and disturbing behaviour that may be upsetting to some readers.

This material is provided for educational and investigative purposes to explore the psychological, social, and cultural factors behind these cases. Reader discretion is advised, especially for those sensitive to themes of violence, trauma, or mental health.

CONTENTS

INTRODUCTION

THERE'S A MOMENT IN ALMOST EVERY POSSESSION case where someone must decide what they're looking at. A child who won't stop screaming. A woman who's stopped eating and speaks in voices that don't sound like her own. A man hearing commands to violence he can't explain. In that moment, interpretation matters more than almost anything else. What you see determines what you do next. And what you do next can save someone's life or end it.

I've walked into prison cells and found satanic symbols drawn in salt on the floor, geometric patterns that took hours of concentration from someone whose mind was fracturing. I've watched a nineteen-year-old sit fully clothed in the shower, talking to the wall, having what seemed like a coherent conversation with something I couldn't see. The next day, he was running naked around his cell, screaming, faeces smeared on the walls, completely unreachable.

As a probation officer, I once had a client bring his invisible friend into a session. Not metaphorically. He was having a full conversation with someone who wasn't there, nodding along to observations only he could perceive. When I asked what his invisible friend was saying, my client looked at me with something like pity. His friend wanted to hurt me, he said. Then he started punching himself in the face. Hard. Repeatedly. I held his arms down to stop him. Later that day, after he'd left my office, he stabbed himself in the stomach.

When you're in the room with someone whose reality has fractured that completely, the question of what you're looking at becomes urgent and practical. Are you seeing evil? Demonic possession? Something supernatural that's taken hold? Or are you seeing severe psychiatric illness, a brain malfunctioning in ways that medicine can explain and treat?

This book is about those moments of interpretation. About the belief systems we use to make sense of suffering that seems inexplicable, and about what happens when the framework we choose leads us catastrophically wrong. I'm not here to prove or disprove whether demons are real. What interests me is what happens when people believe someone is possessed, how that belief shapes everything that follows, and how easily a psychiatric crisis gets filtered through a supernatural lens in ways that prevent help and sometimes cause terrible harm.

The cases span centuries and continents. Some are historical: the possessed nuns of Loudun in 17th-century France, where political machinations used women's symptoms to destroy a priest who'd made too many enemies. Some are more recent: the Maryland boy whose 1949 exorcism became the most famous in American history, inspired *The*

Exorcist, and remained a secret he carried in terror for seventy years. Some happened in living memory, children and adults who died because the people around them saw demons instead of recognising illness, trauma, or entirely treatable medical conditions.

What connects them isn't just possession belief. It's a pattern. Vulnerable people experiencing psychiatric symptoms, neurological conditions, or psychological distress get reinterpreted through a supernatural lens. Isolation and stress break minds in predictable ways. Group dynamics reinforce delusional beliefs. Religious authority overrides medical expertise. Exorcism rituals worsen the symptoms they're meant to cure.

I've spent years trying to understand how ordinary people, people who aren't evil or deliberately cruel, can do terrible things to vulnerable people whilst believing they're helping. How parents can torture their children to death whilst calling it deliverance. How a church can suffocate an autistic boy whilst thinking they're casting out demons. How families can beat mentally ill relatives, whilst convinced they're driving out evil spirits.

The answer, uncomfortable as it is, usually isn't that these people are monsters. It's that they're operating inside belief systems that make violence look like healing and suffering look like spiritual warfare. Once you're inside that framework, especially when everyone around you shares it, getting out becomes almost impossible, even when the evidence that you're wrong is literally dying in front of you.

The human brain breaks in predictable ways under certain conditions. Isolation produces hallucinations. Sleep deprivation causes psychosis.

Trauma creates dissociation. Temporal lobe epilepsy generates religious visions. Every symptom historically associated with demonic possession can be produced through natural mechanisms, without any supernatural explanation required.

When I held my client's arms whilst he tried to punch himself in response to voices I couldn't hear, I had to make an immediate assessment. Exorcism was the last thing on my mind; I used empathy, communication and my counselling skills to aid this client. I chose professionalism, not because I dismiss spiritual realities, but because what I was seeing matched every symptom of acute psychosis with command hallucinations. He got the appropriate care after stabbing himself in the stomach later that evening, and he recovered with a mental health crisis team.

But I've seen other interpretations take hold. I've watched staff debate what they were going to do with the man drawing symbols in salt was possessed or mentally ill. I've heard people argue that a nineteen-year-old talking to a shower wall was under demonic influence. I understand why those interpretations arise. When behaviour seems impossible, when it makes no sense within normal frameworks of human psychology, the supernatural can feel like the only explanation that fits.

This book shows you why it usually isn't, and why it's often dangerous.

We begin with the psychological and neurological mechanisms behind symptoms that get attributed to possession, stress-induced psychosis, traumatic dissociation, delusional systems, epilepsy, and shared hysteria. Not as an academic exercise. As tools for recognising what's actually happening in the cases that follow.

Then come the cases themselves.

Victoria Climbié, tortured to death by her great-aunt in London, who believed the eight-year-old was possessed. Terrance Cottrell Jr., an autistic boy, suffocated during an exorcism in Milwaukee. Anneliese Michel, whose epilepsy and psychosis were treated with sixty-seven exorcisms instead of medical care, starved to death. Roland Doe, the boy whose exorcism inspired *The Exorcist*, lived for 70 years, terrified that someone would discover his identity.

Some cases involve adults whose own religious beliefs became barriers to getting help. Some involve vulnerable people in isolated situations. Joanna Demafelis, a Filipina domestic worker, was found frozen in her employer's freezer after dying during rituals for supposed djinn possession. Kiran Bala was beaten to death by her in-laws in India, who believed she was possessed when she was most likely experiencing postpartum psychosis.

Throughout, I weave in psychological understanding, not to be preachy, but because it makes sense of what otherwise seems senseless. Why did the Loudun nuns keep having symptoms for three years after the man they'd accused was executed? Because mass hysteria doesn't end when its supposed cause is removed. Why did Roland Doe's symptoms stop so abruptly after weeks of exorcism? Because expectation and suggestion are powerful. When authority figures tell you the demons are gone, symptoms often comply.

The pattern that emerges is consistent. Possession beliefs cluster around vulnerable people experiencing explainable crises in contexts where appropriate help is unavailable or culturally out of reach. The traumatised eight-year-old becomes a possessed child needing exorcism rather than an abused child needing protection. The woman with postpartum psychosis becomes demon-possessed rather than medically ill. The autistic boy's differences become a demonic influence rather than a neurodevelopmental condition requiring understanding.

And crucially, the interventions make things worse. Exorcism rituals involve exactly the conditions that worsen psychiatric symptoms: isolation, sleep deprivation, stress, physical restraint, and suggestion that reinforces delusional beliefs. It's self-reinforcing; every failure proves the demons are powerful, and more intervention is needed. There's no mechanism for being wrong. The belief system is sealed from the inside.

That certainty is what makes possession beliefs dangerous.

When my client's invisible friend told him to hurt me, everything about the scene matched the possession narrative: the violence, the self-harm, the sense of malevolent presence. But I chose to see psychosis. That choice meant he got to a hospital rather than an exorcist, got medication rather than prayer, got a chance to recover.

The people whose stories fill this book didn't always have someone making that choice. They had people who saw demons, chose exorcism, and interpreted their suffering through frameworks that prevented help.

Many of them died because of it.

These are their stories. Told as plainly and as honestly as the records allow. They're disturbing, some involve graphic descriptions of abuse and death, but they're true, as true as court documents and psychiatric reports and survivor testimony can make them. These things happened. People died. And the belief systems that led to their deaths are still active.

If this book does what I hope, it will make you more cautious about identifying possession, more willing to seek medical evaluation before spiritual intervention, and more aware of how mental health conditions can look like something else entirely.

Because the moment someone is identified as possessed, everything changes. They stop being someone who might need medical help and become something that needs fighting. Their suffering becomes evidence of spiritual warfare rather than symptoms requiring treatment. Once that framework is in place, saving that person becomes nearly impossible; every intervention is aimed at the wrong thing.

I've seen madness in people's eyes. I've seen symbols drawn in salt by hands guided by fracturing minds. I've seen young men talking to walls, smearing faeces, hurting themselves because voices commanded it. Every time, I had to choose what I was seeing.

I chose illness. I chose medicine. And I watched people recover.

The people whose stories fill this book didn't get that choice made for them.

The demons aren't real. But the harm done in their name is. It's time we faced that truth, whatever it costs us to admit it.

CHAPTER 1

What Breaks A Mind

BEFORE WE GET INTO WHAT HAPPENED TO THESE people, it helps to understand what the human mind does under extreme pressure. Not because you need a psychology degree to follow these stories, but because some of what you're about to read will seem impossible unless you understand what isolation and fear can do to someone's grip on reality.

When someone says they're possessed, when they claim voices are commanding them to violence, when they insist supernatural forces are controlling their actions, the immediate question is always: are they lying or telling the truth? Is this a genuine spiritual experience, mental illness, or manipulation? But that question misses something crucial about how human psychology actually works. The answer is often more complicated than any of those options. Sometimes people genuinely experience things that aren't real. The brain creates perceptions, beliefs, and entire realities that have no external basis but feel absolutely true to the person having them. And those experiences get interpreted through whatever cultural lens is available: demons, government mind control, alien abduction.

The human brain is remarkably good at creating coherent narratives from incomplete information. It's also surprisingly fragile when subjected to conditions it wasn't designed to handle. Isolation, sleep deprivation, and extreme stress- these things don't just make you uncomfortable. They actively break down the brain's ability to distinguish between internal and external stimuli, between memory and perception, between thought and reality.

Stress-induced psychosis

Psychosis isn't one thing. It's a cluster of symptoms: hearing or seeing things that aren't there, believing things that aren't true despite clear evidence to the contrary, thoughts that don't connect logically, and paranoia. Most people assume psychosis only happens to people with serious mental illnesses like schizophrenia. It doesn't. Psychosis can be induced in otherwise healthy people through environmental conditions alone.

Sleep deprivation is one of the most reliable methods. Keep someone awake for seventy-two hours, and they'll start experiencing perceptual distortions. After four or five days without sleep, full-blown hallucinations typically emerge, such as shadowy figures in peripheral vision, sounds that aren't there. After a week, a complete psychotic breakdown becomes almost inevitable. But let them sleep, and the symptoms resolve. The brain breaks under conditions it can't handle; it can also recover when those conditions change.

Sleep deprivation works so reliably because sleep is when the brain processes information, consolidates memories, and clears out metabolic waste. Without it, reality testing deteriorates. The boundary between waking and dreaming blurs. Thoughts normally recognised as internal start seeming external. By day five or six, people often can't tell whether they're awake or asleep, whether something actually happened or they imagined it. This is why sleep deprivation has been used as torture; it destroys someone's grip on reality without leaving physical marks.

Isolation works similarly but takes longer. The human brain needs social input and sensory variation to function properly. Remove those things, put someone in a cell by themselves with minimal stimulation for weeks or months, and the brain starts malfunctioning. It begins to create its own stimulation because it isn't getting enough externally. The auditory cortex starts firing without external input, and the person hears voices. The visual cortex creates images, and the person sees things that aren't there.

These aren't vague, dreamlike experiences. Voices have distinct tones, accents, and personalities. They say things that feel meaningful and directed. Visual hallucinations have detail and presence. To the person experiencing them, they're real. As real as anything else they perceive. Neurologically, they are real: the same brain regions activate as if actual external stimuli existed. The difference is that there's no external source, but the brain can't tell that.

Here's where it gets complicated. When your brain starts producing these experiences, you need to make sense of them. The explanation you construct depends entirely on what cultural lens you have available. If you're in a strictly religious environment, if the only books accessible are religious texts, if your only visitors are chaplains, then interpreting those voices as God or demons makes perfect sense. It's the narrative that fits your available information.

This is why possession claims cluster in certain communities and time periods. It's not that demons are more active there. It's that the cultural lens for interpreting unusual experiences includes the possibility of possession. When people in 17th-century France started hearing voices and having convulsions, demonic possession was a socially acceptable explanation that made sense within their worldview. When people in 1960s America had similar experiences, they were more likely to be diagnosed with schizophrenia. Same symptoms. Different interpretations. Different cultural materials are available to make sense of them.

Trauma and dissociation

Trauma doesn't just create memories. It creates lasting changes in how the brain processes threat, regulates emotion, and experiences the body and the self.

When someone experiences serious abuse, especially repeated trauma over long periods, their brain adapts to survive it. One adaptation is dissociation: the mind splits off parts of experience to make them bearable. During traumatic events, people often report feeling like they're watching from outside their body, like it's happening to someone else. That's dissociation as a protective mechanism. If you can't escape physically, your mind escapes instead.

But dissociation doesn't only happen during trauma. Once the brain learns that response, it can be triggered again in situations that remind you of the original event, even when no actual danger exists. For people with serious abuse histories, dissociation can become almost automatic under stress. And in a dissociative state, perception of reality changes dramatically.

You might lose time and have gaps in memory, where you can't account for what you did. This isn't the same as simply forgetting. It's that the memory was never properly encoded because, during the dissociative episode, normal memory systems weren't functioning.

People can commit acts of violence, hold entire conversations, perform complex behaviours, and have no recollection afterwards. Not because they're lying. Because the dissociative state prevented the memory from forming.

This matters for cases where someone commits violence and claims they don't remember it, that it wasn't them, that something else took control. From the outside, this looks like an obvious lie. Of course, you remember killing someone. But dissociative amnesia is real and documented. Someone can genuinely have no accessible memory of actions they performed whilst in a dissociative state. When you're told you did something horrific but have no memory of it, no sense of having been present, the experience of "something else did it through me" can feel like the only explanation that makes sense.

Dissociation can also fragment your sense of self. You might experience parts of yourself as separate entities with distinct characteristics, ages, and memories. In extreme cases, this becomes dissociative identity disorder, where the sense of having multiple distinct selves becomes fixed and persistent. When people in dissociative states commit violence or harm themselves, they often genuinely don't feel like it was them doing it. From the inside, it feels like something else took over. If the cultural framework available includes possession, that becomes the narrative. "A demon made me do it" might be the closest language someone has for describing a dissociative episode where they lost time, lost control, and did something their conscious self would never choose.

Childhood abuse creates heightened vulnerability for exactly this kind of fragmentation. When trauma happens during the developmental years, when a child's sense of self is still consolidating, severe abuse can prevent that consolidation from happening properly. The psyche fragments to survive. It creates separate self-states to hold different aspects of experience, and those fragments can persist into adulthood as distinct identity states or as a vulnerability to dissociation under stress.

This is why childhood abuse appears in the background of so many possession cases. It's not that abused children are more likely to encounter demons. It's that abused children develop brains wired for dissociation as a survival mechanism, and that dissociative capacity makes them vulnerable later to experiences that feel like external control, like being taken over, like not being themselves. The abuse creates the psychological conditions that later get interpreted as possession.

Delusional systems

Delusions aren't random. They follow predictable patterns and develop through specific stages.

They typically start with anomalous experiences. Something happens that doesn't fit your existing understanding of the world. You hear a voice. You see something strange. You experience a coincidence that seems too specific to be random. Most people have anomalous experiences occasionally and either ignore them or find mundane explanations. But in people under extreme stress, those experiences demand explanation.

The brain doesn't tolerate unexplained phenomena. It wants coherence, narrative, understanding. It creates an explanation. Initially, tentative, maybe I'm stressed, maybe I imagined it. But if anomalous experiences continue, if stress increases, if no alternative explanation becomes available, the tentative explanation becomes conviction.

Then confirmation bias kicks in. Once you have a working theory, your brain starts noticing evidence that supports it and ignoring evidence that contradicts it. A bad night's sleep becomes demonic interference. An argument becomes spiritual warfare. Random aches become physical attacks from evil forces. Each piece of "confirming evidence" makes the belief stronger, and as it gets stronger, it starts reshaping how you interpret everything.

This is the stage where delusions become fixed. You're no longer testing the hypothesis. You're certain. Any contradictory evidence gets reinterpreted to fit. Tell someone demons aren't real, and they conclude that demons are deceiving you, too. If medication reduces symptoms, that becomes proof that doctors are part of the conspiracy. The delusional system becomes self-sealing, immune to contradiction, impossible to reach from the outside.

The specific danger with possession delusions is that they often include moral justification for violence. When someone develops the belief that they're under attack by evil forces, violence against those perceived forces becomes not just acceptable but necessary. "I had to do it" isn't an excuse in these cases. It's a genuine description of how the person experienced the situation. They felt they had no choice because in their delusional reality, they were defending themselves or others against genuine threats.

This is why some people who commit horrific violence whilst psychotic seem baffled afterwards that anyone would think they'd done something wrong. From their perspective, they were heroes fighting evil. That they killed a family member or attacked a stranger gets reinterpreted as having killed a demon or stopped a possessed person from causing harm. The delusional system provides complete moral justification for actions that would otherwise be incomprehensible.

Psychotic depression

Most people think of depression as sadness or a lack of motivation. But severe depression can become psychotic, involving delusions and hallucinations alongside mood symptoms. These delusions typically centre on guilt, worthlessness, persecution, or the body. Someone with psychotic depression might believe they're fundamentally evil, that they deserve punishment, that they've committed unforgivable sins. Combined with religious frameworks, this can manifest as believing you're possessed by demons or damned by God.

The danger is the combination. Delusional thinking plus profound hopelessness plus self-hatred. Someone might develop the belief that they're possessed or cursed and simultaneously feel that death is the only escape. The delusions provide the narrative; the depression motivates action.

Malingering and secondary gain

Not everyone who claims possession is genuinely experiencing psychosis. Some people fake symptoms. Some exaggerate real symptoms for strategic reasons. Some occupy a grey area where genuine experiences are consciously embellished to achieve specific goals.

This is difficult territory. Dismissing genuine symptoms as faking causes serious harm, but taking every claim at face value enables manipulation and prevents appropriate treatment. The truth is that malingering and genuine illness aren't always opposites. Someone can have real psychiatric symptoms and strategically emphasise them when it's advantageous.

In legal contexts, claiming demonic possession can support an insanity defence. In prison, religious experiences might get you access to chaplains, be moved out of isolation, and be seen by a doctor when direct requests for help would be denied. In families and communities, being possessed can bring attention and care that would otherwise be unavailable. These secondary gains don't automatically mean someone is performing, but they create incentives that complicate any assessment.

The best approach is usually to assume genuine distress even when performance is obvious, because the need to perform distress is itself a form of distress. Someone who fakes possession symptoms to escape solitary confinement is still someone being harmed by solitary confinement. Performance and genuine suffering often coexist.

Suggestion and expectation

There's one more mechanism particularly important for cases involving exorcisms, and it's this: suggestion and expectation can create or worsen the very symptoms they're supposed to cure.

When someone is told they're possessed, when they're subjected to rituals designed to drive out demons, when authority figures treat them as if supernatural forces are controlling them, powerful expectations are set. And the brain responds to expectations. If you're told demons are speaking through you, you might start speaking in ways that match what you think demon-speech sounds like. If you're told evil spirits will resist holy water, you might find yourself reacting violently to it because that's what's expected.

This isn't conscious deception. It's the brain conforming to social and psychological expectations in ways the person isn't fully aware of. Someone who's already psychologically vulnerable, already under stress, already having some unusual experiences, can have those experiences dramatically amplified and shaped by an exorcism ritual. The ritual teaches them how possession is supposed to manifest. Their symptoms adjust to match.

This creates a feedback loop. The person manifests symptoms. The exorcists interpret this as proof of possession. They intensify the ritual. The symptoms intensify in response. Each iteration reinforces both the belief in possession and the symptoms that express it. What began as manageable psychological distress becomes a full-blown crisis caused, in part, by the intervention itself.

Shared psychosis

Shared psychosis, folie à deux, or shared psychotic disorder is when a delusional belief transfers from one person to others in a close relationship. It's rare but well-documented, and it explains how entire communities can become convinced of things that aren't true.

It requires specific conditions: constant proximity between the people involved, social isolation from outside perspectives so there's no reality-checking, a dominant individual who is the primary source of the delusion, and a closed belief system that explains why outsiders can't be trusted. In prisons, cults, and isolated religious communities, these conditions are often present simultaneously.

When shared psychosis develops, it spreads rapidly. One person starts hallucinating and interprets the experience as demons or divine messages. They share this with others who are already stressed and vulnerable. Others start having similar experiences partly because they're in the same stressful environment, partly because expectations and suggestions are doing their work. Soon, multiple people are reporting seeing demons, hearing voices, and experiencing possession. Each person's report confirms the others'. The shared belief becomes its own reality within the group.

Breaking it is extremely difficult because any attempt at intervention gets interpreted through the delusional framework. A psychiatrist trying to explain group hysteria gets dismissed as someone deceived by demons. The system has an explanation for every contradiction.

Epilepsy

Perhaps the most overlooked explanation for possession symptoms throughout history. Temporal lobe epilepsy can produce experiences that look exactly like demonic possession to observers who don't understand what's happening neurologically.

Epileptic seizures aren't always the dramatic convulsions most people picture. Temporal lobe seizures can be subtle, brief alterations in consciousness, strange sensations, or automatic behaviours that the person doesn't fully control. But they can also produce vivid hallucinations, profound religious or spiritual experiences, personality changes, and violent outbursts.

During temporal lobe seizures, people commonly report intense religious feelings, a sense of divine presence, visions of religious figures, and hearing voices with spiritual content. These aren't vague or dreamlike. They're vivid, compelling, and often life-changing. People who've had these seizures frequently describe them as the most profound spiritual experiences of their lives, more real than normal reality.

Between seizures, some people with temporal lobe epilepsy develop what's called Geschwind syndrome: a cluster of personality traits including intense preoccupation with religious or moral concerns, compulsive writing, altered sexuality, and circumstantial speech. They see profound spiritual significance in everyday events and feel chosen for special religious purposes.

When you combine the seizure experiences themselves with the between-episode personality changes, someone with temporal lobe epilepsy can present almost exactly like historical and contemporary descriptions of possessed individuals. The seizures look like demonic attacks. The visions and voices sound like demons speaking. The personality changes suggest something has taken over.

And temporal lobe epilepsy is treatable. Anticonvulsant medication can control seizures and often reduce or eliminate the personality changes, too. Someone who looks possessed, who sincerely believes they're under spiritual attack, whose family and community are convinced, might simply need medication to stop their brain from misfiring.

But if their symptoms get interpreted through a possession belief system, if religious intervention is pursued instead of medical treatment, the person continues suffering needlessly. Worse: exorcism rituals are intensely stressful, and stress triggers seizures. The exorcism produces more symptoms, which convinces everyone that the possession is real and more intervention is needed, which creates more stress and more seizures. The actual medical condition goes untreated while the person's health deteriorates.

All of this matters because it shows how easily what appears supernatural can be explained by psychology and neurology operating under extreme or abnormal conditions. When someone claims they're possessed, they might be experiencing genuine hallucinations from isolation-induced psychosis. They might be dissociating due to trauma resurfacing. They might have developed a fixed delusional system. They might have undiagnosed epilepsy. They might be part of a group experiencing shared psychosis. They might be performing symptoms whilst also experiencing real distress. Usually, it's some combination of these, operating together.

None of this proves that demons aren't real. These mechanisms don't rule out the possibility that supernatural forces exist and sometimes influence people. But they do show that you don't need supernatural explanations to account for possession symptoms. Hearing voices. Seeing entities. Feeling controlled by outside forces. Believing you've become someone or something else. Speaking in altered voices. Violent behaviour. Self-harm. All of it can be produced by stress-induced psychosis, fear responses, epilepsy, delusional systems, group dynamics, and suggestion effects. Not easily, not commonly, but predictably, when the conditions are right or when specific medical conditions are present.

Keep that in mind as you read the cases that follow. When you encounter someone who gouged out their own eyes, or murdered their family, or participated in group violence, all whilst claiming demonic influence, the question isn't only whether demons are real. It's whether the specific circumstances they were in (isolation, trauma, sleep deprivation, untreated epilepsy, group pressure) could have produced those symptoms through purely psychological or neurological mechanisms.

Often, when you look closely at the conditions and medical history, the answer is yes.

That doesn't mean their suffering wasn't real. It doesn't mean their experiences weren't genuine. It means that, under pressure or dysfunction, human psychology and neurology produce experiences that people across cultures and centuries have interpreted as possession. Understanding that helps make sense of what seems senseless. It finds the pattern in what appears to be chaos.

The mind breaks. The brain malfunctions. That's the starting point.

Everything else, how we interpret that breaking, what we believe caused it, whether we respond with treatment or with prayer, with compassion or condemnation, comes after.

Keep that in mind as you read what follows.

CHAPTER 11

The Devil Made Me Do It

BROOKFIELD, CONNECTICUT. SUMMER 1980
Brookfield, Connecticut, was the sort of place where people knew their neighbours. Not in that unsettling small-town way you see in films where everyone's hiding something, just ordinary knowing. You'd wave at Mrs Henderson watering her roses, stop for a chat about the weather at the post office, the kind of town where a murder hadn't happened in 193 years.

Until 16th February 1981.

But this story starts months earlier. Summer 1980. An eleven-year-old boy named David Glatzel.

David was Debbie Glatzel's youngest brother. Debbie was twenty-six, worked as a dog groomer, a practical sort of woman who spent her days dealing with anxious terriers and overexcited spaniels. She had a boyfriend, Arne Johnson, though everyone called him Cheyenne. Nice lad. Quiet. Sang in the church choir. They were moving in together, renting this little place, and David, being a good brother, went along with Cheyenne to help clean it up before they moved in.

"I was sweeping," David said years later, and you could still hear something raw in his voice, something that never quite healed. "Just sweeping this bedroom. And I felt... I'm not sure how to put it into words. Like something was watching me."

Kids say things like that. Parents roll their eyes. David's mother, Judy, probably figured he was trying to get out of work. Eleven-year-old boys aren't renowned for enthusiasm about housework. But then he described what he'd seen. A man with big black eyes, a thin face, animal features. Jagged teeth, pointed ears, horns and hooves. "Like the devil from a Halloween costume," Judy told reporters later, and you could hear how she still didn't quite believe she was saying these words aloud.

Your kid sees a devil in an empty house. You tell him to stop messing about, finish sweeping, and let's go home. That's what normal parents do. Except David didn't stop seeing it. The thing kept coming back, night after night, and what started as a child's fright turned into something that would destroy multiple lives and make legal history.

The way Judy Glatzel tells it, David started getting worse. Not just scared-of-the-dark worse. Something else entirely. Night terrors that weren't like ordinary nightmares. Convulsions. Seizures, maybe, except they didn't look like any seizure the doctors had seen. The boy would thrash in bed, and someone, usually his mother or Debbie, had to stay up with him. Every single night. Watching him suffer through these episodes whilst not having the faintest idea what was wrong or how to help.

"He'd start talking in these voices," Debbie said, and she wasn't the type to exaggerate. Practical woman, worked with dogs all day, dealt with reality for a living. "Not like when kids play around and change their voice. Different. Like someone else was using his mouth."

The Glatzel family was Catholic. Deeply Catholic. The kind where you don't just go to church on Sundays, you believe. Heaven and hell, saints and demons, the whole cosmic struggle between good and evil. When David started reciting passages from the Bible he'd never read, and quoting John Milton's Paradise Lost, a book an eleven-year-old had no business knowing existed, let alone memorising chunks of, Judy Glatzel knew what she was looking at. At least, she thought she did.

"I saw marks on his neck," Judy said, her voice dropping to something quieter, more frightened. "Red marks, like fingers. Like someone had choked him. But there was no one there. We were all in the room, watching him. No one touched him."

You can dismiss this. Say the kid was acting out, needed therapy, had some psychiatric disorder. Hell, maybe he did. Dissociative identity disorder can manifest in children, particularly those who've experienced trauma. The human mind has remarkable ways of fragmenting under stress, creating alternate states of consciousness that can seem like entirely different personalities. A child in distress, especially one immersed in religious imagery and language, might unconsciously adopt personas drawn from that cultural framework. The "voices" could be his psyche fracturing, protecting itself, and processing something too overwhelming for a unified self to handle.

But try telling that to a mother watching her son get beaten by invisible hands. Try explaining dissociative disorders and psychogenic symptoms to a family functioning on no sleep, watching a child they love suffer in ways they can't comprehend. The medical explanation might be correct, probably is correct, but it doesn't help in the moment. It doesn't give them anything to do, any ritual or action that might make things better. And humans need to do something when someone they love is in pain. We're not built to just watch and wait whilst symptoms cycle through their course.

That's when the Warrens entered. Ed and Lorraine Warren. If you've seen those Conjuring films, you know them, or at least the Hollywood version. Ed, the demonologist with the calm voice and serious face. Lorraine, the clairvoyant, had that soft manner that made you want to trust her. In real life? More complicated, as most things are.

They'd made their name on the Amityville Horror case a few years back. Depending on whom you ask, they were either genuine investigators of the paranormal or a couple of con artists with a knack for publicity. Probably somewhere in between. They might have truly believed in what they were doing, whilst also being perfectly comfortable profiting from it. Human motivation is rarely pure.

Judy Glatzel went to one of their lectures. She was desperate by this point because nothing else was working. Doctors couldn't help. Priests were sympathetic but uncertain. Her boy was suffering, and she'd try anything, believe anyone, if they could make it stop. After the lecture, she approached them. Told them about David. The Warrens agreed to come.

"The minute I walked in," Lorraine said later, and you could hear the absolute certainty in her voice, "I saw this black, misty form next to him. Like smoke, but darker. That's when I knew we were dealing with something negative."

Ed interviewed David whilst Lorraine observed. The boy complained of being choked by invisible hands, and then, right there in front of them, red marks appeared on his neck. Or so they claimed. It's worth noting that dermatographia, a condition in which the skin becomes inflamed from light scratching or pressure, can leave marks that look remarkably like fingerprints. Stress makes it worse. And David was certainly stressed.

The Warrens didn't hesitate in their diagnosis. Forty-three demons, they said. Not one. Not a couple. Forty-three separate entities had latched onto this eleven-year-old boy. The specificity is interesting, isn't it? Not "many demons" but exactly forty-three. It lends authority, suggests precise knowledge, and makes the claim sound more credible. The difference between someone saying, "I feel ill", and "my temperature is 39.4 degrees." The precision implies expertise.

Getting the Catholic Church to perform an exorcism isn't like in the films. You can't just ring your local priest and say, "My kid's possessed, can you come over Tuesday?" The Church investigates. Thoroughly. They're supposed to exhaust every medical, every psychological possibility first. They don't want to be wrong about this sort of thing. More to the point, they don't want to be seen performing exorcisms on children who are mentally ill. The liability alone would be staggering, never mind the moral implications.

But the Bridgeport Diocese sent priests. Multiple times. They examined David, spoke with the family, and witnessed whatever it was they witnessed. In September and October 1980, they performed what they called "lesser exorcisms." Not the full theatrical ritual you see in films, but close enough. Prayers in Latin, holy water, and commands to unclean spirits. The whole apparatus of Catholic spiritual warfare was deployed against an eleven-year-old boy's suffering.

David's brother Carl would later say this was all bollocks. That the Warrens were manipulating his family, that David had mental health issues no one wanted to address properly. Then there was this darker possibility, the one Carl hinted at in interviews years later. He found a note after their mother died. "The family had their medicine tonight, and everything was good." What does that mean? Carl thinks Judy was drugging them with Sominex, a sleep aid, putting it in their food to calm the household chaos. If that's true, and we'll never know for certain, it might explain some of David's symptoms. Sleep medications can cause vivid hallucinations, memory problems, and behavioural changes. They can make reality feel slippery, uncertain.

But in the moment, in autumn 1980, the family believed. The priests believed, or at least thought, something strange enough was happening to warrant their involvement. And Arne Johnson believed. Which brings us to the worst decision a nineteen-year-old tree surgeon ever made.

Cheyenne was living with the Glatzels by then. He and Debbie were engaged, planning a life together. He loved her family, loved that kid David like a brother. When the exorcisms started, he was there. Supporting Debbie. Trying to help. He watched David suffer. Watched the boy choke and turn blue, watched him convulse and scream in voices that didn't sound human. Watched priests pray over him whilst the kid writhed on the floor.

The human capacity for empathy can be dangerous. We feel other people's pain, especially the pain of those we love, and that feeling drives us to do things we otherwise wouldn't. Cheyenne was watching this child suffer and feeling utterly powerless. Young men especially struggle with powerlessness. They're conditioned to act, to fix, to protect. Just standing there whilst someone hurts goes against everything they've been taught about masculinity, about being useful, about their role in the world.

During one of these sessions, at a church this time, not the house, David started gasping. Choking. His face went blue. No one was

touching him, but it looked for all the world like someone was stran-
gling him.

Cheyenne couldn't take it anymore. "Leave the boy alone!" he
shouted. Not at the priests. Whatever was tormenting David. "Come
on, take me on! Take me instead!"

The words hung in the air. Lorraine Warren's face went pale. She
grabbed his arm, and according to multiple accounts, she wasn't angry.
She was scared. "You shouldn't have done that," she said.

Detective Glen Cooper from Brookfield Police would later testify
about what happened next. The Warrens kept local police informed
about their investigations, which was probably quite smart, considering the situations they walked into. You don't want to be performing
exorcisms and have police show up, thinking something criminal is occurring. Cooper met Lorraine after that session.

"She was upset," Cooper said in his testimony. "Really upset. Not
theatrical, not performing for effect, just genuinely disturbed. She told
me Arne had challenged the demon, invited it in." He paused, and you
can almost see him choosing his words carefully. "She said she had a vision. Serious injury. A death. A knife. She wanted to put us on notice
that a crime could occur."

This was October 1980. Four months before, Alan Bono would
bleed out on the ground outside a dog kennel with five stab wounds to
his chest and stomach.

Lorraine Warren's "vision" could be explained in several ways. If
you're a believer, she had a genuine psychic premonition. If you're a
sceptic, she was either making it up after the fact or, more charitably,
picking up on warning signs. Cheyenne had just made a dramatic,
emotionally charged statement. He was immersed in this world of
demons and possession. He was young, stressed, and sleep-deprived.

Anyone with half a brain could have predicted this situation might lead somewhere dark. Warning, the police were either supernatural insight or simple risk assessment dressed up in mystical language.

Either way, she called it. Four months later, someone was dead.

David got better almost immediately after that session. The night terrors stopped. The convulsions ended. He started sleeping through the night and started acting like a normal kid. The demons were gone, the Warrens said. Driven out by the exorcisms. But symptoms that resolve suddenly tend to have been psychogenic in the first place. Physical illnesses don't vanish overnight. Brain tumours don't spontaneously cure themselves. But psychological conditions, particularly those maintained by environmental factors, can improve dramatically when those factors change. If David's symptoms were a response to family stress, to shared delusion, to the attention and drama of the exorcism sessions themselves, then yes, they could simply stop once the ritual concluded and everyone's expectations shifted.

But Cheyenne started getting worse. "He'd go into these trances," Debbie said. "Just stare at nothing. And then he'd start growling." She stopped, shook her head, aware of how it sounded. "I know how that sounds. But he'd make this noise, this animal sound, and say he saw the beast. The same thing David described. And afterwards, he wouldn't remember any of it."

Cheyenne drove his car into a tree one day. Walked away without a scratch, insisted something else had been driving. His coworkers at Wright Tree Service noticed he seemed off sometimes. Distant. Not quite there. But he kept working, kept living his life. The human ability to function whilst profoundly disturbed is remarkable. We compartmentalise, carry on, because what else can we do?

Martin Minnella, the lawyer who would eventually defend

Cheyenne, later said he'd heard tapes from David's exorcisms. "David Glatzel speaks the names of forty-two demons in Latin," Minnella claimed. "And the police chief was prepared to testify that he'd seen the child levitate."

But that testimony would never make it into court. Because on 16th February 1981, theoretical discussions about demons became brutally, irreversibly real.

It was cold that day. Not brutally cold, but enough that you kept your jacket on. Cheyenne called in sick to work. Didn't feel like climbing trees, trimming branches. Instead, he went to Brookfield Boarding Kennel, where Debbie worked. Their landlord was Alan Bono. Forty years old, managed the kennel. By all accounts, he and Cheyenne got along fine. More than fine, actually. Sometimes, Cheyenne would call in sick to hang out at the kennel with Bono. They were friendly. Which makes what happened next even more difficult to process.

That day, Bono suggested they all go to lunch. Cheyenne, Debbie, Cheyenne's fifteen-year-old sister, Wanda, and Debbie's nine-year-old cousin, Mary. Just a casual meal. Normal day. Except Bono drank. A lot. Multiple witnesses would later talk about the wine bottles, how many he'd gone through. By the time they got back to the kennel in the early afternoon, he was drunk. And his mood had shifted into something ugly.

During lunch, Bono said something obscene about Debbie. Crude enough that it enraged Cheyenne, though he didn't act on it. Not then. He swallowed it, kept quiet, but you could see the tension building. Back at the kennel, Bono's behaviour deteriorated. Aggressive, belligerent, the way drunk men get when they've crossed some invisible line and their inhibitions have dissolved. Debbie took Mary to get pizza to try to defuse things, but someone urged her to come back quickly. Wrong vibe in the air, the sense that something bad was building

When they returned, Bono had grabbed Mary. A nine-year-old child was trying to squirm away, and this drunk forty-year-old man had hold of her and wouldn't let go. Think about that scene for a moment. Really, picture it. A little girl, frightened. A drunk man twice her size. The primal protectiveness that would trigger in anyone who cared about that child.

"Everyone got out of the room except Bono," according to testimony. "He was still holding Mary."

Cheyenne came back downstairs from their apartment. Told Bono to let the girl go. Mary managed to break free and ran to the car, but Bono and Cheyenne were face-to-face now. Debbie is between them, trying to calm things down. Wanda was pulling at her brother's arm, sensing how wrong this was about to go.

Then Cheyenne's whole demeanour changed. "He started growling," the witnesses said. All of them, independently, described the same thing. "Like an animal."

Debbie testified she was standing between them. Never saw the knife. One second, Bono was pounding his fist, yelling. Next, he was on the ground. Cheyenne had pulled out his five-inch pocketknife, the kind any tree surgeon carries for work, and stabbed him. Four times. Five times. The medical examiner's report listed wounds to the chest and stomach. One slash went from Bono's stomach to the base of his heart. That's not defensive. That's not even aggressive. That's rage made physical, violence coming from somewhere deep and primitive.

When it was over, when whatever possessed him, literally or figuratively, had passed, Cheyenne stood there holding a bloody knife with no clear memory of what he'd just done. They ran. Got about two miles before Cheyenne stopped the car.

"I need help," he told Sergeant Gordon Fairchild when police arrived. "I've got a drinking problem."

He was cooperative. Confused. "I think I hurt someone," he said. "I didn't mean to hurt anyone." Back at the kennel, Alan Bono bled out and died. Forty years old. Drunk, yes. Inappropriate, yes. But dead. And there's no coming back from the dead, no second chance to make different choices.

The next day, Lorraine Warren rang the Brookfield Police Department to explain something that probably made the officers' heads spin. Arne Johnson hadn't killed Alan Bono, she said. Not really. The demon had. The same demon that tormented David Glatzel, that Cheyenne had challenged during the exorcism. It had possessed him, taken control, used his body to commit murder.

The case exploded. This wasn't staying local. It went national, then international. "Demon Murder Trial," the papers called it. The Washington Post, The New York Times, and People magazine. Everyone wanted a piece. The Warrens promised lectures, a book, and a film. Money was about to be made, lots of it.

Martin Minnella, a lawyer from Waterbury, offered to take the case for free. Maybe he believed. Maybe he smelled publicity. Maybe both. Human motivation is rarely pure. He flew to England to research two similar cases where possession had been claimed, though neither had actually gone to trial. One case stuck with him. Michael Taylor, 1974. A man murdered his wife after an exorcism went wrong. Didn't claim possession as a defence, but argued that the trauma of the exorcism itself, combined with pre-existing mental illness, had driven him temporarily insane. The jury found the defendant not guilty by reason of insanity.

Minnella thought he could work with that. Build something unprecedented. He planned to bring in exorcism specialists from Europe, subpoena the priests who'd worked with David, and put the Warrens on the stand. Present the audio recordings of the exorcisms, yes, they existed, yes, they're disturbing as hell. Get testimony from the Glatzel family about everything they'd witnessed. Build a case that Arne Johnson, through no fault of his own, had been seized by a force beyond human understanding and compelled to commit an act he would never have done otherwise.

The Catholic Church, naturally, lost its mind. Hired a lawyer specifically to quash any subpoenas of their priests. The last thing they needed was clergy testifying about demons in a murder trial. The liability exposure alone would have been catastrophic. And the theological implications, having Church officials confirm in legal testimony that demonic possession was real and their exorcism rituals had failed to protect someone? That's not a precedent Rome wanted set.

On 19th March 1981, eighteen people sat in the grand jury room in Danbury Superior Court, hearing testimony about what happened at that kennel. Six witnesses. Mary Tennant, nine years old. Cheyenne's sisters Janice and Wanda are eleven and fifteen. Two Brookfield police officers. The medical examiner's report.

Wanda and Janice had given statements. Signed statements. They'd seen their brother stab Alan Bono. Multiple times. There was no question about what happened. Only about why. The grand jury indicted him for murder. State's Attorney Walter Flanagan made it clear this was a homicide case, not an episode of The Twilight Zone. Facts, evidence, law. That's what courtrooms dealt with, not theology.

28th October 1981. Superior Court in Danbury. Judge Robert Callahan presiding. Martin Minnella stood up and entered a plea of not guilty by reason of demonic possession. For the first time in American legal history, anyone had tried it.

Judge Callahan shut it down immediately. "Irrelevant and unscientific," he said. The defence of demonic possession was "simply not relevant" to the proceedings.

Think about what he was saying. Not that demons don't exist, the court wasn't weighing in on theology. The legal system simply couldn't handle this kind of evidence. How do you prove possession? How do you cross-examine a demon? How do you establish reasonable doubt based on supernatural claims? You don't. The American legal system is built on principles of evidence, testimony, and expert witnesses. It requires things that can be tested, verified, and challenged. Supernatural claims, by their very nature, exist outside that belief system. They can't be proven or disproven. They're matters of faith, not fact. And faith, whatever its personal or spiritual value, has no place in a courtroom determining guilt or innocence for murder.

"We were very disappointed," Minnella said later, which is rather an understatement. His entire strategy had been ruled inadmissible. No testimony from the Warrens. No priests. No audio recordings of David's exorcisms. No evidence about the alleged possession at all. The international media that had descended on Brookfield suddenly lost interest. Without the demon angle, this was another murder trial, and those happen every day.

Minnella had to pivot. Self-defence, he argued. Bono was drunk, aggressive, and had grabbed a nine-year-old child. Cheyenne acted to protect Debbie and Mary. But even Minnella admitted it was "half-baked." "The number of wounds like that would negate self-defence," he said years later. "Any one of those blows to the heart could've killed him." Five stab wounds don't say "stopping a threat." They say rage. Loss of control. Something snapping inside.

State's Attorney Walter Flanagan kept it simple. Arne Johnson stabbed Alan Bono to death. Here's the knife. Here are the witnesses. Here's the medical examiner's report. The motive? Either jealousy, there were whispers about Debbie and Bono, rumours of an affair, or just alcohol-fuelled violence that spiralled out of control. Human emotions. Human weakness. No demons required.

Minnella brought in character witnesses. People who'd known Cheyenne all their lives. He was gentle, they said. Kind. Wouldn't hurt anyone. Sang in the church choir, played Little League baseball, and rang his sisters to check on them. "This wasn't him," they said. "This was completely out of character."

Without the possession angle, though, that argument had no foundation. People do out-of-character things all the time. Especially when they're angry, drunk, frightened. Especially when someone's threatening people they love. The psychiatrist Carl Jung talked about the shadow self, the part of our psyche that contains everything we refuse to acknowledge about ourselves. The violence, the selfishness, the capacity for cruelty. We like to think we know ourselves, that we're good people incapable of terrible acts. But the shadow is always there, waiting. Under the right circumstances, the right combination of stress and fear and rage, it emerges. No demons necessary.

The courtroom went quiet when Arne Johnson walked up to testify. Slight lad, curly hair, looking younger than nineteen. Looked like he might cry. He described what he remembered. Seeing Bono grab Mary. Feeling rage. Overwhelming, consuming rage unlike anything he'd ever felt. And then nothing. A blank space where the murder should be.

"I blacked out," he said. "I don't remember drawing the knife. Don't remember stabbing him. I just... I wasn't there."

Dissociative amnesia is real. The brain sometimes protects us from traumatic memories, especially those of our own actions. It's a defence mechanism, like fainting at the sight of blood or going numb after injury. The mind decides we can't handle knowing what we've done, so it hides that knowledge from us. Or he could have been lying. A convenient excuse, claiming not to remember. "Your Honour, I don't recall" is the refuge of the guilty and the genuinely traumatised alike, and courts can't reliably distinguish between them.

The prosecutor poked holes. Had Johnson been drinking? Yes. Was he jealous of Bono? Maybe. Had he been angry about the crude comment Bono made about Debbie? Yes. A drunk, jealous, angry young man kills someone in rage. Tale as old as time. No supernatural explanation required.

Minnella swore there was more to it. Said the lights in the courtroom flickered on the first day of trial. Kept going on and off for no reason. Electrical problem? Maybe. Or maybe something else was watching. But fear and pattern-seeking are deeply intertwined in the human brain. We evolved to spot threats, to find meaning in chaos. Flickering lights in a courtroom could be faulty wiring or a demon's presence, and which one you believe says more about your worldview than about objective reality.

"The case scared us shitless," Minnella admitted later. "I mean, genuinely frightened us."

The jury deliberated for fifteen hours over three days. On 24th November 1981, they came back: guilty of first-degree manslaughter.

Not murder. Manslaughter. Killing in the heat of passion. They'd acknowledged something about this case was unusual, even if they couldn't name what. The distinction matters legally and carries a lighter sentence. The jury was saying: yes, he killed someone. But some factors reduced his culpability. Not demons, they couldn't consider demons. But something.

On 18th December, Judge Callahan sentenced Cheyenne to 10 to 20 years. The maximum sentence for manslaughter. Cheyenne turned to Minnella. "I'm going to spend the rest of my life in prison for something I didn't do. Or something I don't remember doing."

Minnella promised to appeal. Never did. What was the point? The precedent was set. American courts don't do exorcisms.

Arne Johnson served for five years. Got out in 1986 on good behaviour. Model prisoner, by all accounts. Earned his high school diploma and took educational courses. The gentle kid came back once the cage door closed behind him. He'd had to do something terrible to learn he was capable of it, had to live with that knowledge, but he didn't do it again. Whatever had broken in him that day at the kennel, whether demon or psychotic break or simple rage, it was gone.

Debbie waited for him. Visited regularly. They got married whilst he was still in prison, on 30th January 1985. Some kind of romance in that, maybe. Or just stubbornness. She never doubted him. Never thought he'd really killed Bono, not the way prosecutors said. "Arne started showing the same signs my brother did when he was under possession," she told reporters. "You never take that step. You never challenge the devil."

After his release, they built a life. Sherman, Connecticut. Cheyenne worked as a landscaper, later as a construction superintendent. Debbie became a certified nurse's assistant. Two sons. Two grandsons, eventually. Normal life, or as normal as you can get after something like that. Debbie stayed close to Lorraine Warren and contributed to an online radio show about demonology. Never stopped believing in what happened. Cancer took her in 2021.

The Warrens never wavered either. David Glatzel was possessed by forty-three demons. Arne Johnson was possessed when he killed Alan Bono. End of story. In 1983, with Lorraine's help, Gerald Brittle published "The Devil in Connecticut." The Glatzels got $2,000 from the publisher. The Warrens got considerably more, both in money and reputation. They became legends in paranormal circles. The case cemented their status, gave them credibility, or at least the appearance of it.

When Ed died in 2006, Lorraine kept going until her own death in 2019. *The Conjuring* films turned them into folk heroes, Patrick Wilson and Vera Farmiga playing them like saintly crusaders against evil. The third film, "The Devil Made Me Do It," took massive liberties with the Johnson case, adding occult conspiracies and elaborate investigations that never happened. But that's Hollywood. They're not interested in messy, ambiguous truth. They want good versus evil, clear stakes, and a satisfying resolution.

But the real question remained: were the Warrens true believers who'd stumbled onto genuine supernatural phenomena? Or were they opportunists who knew a good story when they saw one and weren't above embellishing for effect? Probably both. Human beings are complicated. We can sincerely believe something whilst also profiting from it. We can be sincere and calculating at the same time. The Warrens might have truly thought they were helping people whilst being perfectly comfortable with the fame and money that came from their work.

David Glatzel's relationship with all this is messy. In the 2023 Netflix documentary "The Devil on Trial," he talks about what happened to him. Describes the entity he saw, the terror, the exorcisms. He believes something real happened. But he's bitter about the Warrens. "Lorraine told me I was going to be a rich little boy from having this book deal," David says, and you can hear the anger. "That was a lie. The Warrens made a lot of money off us. If they can profit off you, they will."

The recordings of David's alleged possessions that appear in the documentary are genuinely unsettling. A child's voice screaming obscenities, speaking in tones that sound wrong. Could be faked. It could be a mental illness. It could be exactly what the Warrens said it was. You decide. I can't tell you what to believe.

Carl Glatzel, the oldest brother, tells a different story. Has been doing it from the beginning. "The murder of Alan Bono? I never thought it was connected to David," he says flatly in the documentary. "There's nothing demonic in this. Arne was very possessive of Debbie. There were rumours she was having an affair with Alan Bono." Jealousy. Alcohol. Violence. Simple as that.

Carl thinks the Warrens were con artists who exploited his family's vulnerability. Thinks David had mental health issues that needed real treatment, not exorcisms. And that note he found after their mother died, "the family had their medicine tonight," suggests something darker happening in that house. In 2006, Carl and David sued the publishers of "The Devil in Connecticut" for invasion of privacy, libel, and intentional infliction of emotional distress. Carl claimed the book falsely portrayed him as abusive. The case eventually settled, details undisclosed.

The Glatzel family is shattered now. Scattered. Siblings don't talk much. David and younger brother Alan still believe in the possession. Carl thinks it was all bollocks. Everyone's stuck with their version, unable to bridge the gap. That's what trauma does to families. It splinters them, leaving everyone with their own interpretation of events and their own way of coping. And sometimes those interpretations are so incompatible that the family can no longer exist as a unit.

Here's what I keep coming back to: we'll never know. Not for certain. Not in the way we can know that water boils at 100 degrees Celsius or that the Earth orbits the sun. This case exists in the murky space between fact and belief, evidence and faith, what we can prove and what we choose to accept.

The physical facts are clear. Arne Cheyenne Johnson stabbed Alan Bono to death on 16th February 1981, outside Brookfield Boarding Kennel. Four to five wounds. The knife belonged to Johnson. Multiple witnesses saw it happen. Johnson fled, turned himself in, and was convicted of manslaughter. Served five years. Built a life afterwards. Those are facts. Everything else is interpretation.

If you believe in the supernatural, and millions do, the evidence is compelling. David exhibited symptoms consistent with possession as defined by Catholic theology. Multiple priests examined him and concluded something supernatural was occurring. The Catholic Church doesn't throw around exorcisms lightly. They investigate thoroughly and rule out medical explanations. The audio recordings exist. You can hear David's voice changing, speaking in tones that don't sound like an eleven-year-old boy.

Then there's the transfer. David's symptoms improved dramatically after Cheyenne challenged the demon. Cheyenne started exhibiting similar behaviours. Lorraine Warren warned police that a violent crime was coming. Four months later, it happened. And Cheyenne himself, no criminal history, gentle kid, sang in the church choir. The murder was brutal, frenzied, and completely out of character. He claimed to have no memory of it.

For believers, this adds up to demonic possession. An external force temporarily seized control of Arne Johnson's body and will, causing him to commit an act he would never have done on his own.

But if you're sceptical, there are mundane explanations that fit the facts as well. David was exhibiting disturbing symptoms, but disturbing symptoms aren't proof of demons. They're proof that something was wrong, likely something medical or psychological. The "speaking in unknown languages" could be glossolalia, in which people produce speech-like sounds that resemble language but lack meaning. The "knowledge he shouldn't have" could have been absorbed from books, films, or conversations he overheard.

The physical marks could be self-inflicted during dissociative episodes. Or even fabricated. Not saying the family was lying, necessarily, but people see what they expect to see, especially in high-stress situations. The priests who performed the exorcisms were likely sincere, but sincerity doesn't equal accuracy. They believed David was possessed because that's what their religious lens told them to look for.

And if Carl's right about the Sominex, if Judy was drugging the family without their knowledge, that could explain a lot. Sleep aids can cause vivid hallucinations, memory problems, and behavioural changes. An eleven-year-old boy given sedatives without knowing it, immersed in Catholic imagery and language, convinced by his family and priests that he's possessed, his mind could have created exactly the symptoms everyone expected to see.

As for Cheyenne, he witnessed multiple traumatic exorcism sessions. Watched a child he cared about suffer. The power of suggestion in those circumstances is enormous. If everyone around you keeps saying you're possessed, if you're immersed in this world of demons and spiritual warfare, if you're young and scared and desperate to help, your mind can start playing tricks. Then add jealousy. Cheyenne was possessive of Debbie. There were rumours about her and Bono. Add alcohol, add Bono's aggressive behaviour with Mary, add months of stress and sleepless nights, and you have a recipe for violence. The "blackout" Cheyenne described isn't uncommon in crimes of passion. The brain sometimes protects us from traumatic memories of our own actions.

For sceptics, this is a case of mental illness misdiagnosed as supernatural possession, exploited by the Warrens for publicity and profit, defended by a clever lawyer looking for an angle. Tragic, but ultimately human.

Maybe it's both. Maybe it's neither. Maybe there's a truth here that doesn't fit neatly into either category. What if David was genuinely suffering from a psychiatric disorder and the exorcisms, whilst medically inappropriate, actually helped him through the power of belief? Placebo effects are real. Ritual and faith can have profound psychological impacts, even if the underlying theology is questionable.

What if Cheyenne was suggestible enough that witnessing the exorcisms created a self-fulfilling prophecy? He believed he'd invited a demon in, so he started experiencing symptoms consistent with possession, which reinforced the belief, which intensified the symptoms, until the boundary between psychological distress and genuine altered consciousness became impossible to distinguish.

What if the murder had multiple causes? Jealousy and alcohol created the volatile situation, but Cheyenne's fractured mental state from months of trauma made him less able to control his response. Not possession, but not simple jealousy either. Something more complex than either explanation allows.

Chris Holt, director of "The Devil on Trial," said something that's stuck with me: "I sat down with David and Arne and Alan and Carl for hours on end, and their stories never changed. I think they were telling me the truth, but it's their interpretation, not a hard fact. They believed what they were saying."

Truth and belief aren't always the same thing. But they're not always different either.

Judge Robert Callahan's 1981 ruling set a precedent that still stands. American courts will not entertain supernatural explanations for criminal behaviour. No one has successfully argued demonic possession as a defence since. The door the Johnson case tried to open slammed shut and locked tight.

And maybe that's right. Maybe the legal system needs bright lines, clear boundaries. We can't have people claiming demons, ghosts, alien abductions, divine commands as defences for murder. The law needs to function on principles of evidence and reason that can be tested, verified, and argued. Otherwise, every crime becomes a question of competing beliefs, and justice becomes impossible.

But something nags at me about this case. Something uncomfortable. Cheyenne served his time. He was, by all accounts, a model prisoner. The violent rage that possessed him, whether literally or figuratively, never returned. He built a good life, was a good husband, and a good father. The people who knew him best never doubted that something had been wrong that day, that the Cheyenne who killed Alan Bono wasn't the real Arne Johnson.

David still carries the weight of being the "possessed child" whose demons allegedly drove his sister's boyfriend to murder. Real or not, that's a hell of a thing to live with. And the Warrens built an empire on cases like this, convinced thousands that the supernatural was real, dangerous, and needed confronting.

The trial of Arne Cheyenne Johnson stands alone in American legal history. One time, one case, one moment when the supernatural crashed into the courtroom and was politely but firmly escorted out. It won't happen again. The precedent is set.

But the questions remain. About evil, about responsibility, about free will and what we're capable of when something inside us takes control. The devil made me do it, Arne Johnson claimed. The court said no. But he's the one who has to live with what his hands did that day.

And forty years later, none of us, not the believers, not the sceptics, not the lawyers or the family or the witnesses, can say with absolute certainty what really happened in Brookfield, Connecticut. Maybe we're not supposed to know. Maybe some things are meant to stay in that grey space between faith and doubt, between what we can prove and what we choose to believe.

The devil made me do it. Or maybe the devil was never there at all. Or maybe the devil doesn't need to possess anyone to make them do terrible things. Maybe we're capable of that all on our own. That's the thought that keeps me awake sometimes. Not the possibility of demons, but the certainty of what human beings can do to each other without any supernatural intervention whatsoever. We contain the capacity for extraordinary evil, and we don't need devils to explain it. We just need stress, fear, rage, and the right circumstances. That should terrify us more than any possession story ever could.

CHAPTER III

The Exorcism That Created A Killer

OSSETT, WEST YORKSHIRE. AUTUMN 1974.

A market town where coal seams met woollen mills, where terraced houses lined streets named after long-dead industrialists, where people kept themselves to themselves mostly, but would nod if you passed them buying bread at the corner shop. Not the sort of place where anything much happened. Certainly not the sort of place where a man would tear his wife's face from her skull with his bare hands.

But that's what happened. And the question everyone's been asking for fifty years isn't whether it happened, we know it did, but why. Why would a mild-mannered butcher, a father of five, commit an act of violence so extreme it made hardened police officers physically sick?

The answer, depending on whom you ask, involves either demons or the catastrophic mishandling of severe mental illness. Or possibly both. Or possibly something we don't have the language to properly describe.

Michael Taylor was thirty-one years old in 1974. Worked as a butcher when his back allowed it, which wasn't often after an injury a few years earlier had left him with chronic pain. The kind that doesn't just hurt your body, it eats away at your sense of self. He couldn't work properly, couldn't provide for his family the way he thought a man should. His wife Christine held everything together whilst he dealt with the pain and the black moods that came with it, that creeping depression that follows chronic illness like a shadow.

Neighbours on their street in the Havercroft district described him as mild-mannered. Kind, even. The sort who'd help you shift furniture if you asked, who kept his garden tidy, who clearly loved his kids. Michael and Christine weren't what you'd call religious. They lived within a few miles of several churches; everyone in Yorkshire seemed to belong to a denomination, but the Taylors never really found the time to attend. Which, in a town like Ossett, where church-going was still fairly standard, made them stand out a bit.

Barbara Wardman, a friend of Michael's, had a theory about his depression. Nothing to do with chronic pain or inability to work properly, at least not directly. Spiritual forces, she reckoned. What he needed was a bit of faith, something to believe in, something bigger than himself to give meaning to the suffering. She'd recently discovered a church group that was different from the usual stuffy congregations. The Christian Fellowship Group, they called themselves. Barbara invited Michael and Christine to come along just once to see what they thought.

Michael and Christine went to be polite, expecting the usual church crowd, all judgment and hymns and no warmth. Instead, they found Marie Robinson.

She was twenty-two years old. Lay preacher. Charismatic in every sense of the word. When Marie spoke about God, about the Holy Spirit, about the power of faith made manifest in ordinary people's lives, you listened. You couldn't help it. The group she led wasn't like traditional churches with their fixed liturgies and quiet prayers. This was Charismatic Christianity, with people speaking in tongues, casting out demons, and performing miraculous healings. The power of God moving through people, changing them, saving them.

Michael and Christine Taylor converted after that first meeting. Just like that. Found themselves caught up in something that felt real, felt powerful, felt like it might actually help with the depression eating away at Michael for so long. And maybe it did help, at first. Having community, having purpose, having something to believe in when you're struggling with chronic pain and depression, that can be genuinely therapeutic. The human need for meaning is profound, particularly when life feels meaningless.

Michael threw himself into the Fellowship. Started attending every meeting, every gathering. The more time he spent with Marie Robinson, the more devoted he became. Not just to the faith. To her.

"He's spending too much time at that church," Christine said to friends. Worried, maybe. Or sensing something she couldn't quite name yet, that particular instinct women develop when their husbands start paying too much attention to someone else.

The private prayer sessions started soon after. Michael and Marie would sit facing each other for hours, sometimes eight, making the sign of the cross over and over. They believed doing this would nullify the evil power of the full moon. Think about that for a moment. Eight hours of repetitive ritual designed to ward off lunar evil. The line between religious devotion and obsessive behaviour can be remarkably thin, and Michael had crossed it without noticing.

Everyone in the Fellowship could see what was happening. Michael Taylor had fallen completely under Marie Robinson's spell. Whether it was romantic, spiritual, or some strange mixture of both, he was obsessed. And when he wasn't with Marie, his moods got darker. More withdrawn, more sullen, more argumentative. He'd lash out at Christine and the children over nothing. The depression was worse, not better. The faith that was supposed to heal him seemed to be making everything worse.

Group psychology is a strange thing. When you're part of a tightly knit community with a charismatic leader, normal social feedback mechanisms break down. Behaviour that would seem obviously concerning to outsiders feels completely normal within the group. No one in the Fellowship told Michael his obsession with Marie was unhealthy. They interpreted it through their spiritual framework, saw it as devotion to God rather than what it was: a mentally unwell man fixating on a young woman half his age, whilst his marriage crumbled.

It came to a head at a Fellowship meeting held at the Taylor house. The congregation gathered, maybe twenty people, singing and praying and speaking in tongues the way they did. At some point during the service, Michael started acting strangely. Shaking violently, shouting garbled words that might have been glossolalia, speaking in tongues as the Charismatics called it, or might have been something else entirely. The group got nervous. This didn't feel like the Holy Spirit moving through him. This felt wrong, felt dangerous.

Then Mavis Smith, one of the members, suddenly burst into tears. Couldn't stop crying, didn't know why, just overwhelmed by something she couldn't name. Marie Robinson knelt before her immediately, placed her hands on Mavis's head, and began to pray loudly. An exorcism, Christine and Michael realised. Right there in their front room. Mavis started writhing, swearing at Marie, telling her she hated her, to leave her alone. The demon speaking through her, Marie said. Fighting back against deliverance.

Christine had seen enough. Later that evening, at another meeting, she stood before the entire congregation and said what needed to be said. "Michael's relationship with Marie Robinson is carnal."

Silence. Absolute silence. You could hear people breathing, hear the clock ticking on the mantelpiece. Then Michael's whole face changed. The group would talk about this moment for years afterwards. How his features seemed to shift, become bestial. How something else looked out through his eyes. Whether that was demonic possession or a psychotic break or just rage and humiliation at being called out in front of everyone, we'll never know for certain. But everyone present saw something change in Michael Taylor that night.

The elders of the Fellowship suggested that Michael and Marie go upstairs to sort it out. Private like. Work it out between them. Which, in retrospect, was possibly the worst decision anyone could have made. What happened in that bedroom depends on whom you ask. Michael made a pass at Marie; that much is certain. She rejected him, also certain. When they came back downstairs, Michael proclaimed a "victory for the Lord."

But something had broken inside him. Minutes later, he attacked Marie Robinson. Verbally at first, screaming at her in tongues, then physically, striking her whilst she screamed back at him. The congregation had to restrain him whilst he thrashed and shouted. "I suddenly glanced at Mike, and his whole features changed," Marie said later, her voice still shaken. "He looked almost bestial."

The next day, Michael received absolution from Marie Robinson. Forgiven. Christians forgive, after all. Turn the other cheek. But the congregation couldn't forget what they'd seen. His behaviour got worse after that night. More erratic, more violent. Speaking in strange voices, claiming to feel evil inside him, having outbursts of rage that seemed to come from nowhere.

The local vicar got involved. Several ministers examined Michael. They all reached the same conclusion. Demonic possession. Not mental illness, not psychosis, not the obvious psychiatric crisis that was unfolding. Demons. Multiple demons. Over forty of them, by their count.

Midnight. Saturday, 5th October 1974. St Thomas's Church, Gawber. Two ministers led the ritual. Father Peter Vincent, Anglican priest, and Reverend Raymond Smith, Methodist clergyman. They'd got permission from the Bishop of Wakefield himself. This wasn't some fringe nonsense or a backroom exorcism performed by amateurs. This was official Church business, sanctioned at the highest levels.

Michael and Christine Taylor arrived with members of the Fellowship. Michael knew what was coming. Believed in it, even. Believed something evil had got inside him and needed to be cast out. Maybe he was right, in a way. There was something deeply wrong inside him, something that needed treatment. Just not the kind of treatment he was about to receive.

They tied him to the floor of the church. Had to. He started thrashing almost immediately, convulsing, spitting. A crucifix was jammed into his mouth. Holy water poured over him until he was completely soaked, until he was choking on it. The exorcism lasted eight hours.

Think about what that means. Eight hours. Through the night, Father Vincent and Reverend Smith worked, along with the congregation bearing witness. Calling out the demons, commanding them to leave, wrestling with whatever forces had taken hold of Michael Taylor. By their count, they expelled over forty demons. Demons of incest, bestiality, blasphemy, and lewdness. Demons with names, demons without. One after another dragged out of him, kicking and screaming, if you believed what they said afterwards.

From a psychological perspective, eight hours of that kind of ritual is torture. Doesn't matter if you call it spiritual warfare; it's still torture. A man tied to the floor, restrained, having objects forced into his mouth, being shouted at by multiple people simultaneously, drenched in water, subjected to intense sensory overload and emotional manipulation. If Michael Taylor wasn't psychotic before the exorcism started, eight hours of that would certainly push anyone towards a break with reality.

By eight o'clock Sunday morning, 6th October, the priests were exhausted. Couldn't continue. They were only human, after all, and they'd been performing an intensely demanding ritual all night. Michael lay on the floor, still tied down, drenched in sweat and holy water, mumbling to himself. Whether he was better or worse than when he'd arrived, nobody could really say.

"We've got most of them," Father Vincent said. "Only three left now."

Three demons. Violence. Insanity. Murder.

Let that sink in for a moment. The priests identified, by name, that the demon of murder remained inside Michael Taylor. They knew it was there. They told him it was there. And then they said, "Go home. Rest. We'll finish this later. Don't worry."

Don't worry. The demon of murder is still inside you, but don't worry about it. Get some sleep, we'll sort it out later.

One woman in the congregation, Margaret Smith, grabbed Father

Vincent's arm. "Don't let him leave," she begged. "Please. I've had a warning. From God. The demon of murder is going to escape. It's going to kill Christine."

Father Vincent dismissed her concerns. They'd done good work that night. Cast out over forty demons. Three more wouldn't matter. Michael just needed rest, and frankly, so did the priests. Human exhaustion trumped divine warning. Michael and Christine Taylor left St Thomas's Church around eight in the morning. Got home about half past. Both of them were exhausted, traumatised, barely able to think straight after eight hours of that ritual. Christine must have been terrified, watching her husband subjected to that ordeal all night. Michael must have been completely dissociated from reality, convinced he had demons inside him, and told that the demon of murder was still there.

Less than two hours later, Christine Taylor would be dead.

Police Constable Ian Walker got the call at 9:45. Someone had seen a man wandering the streets naked, covered in what looked like red paint. Probably a prank, the caller thought. Students, maybe. Still, worth checking out.

Walker found Michael Taylor stumbling through the streets of Ossett in broad daylight. No clothes. Covered head to toe in blood. Not paint. Blood. Fresh blood, still wet, covering his hands, his face, his entire body.

"It is the blood of Satan!" Michael was shouting. "Released! I am released! It is done!"

Walker arrested him without incident. Michael wasn't resisting, wasn't violent anymore. Just kept muttering about being released, about evil being destroyed, about victory over Satan. He got into the patrol car peacefully, still covered in his wife's blood, still convinced he'd done something holy.

Another officer went to the Taylor house to check on Christine. The senior policeman who arrived first looked green. Pulled the younger officer aside before he could go in. "You don't want to see this one, son," he said, and his voice was shaking. "I've seen nothing like it before, and I've seen a few. It's the wife. She's got no... he's ripped at her, son. It's a right mess in there. There's not much of her left. You don't want to see it."

But the younger officer did see it. Had to. It was his job. Christine Taylor lay in the bedroom. Her face had been torn from her skull. Eyes gouged out. Tongue ripped from her mouth. Chunks of flesh and spatters of blood covered the walls, the floor, the bedding. The level of violence was incomprehensible, the kind of thing you read about in medieval torture manuals, not something that happens in a terraced house in West Yorkshire in 1974.

In another room, they found the family dog. Strangled. Dismembered. Limbs scattered about as if someone had just torn the animal apart in a frenzy, rage needing an outlet after Christine was already dead.

No murder weapon. Michael Taylor had done all this with his bare hands. He'd been home less than two hours when it happened. Less than two hours after the priests told him everything would be fine, that they'd finish the exorcism later, that he should go home and rest. The demon of murder, Margaret Smith had warned. It's going to kill Christine. She'd been right.

March 1975. Crown Court. The case that shocked the nation. Husband murders wife after all-night exorcism. Priests claim they left three demons inside him, including the demon of murder. Did they create a killer or fail to stop one?

The prosecution kept it straightforward. Michael Taylor murdered his wife. The physical evidence was overwhelming. The brutality was undeniable. The question wasn't whether he'd done it; everyone agreed he had. The question was whether he was responsible for his actions. Whether he'd been in his right mind when he tore Christine's face off. Whether this was murder or something else.

The defence, led by Mr Ognall QC, had a more complicated argument to make. Their client had committed the crime, yes. No one was disputing that. But the Christian Fellowship Group and the exorcism had destroyed an already fragile mind. "Neurotics feeding neurosis to a neurotic," Ognall called it, and it's a phrase that's stuck with me because it captures something true about how vulnerable people get exploited by religious groups.

"I am aware," Ognall said in court, his voice heavy with something between anger and sorrow, "that it is going to be extremely difficult for members of the jury to imagine how anyone in the year 1974 could seriously suggest that a human being could be possessed by the devil or evil spirits. But that is what the defendant was led to believe by this prayer group."

The defence argued that the Fellowship had been more cult than church. That Marie Robinson's charismatic leadership had constituted a form of mind control, not in the Hollywood sense but in the very real psychological sense of undue influence over vulnerable individuals. That Michael Taylor, already struggling with depression and chronic pain, had been easy prey. That the exorcism itself, eight hours of psychological and physical torment, had pushed him into full psychosis.

Psychiatrists testified. Michael Taylor had been suffering from acute schizophrenia, they said. Whether it had been developing for years or whether the stress of the Fellowship had triggered its emergence, they couldn't say. But by the time of the exorcism, he was deeply unwell. And the exorcism hadn't cured him. It had made everything catastrophically worse. Taken a man on the edge and shoved him straight over.

"The intense psychological torment he experienced that night," one clinical psychologist stated, "was the direct cause of his actions the following morning."

Think about the psychology of what happened. Michael Taylor spent eight hours being told he was possessed by over forty demons. The demon of murder was identified, named, and given reality through that naming. Then he was sent home, whilst, according to everyone present, he still contained that demon. His psyche had been told, in the most dramatic and traumatic way possible, that he contained murderous evil. That the demon of murder lived inside him. That it was still there, waiting.

Self-fulfilling prophecy doesn't quite capture it. It's more like programming. You take someone already mentally unwell, subject them to hours of ritual that reinforces a belief in demonic possession, tell them specifically that the demon of murder remains inside them, then send them home exhausted and traumatised. What do you think is going to happen?

Michael himself gave testimony. Tried to explain what he'd felt. The evil inside him. The voices. The sense of something else using his body. When he'd attacked Christine, he said he'd been trying to destroy the evil in her. Hadn't seen his wife at all. Had seen a demon wearing her face. "Released," he kept saying. "I was released. The evil in her had to be destroyed."

Whether this was a genuine psychotic delusion or the logical endpoint of eight hours of being told he was possessed, it doesn't really matter. The effect was the same. Michael Taylor killed his wife, believing he was destroying a demon. The exorcism had permitted him, had given him the belief system, had told him exactly what evil looked like and what needed to be done about it.

Father Peter Vincent also testified. Unrepentant. Yes, they'd performed an exorcism. Yes, they'd identified over forty demons. Yes, they'd sent Michael home with three still inside him. But they'd been dealing with genuine demonic possession, he insisted. The ritual was necessary. Their only mistake was stopping before the work was complete. If they'd continued for another hour, two hours, however long it took, Christine would still be alive.

The Church of England, watching this unfold with growing horror, stayed mostly quiet. Let their clergy speak for themselves. The Archbishop of Canterbury, Donald Coggan, eventually condemned what he called the "reckless approach" of the Fellowship, but did so carefully, without directly attacking the practice of exorcism itself. Because the Church of England still performs exorcisms. Still believes, in some capacity, that demons are real and can possess people. They have more rigorous protocols now. More oversight. More medical evaluation first. Lessons learned from Ossett, even if those lessons didn't extend to abandoning exorcism entirely.

The jury deliberated and reached their verdict: not guilty by reason of insanity. Michael Taylor had certainly killed his wife in the most horrific way imaginable, but he had not been in his right mind when he'd done it. The exorcism, the Fellowship, the obsession with Marie

Robinson, the underlying mental illness, all of it had combined to create a temporary psychosis that robbed him of sanity.

Two years in Broadmoor Hospital, the high-security psychiatric facility. Then another two years in a secure ward at Bradford Royal Infirmary. Four years total before they released him back into society, deemed no longer a danger to the public.

None of the members of the Christian Fellowship Group faced any charges. Marie Robinson walked free. Father Peter Vincent got promoted the following year. His career didn't suffer from his role in a woman's brutal murder. The Church protected its own.

Michael Taylor, the man who'd torn his wife's face off with his bare hands, served four years and then disappeared into anonymity. Or tried to.

Here's what the official records show. Michael Taylor was diagnosed with acute schizophrenia. The exorcism had triggered a psychotic break in a man already suffering from mental illness. The Fellowship Group had exploited his vulnerability, his depression, his desperate need for something to believe in. The ritual itself, eight hours of physical and psychological torture disguised as spiritual healing, had destroyed whatever stability he had left. That's the medical explanation. The rational one.

But there's another version, whispered in certain circles, believed by people who think the material world doesn't explain everything. Michael Taylor was genuinely possessed by over forty demons. The exorcism worked, mostly. Cast out the majority. But exhaustion made the priests stop before finishing the job. They left three demons behind. Violence. Insanity. Murder. Those three demons, unchecked, drove Michael to kill his wife within hours of returning home. The tragedy wasn't that the exorcism happened, from this perspective. The tragedy was that it didn't finish.

Pick whichever version makes sense to you. The courts picked the first one. Dr Milne at Broadmoor initially diagnosed acute schizophrenia, then reversed his decision. His final opinion was that the Fellowship Group had created Michael's insanity. Not discovered it, not revealed it. Created it. Whatever Michael had been before joining that church, the church had broken him.

After his release, Michael moved back to Ossett. Tried to rebuild something resembling a life. Attempted suicide four times, according to reports. Whatever had happened to him, whatever he'd done, he couldn't escape it. The guilt, the memories, the knowledge of what his hands had done, followed him. You don't tear your wife's face off and then just move on with your life.

July 2005. Thirty-one years after Christine's murder. Michael Taylor made headlines again. Arrested for indecently assaulting a teenage girl. Convicted. Sent to prison.

A week into his sentence, he started exhibiting strange behaviour. The same kind of erratic conduct that had preceded Christine's murder in 1974. Speaking in odd voices, violent outbursts, and claims of feeling evil inside him. The prison authorities didn't mess about. Sent him straight for medical evaluation. When he appeared before the court again, they ordered him into medical treatment rather than continuing his prison sentence.

Four attempted suicides. A second crime decades later. Recurring psychiatric episodes. Whatever had broken inside Michael Taylor in 1974 had never properly healed. Was that because the three demons were still inside him, as believers might say? Or because trauma and mental illness don't just disappear, no matter how much treatment you receive?

More than fifty years on, the case of Michael Taylor still divides opinion. Mental health professionals see it as a tragedy that could have been prevented. Michael showed clear signs of serious psychiatric illness. Depression that had gone untreated for years. Possible schizophrenia developing. Obsessive behaviour. Dissociative episodes. What he needed was proper medical intervention. Medication, therapy, and medical care. What he got instead was eight hours of ritual torture that convinced him he was possessed by demons.

The power of suggestion in someone already mentally fragile is enormous. If everyone around you keeps saying you're possessed, if priests are screaming at you and drowning you in holy water and jamming crucifixes in your mouth, if you're already suffering from delusions and paranoia, your mind will create the reality you're being told to expect. The exorcism didn't cure Michael Taylor. It destroyed him. Took whatever tenuous grip on reality he had left and obliterated it.

From this view, the Christian Fellowship Group and the priests who performed the exorcism bear significant responsibility for Christine Taylor's death. They took a vulnerable, mentally ill man and subjected him to a ritual that pushed him past the breaking point. The demon of murder wasn't cast out during the exorcism. It was created by it.

Believers in demonic possession look at the same case and see something different. A man who was genuinely possessed by over forty demons. A Fellowship Group that recognised the possession and tried to help. An exorcism that nearly worked but was stopped too soon. The priests had warned Michael that three demons remained. Margaret Smith had received a divine warning that the demon of murder would kill Christine. They knew he was still dangerous. Their mistake wasn't performing the exorcism, from this perspective. Their mistake was letting him leave before it was finished.

Father Peter Vincent never wavered from this position. Until his death, he believed absolutely that Michael Taylor had been possessed, that the exorcism was the right response, and that the only error was stopping before the job was complete. No regrets, no second thoughts, no acknowledgement that maybe they'd taken a sick man and made him exponentially worse.

Maybe the truth is somewhere between these extremes. Maybe Michael Taylor was mentally ill, and the exorcism made it worse. Maybe the Fellowship Group truly believed they were helping, but their methods were dangerous and irresponsible. Maybe everyone involved meant well, and the outcome was still catastrophic. Good intentions don't prevent tragedy. Sometimes they cause it.

The Archbishop of Canterbury condemned the Fellowship's approach but not the practice of exorcism itself. The Church of England continues to perform exorcisms, but now with more rigorous protocols. Psychiatric evaluation first. Medical explanations ruled out. Multiple levels of approval required. They learned something from Ossett, even if they didn't entirely change their minds about demons.

The courts learned something, too. When the next case came along, when Arne Cheyenne Johnson tried to use demonic possession as a defence for murder in America seven years later, judges could point to Michael Taylor. Could say, we've been down this road before. We know where it leads. Mental illness exists. Demons, legally speaking, do not.

The Michael Taylor case refuses to stay buried. Keeps resurfacing in documentaries, podcasts, and books. The horror of it, the grotesque violence, the theological questions it raises, all of it too compelling to ignore. David Peace used it in his novel *Nineteen Seventy-Seven*, renaming Taylor as Michael Williams but keeping the essential horror intact. The case gets mentioned in *The Conjuring: The Devil Made Me Do It*, though only in passing. Hollywood prefers the American version of this story because it went to trial with the possession defence. But the Taylor case asks harder questions.

If you sincerely believe in demonic possession, when is an exorcism appropriate? How do you distinguish between mental illness and supernatural affliction? What safeguards should exist? And if an exorcism goes wrong, who's responsible? If you don't believe in demons, what do you do about people who do? How do you protect vulnerable individuals from religious practices that might harm them? Do you ban exorcisms entirely, or just regulate them more strictly? And what about religious freedom?

There are no easy answers. The Michael Taylor case proves that.

Marie Robinson disappeared from public record after the trial. No interviews, no statements, no trace of her in any accessible documentation. The charismatic young lay preacher who'd led the Fellowship, who'd performed exorcisms in people's front rooms, who'd rejected Michael Taylor's advances and inadvertently triggered his breakdown, vanished into anonymity. Whether she still believes Michael was possessed, whether she feels any responsibility for what happened, we'll never know.

The five Taylor children grew up without their mother and, effectively, without their father. The trauma of what happened that October morning rippled through their lives in ways we can only imagine. Did they believe their father was possessed? Did they think he was simply mentally ill? How do you make sense of something like that when you're a child?

The Christian Fellowship Group continued for a while after the trial, then quietly dissolved. The case had made them notorious. Hard to recruit new members when everyone associates you with a brutal murder.

Ossett itself still carries the stain. *The Exorcist* Murder, they call it locally. Fifty years on, and people remember. Point out the house where it happened. Tell the story to newcomers with a mixture of horror and fascination. St Thomas's Church still stands in Gawber. You can visit it if you want. Sit in the pews where the congregation gathered that night. Stand in the space where they tied Michael Taylor to the floor and spent eight hours trying to save his soul. The church keeps no plaque, no memorial, nothing to mark what happened there. Why would they? It's not something to celebrate. It's something to forget.

In the end, the Michael Taylor case is a Rorschach test. What you see in it reveals more about your worldview than it does about what actually happened. The physical facts are undisputed. Michael Taylor killed his wife in the most horrific way imaginable, less than two hours after an eight-hour exorcism. He was found not guilty by reason of insanity. He spent four years in medical care, was released, struggled with mental illness for decades, committed another crime, and eventually disappeared from public view.

Christine Taylor is dead. Five children lost their mother. A community was traumatised. The Church of England was forced to reckon with the dangers of exorcism performed without adequate safeguards. Whether demons were involved or not almost doesn't matter at this point. The damage was real either way.

Michael Taylor, if he's still alive today, is in his eighties. Carrying the weight of what his hands did that morning for over fifty years. Whether he was possessed or psychotic, whether the exorcism helped or hurt, whether the Fellowship saved him or destroyed him, he's the one who has to live with Christine's death. Those four suicide attempts suggest living with it wasn't possible.

The three demons that remained. Violence. Insanity. Murder. Maybe they were real entities, supernatural forces that the priests failed to cast out. Maybe they were just names for the darkest parts of human nature, the capacity for violence that lives in all of us, waiting for the right conditions to emerge. Or maybe they were both. Maybe the line between psychological breakdown and spiritual possession is thinner than either scientists or priests want to admit.

What I keep coming back to is this: it doesn't matter if you believe in demons or not. What matters is that a vulnerable man with mental illness was subjected to a ritual that destroyed what was left of his sanity. What matters is that Christine Taylor died because priests were too exhausted to finish what they'd started. Margaret Smith's warning was ignored because everyone involved was so convinced they were fighting spiritual evil that they couldn't see the mental health emergency unfolding right in front of them.

The exorcism didn't fail because demons are real, and three were left behind. It failed because you can't cure schizophrenia with holy water and crucifixes. You can't treat psychosis with eight hours of ritual torture. All you can do is make it worse. And that's exactly what happened in St Thomas's Church that October night. They took a sick man and broke him completely. Two hours later, Christine paid the price.

Fifty years on, we still argue about what really happened. But

Christine Taylor is still dead. And that's the only fact that really matters.

CHAPTER IV

The Girl Who Starved For God

KLINGENBERG AM MAIN, BAVARIA. SUMMER 1976.
The autopsy report was clinical, as these documents always are. Precise, detached, the kind of language that drains all humanity from what it describes. Cause of death: advanced emaciation due to severe malnutrition and dehydration. Weight at time of death: 68 pounds, though some reports said 66. Age: 23 years old.

What the autopsy didn't say, what couldn't be captured in medical terminology, was how Anneliese Michel's knees had been shattered from genuflecting hundreds of times a day. How her body was covered in bruises and bedsores. How her hair had started falling out in clumps. How she'd spent the last months of her life eating spiders and coal and licking her own urine off the floor whilst two Catholic priests performed exorcism rites and her parents watched and prayed and did nothing to stop it.

The words carved on her tombstone read: "It is finished." Es ist vollbracht. Christ's last words on the cross. Her parents chose that inscription deliberately, seeing their daughter's death not as a tragedy but as completion, holy suffering that had reached its necessary end.

But the story starts much earlier, in a family where devotion to God wasn't just faith. It was everything.

Anna Elisabeth Michel was born on 21st September 1952 in Leiblfing, a tiny village in rural Bavaria. Everyone called her Anneliese. She was the third daughter of Josef and Anna Michel, wealthy mill owners who took their Catholicism seriously in the particular way that wealthy Bavarian families did. Josef had once wanted to be a priest. Three of his sisters were nuns. The household ran on prayer and discipline and the kind of rigid piety that turns ordinary life into constant penance.

Anneliese and her three sisters weren't allowed to play with other children much. Most of their time was spent indoors, praying. Mass twice a week wasn't enough for the Michels. Prayer permeated everything. Suffering, they believed, was holy. Sacrifice brought you closer to God. Pain was a gift. This wasn't unusual theology for strict Catholics, but the Michels took it further than most. Made it the centre of their existence.

The girl was sickly from the start. Measles, mumps, scarlet fever. Always thin, always pale, always a bit fragile. Her university thesis, written shortly before her death, focused on the phenomenon of fear. Hold that thought. A young woman choosing to write about fear, to study it academically, to try to understand the thing that was probably consuming her from the inside. Her roommate at Würzburg University would later describe her as withdrawn, timid, intensely religious. "Afraid of life," someone said. "Like she was waiting for something terrible to happen."

At sixteen, something terrible did happen.

One ordinary day at school in 1968, Anneliese blacked out. Not fainted, that's too gentle a word. Blacked out. When she came to, she was wandering around in a trance with no memory of how she'd got there, no sense of the time that had passed. Her friends said she looked possessed, though they used that word lightly then, the way teenagers do when something frightening happens and they don't have better language for it.

A year later, another episode. Woke up in a trance, wet the bed, then her body went rigid and started convulsing. Shaking uncontrollably whilst foam gathered at her mouth. Her parents were terrified. This wasn't something prayer could immediately fix, though they certainly tried.

The neurologist's diagnosis was straightforward: temporal lobe epilepsy. A type of seizure disorder that affects the part of the brain responsible for emotions, memory, and perception. It's not uncommon. It's treatable. The doctor prescribed Dilantin, an anti-convulsion medication that worked for most people.

It didn't work for Anneliese.

By 1970, she'd had a third seizure whilst staying at a psychiatric hospital for treatment. They added more medications. Tegretol is an anticonvulsant. Periciazine is an antipsychotic. Nothing helped. The seizures continued, and worse, new symptoms appeared. She started seeing things. "Devil faces," she called them. Grotesque demonic visages appeared at random times throughout the day. She'd be sitting in class or walking down the street, and suddenly there they'd be, leering at her, mocking her. Only she could see them. The doctors called them hallucinations, a known symptom of temporal lobe epilepsy. Visual distortions, terrifying but explicable, a misfiring in the brain's temporal lobe creating images that weren't there.

In 1973, Anneliese enrolled at the University of Würzburg to study education. She wanted to be a teacher, to work with children. Her classmates remembered her as quiet, very religious, and mostly keeping to herself. The walls of her dormitory room were covered in pictures of saints. A holy water font by the door. Rosary beads are always close at hand. Not unusual for a devout young woman, but the intensity of it unsettled some people.

Behind the pious facade, something was deteriorating. By 1973, the hallucinations had evolved into something worse. Voices. Not just any voices, but voices that told her she was damned. That she would rot in hell. That the devil was inside her. She smelled things too, burnt faeces she told her doctors, a smell so overwhelming it made her gag. And oddly, people around her sometimes smelled it too, which shouldn't have been possible if it was a hallucination. Olfactory hallucinations can be shared in groups under certain conditions, particularly when suggestion and expectation are high, but the phenomenon remains poorly understood.

Depression set in. Heavy, crushing depression that the medications couldn't touch. She became suicidal, tried to kill herself multiple times, even though she knew, as a devout Catholic, that suicide was an unforgivable sin. Something stronger than her faith was pushing her towards death. The doctors were baffled. Five years of psychiatric medications, endless adjustments to dosages and combinations, and nothing was working. If anything, Anneliese was getting worse.

Then she started developing an intense aversion to religious objects. Couldn't walk past a crucifix without feeling physical pain. Claimed the sacred images burned her skin, that looking at them was agony. A family friend took her to an unauthorised shrine in San Damiano, Italy. Anneliese couldn't enter, couldn't even approach the holy spring to drink the water. Being near the sacred site caused her distress.

The friend became convinced this wasn't a mental illness. This was demonic possession. Anneliese's mother, Anna, latched onto this explanation. It made sense to her in a way the doctors' diagnoses didn't. Mental illness, psychiatric disorders, chemical imbalances in the brain, all that modern medicine nonsense that never seemed to help. Her daughter was possessed. Obviously. Look at her behaviour. Look at her symptoms. The devil had got inside her little girl.

In September 1973, during a visit with Dr Luthy, a neurologist, Anneliese described her visions in detail. The demonic faces tormenting her. The voices telling her she was damned. "The devil is inside me," she said. Dr Luthy, to his credit, didn't immediately dismiss this as psychosis. He suggested the family consult a Jesuit, not instead of medical treatment but in addition to it. He was trying to be respectful of their faith whilst continuing the medical intervention. But the Michels heard what they wanted to hear. A doctor, a man of science, telling them to seek religious help. Permission to pursue the explanation they'd already decided was correct.

Getting the Catholic Church to approve an exorcism isn't simple, at least not officially. There are protocols, investigations, and requirements. Medical explanations must be exhausted first. The Church doesn't want to be wrong about these things, doesn't want to perform exorcisms on people who just need proper medical care. But the Michels were persistent, wealthy, and well-connected. And Anneliese's symptoms were, from a certain perspective, textbook possession.

By 1975, her behaviour had become extreme. She barely slept. When she did eat, which was rare, she'd consume spiders, flies, bits of coal. She licked her own urine off the floor. She destroyed crucifixes, tore holy pictures from the walls. She'd run through the house naked, screaming obscenities in guttural voices that didn't sound remotely like a young woman from Bavaria. She performed what witnesses described as 400 to 500 deep knee bends in a single day. Where the strength came from, given that she was barely eating, no one could explain. Witnesses were convinced it was supernatural. Medical professionals would point to adrenaline, to the way psychosis can temporarily override normal physical limitations, and to the fact that witness accounts are notoriously unreliable about numbers.

Father Ernst Alt, the local pastor, examined Anneliese multiple times throughout 1975. At first, he was sceptical. Mental illness seemed the obvious answer, and he'd been trained to look for natural explanations before jumping to supernatural ones. But the more time he spent with her, the more convinced he became that something beyond psychiatric illness was occurring. Whether he truly believed this or whether the family's certainty and the dramatic symptoms wore down his scepticism, we'll never know. But by August 1975, he was writing to Bishop Josef Stangl of Würzburg, requesting permission to perform an exorcism. Specifically, the major rite of exorcism according to the Rituale Romanum, the 1614 Roman Ritual, which hadn't been widely used in centuries.

Father Adolf Rodewyk, an elderly Jesuit and experienced exorcist, was asked to examine Anneliese. He declined initially due to his age, but put the family in contact with another Jesuit. In September 1975, Father Rodewyk visited anyway, accompanied by Alt. He observed Anneliese carefully, took detailed notes, and wrote a report to Bishop Stangl. The report, described later as "unintelligible to third parties," argued in favour of genuine demonic possession. Rodewyk urged Stangl to allow the major exorcism ritual to proceed.

Bishop Stangl hesitated. This was dangerous territory, legally and theologically. But eventually, he gave his permission with one critical condition: total secrecy. No publicity, no media attention. Just quiet prayers to help a suffering young woman. The Church was trying to protect itself, creating plausible deniability so that, if things went wrong, it could distance itself from the decision.

Father Arnold Renz, a Salvatorian priest and former missionary to China, was assigned to perform the exorcism alongside Father Alt. The first session was scheduled for 24th September 1975. Anneliese's parents stopped consulting doctors at her request. She no longer wanted medical treatment. She wanted the demons out. And her parents, convinced that their daughter's suffering was spiritual rather than medical, respected that choice. They stopped the medications, stopped the psychiatric appointments, and committed fully to the exorcism as the solution.

Sixty-seven exorcisms over ten months. One or two sessions per week, each lasting up to four hours. They recorded forty-two audio tapes. The tapes still exist. You can find them online if you're curious, though fair warning, they're disturbing in a way that stays with you.

During the first exorcism, six demons allegedly revealed themselves through Anneliese's voice. Lucifer, Judas Iscariot, Cain, Nero, Adolf Hitler, and Valentin Fleischmann, a disgraced priest who'd been excommunicated centuries earlier. Anneliese, or the demons speaking through her, provided accurate details about Fleischmann's life that supposedly she had no way of knowing. Believers point to this as proof of possession. How else would she know? Sceptics note that the information about Fleischmann was available in historical texts, that Anneliese was an educated young woman who'd spent her life immersed in Catholic history, that people in psychotic states can access and recombine information in ways that seem impossible but aren't supernatural.

On the tapes, you can hear her voice change. Dropping into deep, guttural growls. Speaking in different tones, different personalities. "We are the demons," she'd say, using the plural. Hitler's voice would shout "Heil!" Judas would complain that Hitler was unbearable in hell because he wouldn't stop bragging about his achievements. They'd argue amongst themselves, jostling for dominance, creating this horrifying theatre of evil personalities fighting for control.

"People are stupid as pigs," Hitler's voice said through her mouth on one recording. "They think it's all over after death. It goes on."

The priests would restrain her during these sessions. Had to, they said, because she'd thrash violently, try to hurt herself, claw at her own face. They'd recite the ancient Latin prayers, command the demons to leave in the name of Christ, and throw holy water on her. Hour after hour after hour. And Anneliese would scream and growl and speak in those voices, and everyone present would become more convinced that they were witnessing genuine possession.

Anneliese began speaking about dying to atone for the wayward youth of the day and the apostate priests of the modern Church. She wanted to be a sacrifice, she said. Suffering for others' sins, the way Christ had suffered on the cross. It was holy, she believed. Necessary. Her pain had meaning, had purpose. This theological system, this idea of redemptive suffering, is deeply embedded in Catholic tradition. But taken to its extreme, it becomes justification for refusing help, for embracing agony, for choosing death.

She stopped eating almost entirely. What little she consumed was hardly food. Insects, coal, things that would make anyone ill. Her body began to waste away, and the priests and her parents interpreted this as evidence of the demons' hold on her. The evil was destroying her from within, they thought. They needed to pray harder, exorcise more aggressively, break the demons' grip. It didn't occur to them, or they refused to accept, that their daughter was starving to death right in front of them.

In a letter to Father Alt from 1975, Anneliese wrote: "I am nothing; everything about me is vanity. What should I do? I have to improve. You pray for me." To another priest: "I want to suffer for other people, but this is so cruel." She was telling them, in her own words, that the suffering was unbearable. That she needed help. But her pleas were filtered through the exorcism framework, interpreted as spiritual struggle rather than a medical emergency.

Father Renz wrote to Bishop Stangl as Anneliese's condition deteriorated, warning that she was getting worse, that her physical state was alarming. The bishop never responded. Whether he didn't receive the letters or chose not to engage, we don't know. But his silence implicitly allowed the exorcisms to continue.

Week after week, month after month. Anneliese's knees shattered from the constant genuflecting. Bones breaking, tendons ripping, but she kept kneeling. Kept praying. Kept begging God to cast out the demons. By spring 1976, she was emaciated. Her hair was falling out. Her skin had taken on a translucent quality, stretched too tight over her bones. She weighed less than 70 pounds. Bedsores covered her body from lying in bed, and she was too weak to move. She had pneumonia, but no one called a doctor.

Father Alt later testified that he never considered her dangerously ill. That if he had, he would've immediately called for medical assistance. Which is either a lie or evidence of such profound negligence and delusion that it amounts to the same thing. Anyone with eyes could see Anneliese was dying. Father Renz was more honest about his indifference. "The exorcism ritual expressly states that clergymen should not burden themselves with medical matters," he said. The 1614 Rituale Romanum said the exorcist should leave medical care to physicians. Since there were no physicians involved, since they'd deliberately excluded medical professionals, Renz apparently felt absolved of responsibility for what was happening to her body.

30th June 1976. The sixty-seventh exorcism. Anneliese weighed somewhere between 66 and 68 pounds. Her body was shutting down. Organ failure had begun. She was too weak to stand on her own and had to be supported by her mother just to remain upright during the prayers.

Her last words, recorded on tape: "Please, absolution." Then: "Mama, stay with me. I am afraid."

Not the demons speaking. Not Hitler or Judas or Lucifer. Just Anneliese, a terrified young woman who knew she was dying and wanted her mother beside her at the end.

The next morning, 1st July, around eight o'clock, Anna Michel found her daughter dead in bed. The body that had carried her for twenty-three years had finally given up. The autopsy was clear. Malnutrition and dehydration. She'd been in a semi-starvation state for almost a year. Even a week before her death, aggressive medical intervention could have saved her. Force feeding, hospitalisation, basic care. Instead, they'd prayed over her whilst she starved to death.

The local prosecutor launched an immediate investigation. This wasn't a mysterious death or a tragic accident. This was, potentially, a crime.

In March 1978, nearly two years after Anneliese's death, the trial began in the district court at Aschaffenburg. It drew massive media attention. National newspapers, television cameras, and international interest. The Exorcism Trial, they called it. Four defendants: Josef and Anna Michel, her parents. Father Ernst Alt and Father Arnold Renz, the exorcists. All were charged with negligent homicide.

The Michels hired Erich Schmidt-Leichner, the famous lawyer who'd defended Nazis at the Nuremberg trials. Interesting choice, revealing something about how they viewed themselves: as victims of persecution, defenders of faith in a secular age. The Church paid for the priests' defence counsel, standing by their clergy whilst maintaining just enough distance to protect the institution.

The prosecution's argument was straightforward. Anneliese Michel had suffered from epilepsy and psychosis. The exorcisms had prevented her from receiving necessary medical treatment. The defendants had watched her starve to death for over ten months and done nothing to stop it. Medical experts testified. Dr Luthy, her neurologist, explained temporal lobe epilepsy, how it can cause hallucinations, religious obsessions, and personality changes. All of Anneliese's symptoms fit a known mental health condition. The medications she'd been prescribed had side effects, true, including depression and suicidal thoughts. But stopping the medication entirely whilst subjecting her to traumatic religious rituals had been catastrophic.

The autopsy report was entered into evidence. Advanced emaciation, multiple broken bones, pneumonia, bedsores. A body that had been systematically destroyed through neglect disguised as spiritual care. Psychiatrists explained how the exorcisms had likely reinforced her delusions. When authority figures, priests, people she trusted absolutely, confirmed that demons were inside her, it validated her psychotic beliefs. Made them more real, harder to escape from. Instead of helping her distinguish between hallucination and reality, the exorcisms erased that boundary.

The prosecution played some of the audio tapes in court. The room went silent as they listened to Anneliese's voice dropping into those guttural growls, claiming to be Hitler, Judas, Lucifer. Screaming, barking like an animal, crying. "This," the prosecutors argued, "is what untreated psychosis sounds like. Not demons. Mental illness that needed medical intervention, not mediaeval rituals."

They called witnesses who'd seen Anneliese in her final weeks. The wasting body, the broken mind. She'd needed to be carried everywhere because she was too weak to walk. Why hadn't anyone called an ambulance? Why hadn't anyone forced her to eat? Why had four adults watched a young woman slowly die and convinced themselves it was God's will?

The defence argued that the exorcism was legal under German law. The Constitution protected citizens in the unrestricted exercise of their religious beliefs. Their clients had been acting in good faith, in accordance with their sincere religious convictions, with the full approval of the Catholic Church. Schmidt-Leichner played more of the audio tapes, not as evidence of psychosis but as evidence of possession. "Listen to the demons arguing," he insisted. How could a young woman from rural Bavaria know accurate details about Valentin Fleischmann, an obscure excommunicated priest from centuries ago? How could she speak in multiple voices simultaneously?

Eyewitnesses testified about phenomena they'd observed. Anneliese levitating during seizures, her body rising from the bed without physical support. Her superhuman strength, whilst being restrained, was required.

multiple people to hold her down. The 400 to 500 deep knee

bends she could perform in a day, despite eating almost nothing. Father Renz testified about the six demons, described how they'd identified themselves, how they'd spoken through Anneliese, and how they'd fought against the exorcism. He was unrepentant. They'd been trying to save her soul. That her body failed was tragic, but secondary to the spiritual battle being waged.

The defence argued that Anneliese herself had requested the exorcisms, had refused medical treatment, and had wanted to suffer as atonement for others' sins. She'd been of sound mind when making those decisions, they claimed, exercising her religious freedom. The judges weren't impressed by this argument. A woman in the grip of psychotic delusions cannot give informed consent to her own starvation.

On 21st April 1978, the court returned its verdict. Guilty. All four defendants were convicted of negligent homicide. The sentences were remarkably light. Six months in prison, immediately suspended. Three years' probation. Fines. The court explained its leniency. The defendants had acted out of sincere religious belief, not malice. They'd honestly thought they were helping. Anna and Josef Michel, the judges said, had "suffered enough" with the loss of their daughter. German law allows for exemption from punishment when the perpetrators have already endured significant consequences from their actions.

Still, guilty. The legal system had spoken. Anneliese Michel had died from neglect, and four people bore responsibility for that neglect. All four appealed initially, then quietly dropped their appeals. The conviction stood.

Bishop Stangl issued a statement afterwards. Carefully worded, legally vetted. Exorcism, he explained, was meant to be nothing more than a prayer for a person who feels at the mercy of forces beyond their control and cannot pray for themselves. Any necessary medical help must accompany it. Always. He warned that talk of the devil intended to strike terror rather than arouse confidence in God was contrary to the spirit of the New Testament. Misconceptions about demonic possession, he reminded everyone, had played a disastrous role over the centuries. Right there in Würzburg, in the 17th century, 300 people had been burned as witches for trafficking with the devil.

The subtext was clear: we made a mistake. This shouldn't have happened. Later, the Catholic Church quietly recanted its finding that Anneliese Michel had been possessed. Mental illness, they decided. Not demons. In 1999, the Vatican issued a revised exorcism formula after a German commission had spent years petitioning for changes. The Germans had been particularly concerned about the practice of directly addressing demons during exorcisms, the "I command thee, unclean spirit" language that confirmed to mentally ill people that their delusions were real. They argued that this confirmation by an authority figure did tremendous damage, reinforcing psychosis rather than breaking it.

The Vatican's revised ritual still allowed for direct address to demons. The Germans didn't get everything they wanted. But the protocols became more rigorous. More medical evaluation, more medical oversight, more safeguards. Too late for Anneliese, obviously.

The Michels never expressed regret. "I don't regret it," Anna Michel said after her daughter's death. She believed, absolutely, that Anneliese had been possessed. That the exorcisms had been necessary. That her daughter had died a martyr, sacrificing herself for the sins of her generation. The grave became a pilgrimage site, not officially sanctioned, but pilgrims came anyway. Catholics who believed Anneliese had been a saint, that her suffering had been holy, and that she could intercede for lost souls from heaven.

Fresh flowers still appear on the tombstone decades later. People pray there, light candles, and leave notes asking for her help. The people of Klingenberg don't much like it. "The town is ashamed," a local woman said years later. "People don't want to talk about it. There's a feeling it was the parents' fault because they were so religious they didn't see what was happening."

When *The Exorcism of Emily Rose* was released in 2005, a loosely based adaptation of Anneliese's story, the town worried that more pilgrims would come. They did, not in huge numbers, but enough to keep the story alive, keep the shame fresh. Anna Michel welcomed the pilgrims. Their presence reaffirmed her faith, validated her belief that her daughter's death had meaning. That it hadn't been a waste. That those ten months of suffering and starvation had been part of God's plan. She died still believing her daughter had been possessed by demons.

The audio tapes are online now. Forty-two recordings from the exorcism sessions. You can listen if you want, though I'm warning you, they're genuinely disturbing. Anneliese's voice changes throughout. Sometimes it's her recognisable young woman's voice, frightened, begging. Sometimes it drops into deep, guttural growls that sound inhuman. She screams, barks, and laughs in ways that make your skin crawl. The demons argue with each other on the tapes. Hitler shouting about how stupid people are. Judas calls Hitler a "big mouth" with "no real say" in hell. They mock the priests, resist the exorcism, and promise violence.

Believers hear these tapes and hear demons. Absolute proof of possession. No young woman could produce those sounds, speak in those voices, know those things without supernatural influence. Sceptics hear the tapes and hear severe mental illness. Psychosis manifests as dissociative identity disorder. Glossolalia, speaking in tongues, is a known psychological phenomenon. The power of suggestion, religious delusion, and untreated epilepsy combine to create horrifying symptoms.

Both groups are looking at the same evidence and reaching opposite conclusions. That's the thing about cases like this. The facts don't speak for themselves. Your interpretation depends entirely on what you're willing to believe is possible.

Dr Luthy and other neurologists who examined Anneliese were clear. Temporal lobe epilepsy combined with psychosis explained everything. Temporal lobe epilepsy affects the part of the brain responsible for processing sensory input, memory, and emotion. Seizures in this region can cause vivid hallucinations, both visual and auditory. Feelings of overwhelming dread or religious ecstasy. Out-of-body experiences. The sensation of a presence in the room. Smells that aren't there, like the burnt faeces Anneliese reported.

Some patients with temporal lobe epilepsy develop Geschwind syndrome, characterised by hyperreligiosity, hypergraphia (compulsive writing), and altered sexuality. Anneliese had all these symptoms. Her walls were covered in religious images. Her obsessive letter writing. Her confusion about sexuality and sin. The psychosis, likely triggered or exacerbated by the epilepsy, created the delusions of demonic possession. The voices telling her she was damned. The visual hallucinations of devil faces. The belief that evil forces were controlling her.

The medications she'd been prescribed, whilst meant to help, had side effects. Depression, suicidal ideation. But stopping the medication entirely didn't cure her. It made everything worse, removing the chemical buffer that was keeping her somewhat stable. Then came the exorcisms, authority figures confirming that her delusions were real. Spending hours reinforcing the belief that demons were inside her, that her suffering was supernatural rather than medical. It was the worst possible intervention for someone in her condition.

The starvation was potentially anorexia nervosa, a condition that was rising rapidly in Germany during this period. Or possibly a psychotic fixation on suffering as atonement. Or both. Either way, it was treatable. Force feeding, psychiatric unitisation, and proper medical care. Instead, she starved to death whilst four adults watched and prayed.

Some Catholics still believe Anneliese was genuinely possessed. That the sixty-seven exorcisms eventually worked. That she died not from starvation but from being released from demonic control, her body too damaged by months of spiritual warfare to survive. Father Renz maintained until his death that the demons had been real. That they'd identified themselves accurately. That Anneliese had provided information about Valentin Fleischmann that she couldn't have known naturally.

From this perspective, the tragedy isn't that the exorcisms happened. It's that modern scepticism undermined spiritual warfare at a critical moment. Bishop Stangl's later recantation, the Church declaring it was mental illness after all, that's just institutional cowardice. The hierarchy protects itself from bad publicity rather than standing by the truth. Anneliese Michel was a martyr, some believe. A saint. Her suffering was holy. Her death saved souls.

What nobody wants to say aloud is that neither the medical nor the spiritual explanation fully accounts for everything that happened. The medical explanation struggles with some of the specifics. How did

Anneliese know accurate details about Valentin Fleischmann? How did she perform 500 deep knee bends in a day whilst starving? The spiritual explanation struggles with other questions. If the exorcisms were working, why did Anneliese's condition deteriorate so catastrophically? Why would God allow a young woman to starve to death whilst priests prayed over her?

Maybe the truth is that multiple things were happening simultaneously. Anneliese had epilepsy and psychosis. The exorcisms reinforced her delusions and made the mental illness worse. Her strict religious upbringing created a framework where suffering was holy and medical help was weakness. And possibly, though I'm sceptical, something else was present too. Something that doesn't fit neatly into either category.

Or maybe not. Maybe it was a young woman with severe, untreated mental illness and a family too religious to see they were killing her.

"It is finished." That's what her tombstone says. Es ist vollbracht. Christ's last words on the cross. Anneliese's parents chose that inscription deliberately, saw their daughter's death as completion, sacrifice, holy suffering that had reached its necessary end. The words carry terrible ambiguity. Finished how? The suffering finished. The exorcism finished. Her life is finished. All of the above, perhaps.

Anneliese Michel was twenty-three years old when she died. She'd spent seven years suffering from a condition that destroyed her mind and body. Whether that condition was epilepsy and psychosis, or demonic possession, or some horrifying combination of both, the outcome was the same. A young woman starved to death whilst the people who should have protected her convinced themselves it was God's will.

Four people were found guilty of negligent homicide. Received suspended sentences. Walked free. The Catholic Church recanted its finding of possession, changed its exorcism protocols, and moved on. Klingenberg carries the shame quietly. In the decades since, Anneliese's story has been told and retold. Three films, countless documentaries, books, and podcasts. She's become a symbol, a cautionary tale, a piece of evidence in an ongoing argument about faith versus science.

But she was a person. A young woman who loved saints and prayer and her family. Who studied education at university? Who wrote a thesis about fear? Who was, by all accounts, intensely devout and deeply frightened. She deserved better than what happened to her. Whether you believe she was possessed by demons or suffering from mental illness, that much is certain. She deserved medical care, compassion, and intervention. She deserved to be saved, not watched whilst she slowly died.

The audio tapes remain online. Her voice, frozen in those moments of extremity, still screaming and growling and begging for absolution. People listen and make their determinations. Demons or delusion. Possession or psychosis. Perhaps the only honest answer is we don't know. We can't know. The line between mental illness and spiritual affliction, if such a line even exists, is too blurred for certainty.

What we do know is this: Anneliese Michel died in agony. Her parents and two priests were convicted of letting it happen. The Catholic Church admitted it had made a terrible mistake. And fifty years later, fresh flowers still appear on her grave whilst the town tries to forget.

Es ist vollbracht. It is finished. But the questions remain, and they always will.

CHAPTER V

The Devils Of Loudun

L OUNDUN, FRANCE, SUMMER 1634

Urbain Grandier was a French Catholic Priest who was burned at the stake in 1634 after being convicted of witchcraft.

A court judgement carried out by the authorities burned Urbain Grandier alive in the public square whilst six thousand people watched. But before they lit the fire, they tortured him. Shattered his legs with red-hot iron boots filled with spikes, the kind of torture device that was usually fatal on its own, but they used it anyway because he was going to die regardless. Refused him the last rites. Denied him the Kiss of Peace, that ancient Christian blessing reserved for the dying. Then tied him to a stake and set him alight.

His crime, according to the seventeen judges who convicted him, was using black magic to bewitch an entire convent of nuns. Sending demons to possess them. Making a pact with Satan himself. The real crime, the one nobody said aloud in that courtroom, was simpler. He'd made too many powerful enemies. Slept with too many important men's wives and daughters. Written too many satirical pamphlets mocking Cardinal Richelieu, the most powerful man in France. Stood in the way of demolishing Loudun's fortifications, which Richelieu very much wanted demolished for political reasons that had nothing to do with demons.

The possessed nuns were just the excuse. Convenient, dramatic, impossible to disprove in an era when nobody really understood how mass hysteria worked or what group psychology could do to people locked in a building together. Perfect cover for political murder dressed up as religious justice.

But before we get to the burning, before the torture and the trial and the public spectacles of exorcism that drew thousands of spectators from across France like it was a theatre, we need to understand who Urbain Grandier was. Whether you believe he was an innocent man destroyed by political machination or a genuine sorcerer who got what he deserved depends entirely on what you think about the man himself.

Grandier was born in 1590, educated by Jesuits at the college in Bordeaux, ordained young and given the parish of Saint Pierre du Marché in Loudun in 1617. His uncle had influence with the Jesuits, pulled strings, and got him the position. Not unusual for the time. The Church ran on patronage and family connections as much as on piety, maybe more so.

He was brilliant. Everyone agreed on that, even his enemies. Charismatic preacher, eloquent writer, quick wit. Handsome too, which didn't hurt. Dark eyes, strong features, the kind of presence that filled a room when he entered it. The problem, if you can call it that, was that he knew all this. Carried himself with the confidence of someone who'd never been told no, who'd never learned to keep his head down, his opinions quiet, his ambitions modest.

In an era when keeping your mouth shut and your thoughts to yourself was how you survived, when criticising the powerful could get you disappeared, Urbain Grandier couldn't help but speak his mind. He wrote treatises attacking priestly celibacy, arguing that forcing priests to be celibate was unnatural and led to corruption. Published pamphlets criticising Church policies. Made jokes about Cardinal Richelieu, which was roughly equivalent to publicly mocking Stalin in Soviet Russia. Spectacularly unwise.

The women loved him. Absolutely adored him. He had affairs with half the noblewomen in Loudun, or so the rumours said. Definitely got Philippe Trincant pregnant, which was particularly awkward because she was the daughter of Louis Trincant, the king's prosecutor. She had to be quietly married off to someone else with a bastard in her belly, whilst everyone pretended not to notice.

Her father, Louis Trincant, never forgave that humiliation. Keep that name in mind. It becomes important later. Grandier fathered other children, too, kept mistresses, wrote love letters that got passed around and laughed over at dinner parties. He wasn't subtle about any of it. Seemed to think his position, his connections, and his charm would protect him from consequences.

For a while, they did. In 1630, the ecclesiastical court finally moved against him. Tried him for immorality and sacrilege. Found him guilty. Banned him from serving as a priest in the Diocese of Poitiers for five years, from Loudun forever. Grandier appealed, called in favours, got witnesses to retract their statements, and had the case dismissed "without prejudice should new evidence be presented." The judges left that loophole deliberately. They knew Grandier. He wasn't going to stay down.

He didn't. Came back to Loudun as if nothing had happened. Started harassing everyone who'd testified against him, demanding legal restitution, making enemies of people who'd have been happy to let bygones be bygones if he'd just quietly disappeared. His friends begged him to leave town. Start fresh somewhere else. Anywhere else. He ignored them. Stayed in Loudun. Kept preaching, kept writing, kept sleeping with married women and making powerful men look like fools.

Fatal mistake.

The Ursuline convent opened in Loudun in 1626. Sixteen nuns, most of them young, most from noble families that had fallen on hard times. Being sent to a convent wasn't always a religious calling in 17th-century France. Often, it was what you did with daughters you couldn't afford to marry off properly, daughters who were too plain or too difficult or just surplus to requirements in families that could only afford dowries for the older girls.

The nuns were bored. Restless. Stuck in that building, praying and doing needlework whilst life happened outside the walls. They gossiped constantly, the way people do when they're trapped together with nothing else to occupy their minds. About everything, but especially about the handsome priest who was allegedly bedding half the town. Jeanne des Anges, the prioress, was twenty-five when she became Mother Superior in 1627. Born Jeanne de Belcier, daughter of a baron, she'd had an accident as a child that left her with a hunchback and stunted growth. Not attractive by the standards of the day. Probably why her family shunted her off to the convent rather than trying to find her a husband.

In her autobiography, written years later after all of this was over, Jeanne described herself with brutal honesty. Said she'd deliberately made herself indispensable to the previous prioress through "ingratiating behaviour," which is a polite way of saying manipulation. Admittedly, she faked states of ecstasy and rapture to seem more spiritual than the other nuns. Confessed she was vain, vindictive, desperate for attention in a place where attention was currency, and she had very little else to trade on.

And obsessed with Urbain Grandier. "When I did not see him, I burned with love for him," she wrote, "and when he presented himself to me, I lacked the faith to combat the impure thoughts and movements that I felt." Except that Grandier never presented himself to her. Not really. She'd seen him from afar, heard stories about his conquests, and built up this elaborate fantasy in her head. Five years of obsession, growing more intense, more consuming, feeding on itself in the confines of that convent where there was nothing to distract her from it.

Their previous spiritual director, Father Moussault, died in 1632. The convent needed a new confessor. Jeanne suggested Grandier. He turned them down. His reasons for refusing aren't entirely clear. Maybe he was too busy with his own parish. Maybe he sensed something unhealthy in the way the prioress looked at him. Maybe he just didn't fancy adding convent duty to his already complicated life. Whatever his reasons, he said no. Recommended that they ask Canon Jean Mignon instead.

Jean Mignon was Louis Trincant's nephew. Louis Trincant, whose daughter Grandier had impregnated and humiliated. Jean Mignon, who'd testified against Grandier in the 1630 trial. Jean Mignon, who hated Urbain Grandier with the kind of bitter resentment that festers over years, that turns into something dark and patient. Mignon accepted the position. Became spiritual director to sixteen frustrated, gossipy young nuns who spent their days talking about the priest who'd rejected them.

Do you see how this is going to end? Because everyone involved probably should have.

September 1632. Exactly a year after Loudun had been devastated by plague. Three thousand seven hundred dead out of fourteen thousand residents. Nearly a third of the town. Doctors had fled because there was nothing they could do. The convent had closed its doors and stopped giving alms to the poor. Trauma hung over the town like smoke, that particular collective grief that comes after disaster when everyone's lost someone, and nobody knows how to process it.

That's when the apparitions started. 22nd September, according to ecclesiastical records. Three nuns, Jeanne des Anges, Sister de Colombiers, and Sister Marthe de Saint Monique, were visited during the night by an apparition of "a man of the cloth" asking for help. Father Moussault, the dead confessor, Jeanne said. Except the ghost looked like Urbain Grandier. And instead of asking for help, he was trying to seduce her. Caressing her, telling her he loved her, pressing her to have sex with him.

She told the other nuns. They started having similar dreams. Spectral men wandering the convent at night. Shadowy figures that looked like Grandier, like Moussault, like other priests from the town. Always trying to seduce them. Always whispering obscenities. The nuns began behaving strangely. Fits of uncontrollable laughter that would go on for hours. Sudden violent rages. Speaking in odd voices. Crawling around on all fours, barking like dogs. Convulsing. Screaming profanities that shocked even the servants who'd heard plenty in their lives.

Canon Mignon did nothing to discourage any of this. Quite the opposite. He reinforced it, shaped it, and gave it theological meaning. Told the nuns these were incubi, demons sent by Satan to corrupt them. That they were being attacked by evil forces. And who, he asked during confession, leading questions that weren't subtle at all, who might be sending these demons?

The nuns knew the answer he wanted. Started saying the name. Urbain Grandier. The handsome priest who'd rejected them, who'd humiliated their spiritual director's uncle, whom everyone in town loved to gossip about. Urbain Grandier was bewitching them. Obviously. Physical evidence appeared. Hawthorn branches materialised in Jeanne's hands, passed there by ghostly fingers, she said. The nuns went into full convulsions. Writhing, shrieking, blaspheming. On 5th October 1632, the first exorcisms were conducted. Within weeks, they'd become public spectacles.

Imagine the scene. A scaffold was erected in the centre of Loudun. Nuns tied to chairs, writhing and screaming. An exorcist in full ceremonial robes commanding the demons to reveal themselves. Thousands of people were watching, packed into the square, necks craning for a better view. Vendors selling food. Children sitting on their fathers' shoulders. This wasn't a secret. This was entertainment, and the church deliberately made it entertainment. Turned possession into proof of Catholic doctrine, a demonstration of priestly power over evil. Better than any play you could see in Paris.

The nuns performed brilliantly. Contorted their bodies in ways that looked impossible, though anyone who's seen a gymnast or studied what the human body can actually do knows it's not supernatural, just unusual. Spoke in deep, guttural voices claiming to be Asmodeus, Leviathan, Behemoth, Astaroth. Demons with names from demonology texts, demons the audience recognised from sermons and scripture. They demonstrated the classic signs of possession that everyone knew about. Superhuman strength, allegedly, though no one ever measured it properly or considered that adrenaline and fear can make people remarkably strong. Speaking in tongues, though, when tested, they couldn't conjugate basic Latin verbs, which proper demons should have managed easily according to Church doctrine. Aversion to holy objects, though that's simple enough to fake if you're motivated.

They accused Grandier. Named him repeatedly. Said he'd thrown roses over the convent wall, enchanted with demonic spells. That he'd made a pact with Satan. That he'd sent the demons to torment them sexually, to steal their virtue, to corrupt their souls. The crowds ate it up. This was better than the theatre because it was real, or seemed real, which is all that mattered. Real nuns, actually possessed, named a real priest as their tormentor. The theological implications were staggering. The entertainment value was through the roof.

Grandier demanded to confront them. Insisted on being allowed to address the demons himself. When he did, he exposed the fraud almost immediately. Asked the demons questions in Latin. They couldn't answer. Asked them in Hebrew. Nothing. The demons of Loudun, it turned out, were remarkably monolingual, which is a problem when Church law clearly states that demons speak all known languages fluently. These demons clearly didn't. Which meant either they weren't demons, or the whole thing was a theatre.

The exorcists pressed on anyway. They had their orders, not from God but from more earthly powers.

Sister Jeanne provided the most damning testimony. During one particularly dramatic exorcism, she vomited up "evidence." The ashes of a consecrated wafer. A child's heart, allegedly from a witch's sabbath ritual. Semen, supposedly Grandier's. And a copy of Grandier's pact with the devil, signed by him and several demons. How convenient that a demon would swallow these items, that Sister Jeanne would vomit them up right when the exorcists needed proof. How theatrically perfect.

In May 1634, another document appeared. The demon Leviathan, speaking through Jeanne des Anges, produced a signed pact. Written backwards, in Latin with scribal abbreviations. On the left side, Grandier's signature. On the right, the signatures of Asmodeus, Leviathan, and other demons. The document exists. You can see photographs of it in historical archives. Whether Grandier actually signed it, or whether it was forged, or whether he signed it under torture later, nobody knows for certain. The handwriting analysis is inconclusive. It could be his. It could be a skilled forgery.

Doesn't really matter by that point, does it? Grandier's fate was sealed the moment Cardinal Richelieu decided he needed to go.

Cardinal Richelieu. The Chief Minister of France, the power behind King Louis XIII's throne, was arguably the most dangerous man in Europe. The kind of person you absolutely did not want as an enemy because he had the resources and ruthlessness to destroy you completely. Urbain Grandier had made an enemy of him years earlier with satirical pamphlets mocking Richelieu's policies. The Cardinal never forgot. Men like Richelieu don't.

In 1633, Jean de Laubardemont was sent to Loudun to demolish the town's fortifications. Part of Richelieu's plan to consolidate royal power and eliminate potential strongholds that could resist the

Crown. Loudun's walls were militarily significant. They had to come down. The town militia refused. Urbain Grandier led the resistance, citing the king's previous promise that Loudun's fortifications wouldn't be touched.

Laubardemont returned to Paris empty-handed. Reported to Richelieu about the failed mission, the priest causing problems, and oh, there's this business with possessed nuns accusing him of witchcraft. Richelieu's interest was immediate. Witchcraft. Possession. A priest making deals with Satan. This was perfect. Not just a way to remove an irritating opponent but a demonstration of royal and ecclesiastical power. A warning to anyone else who might resist.

In November 1633, Laubardemont was commissioned to investigate the possessions. Given extraordinary powers that superseded local authority. Grandier was arrested and taken to the prison at Angers. Letters were sent from Loudun to Paris by the town's officials, pleading for Grandier's innocence and calling the possessions an "imposture." Those letters were intercepted. Never reached their destination. On 31st May 1634, Laubardemont returned to Loudun with a decree from the King's Council. He had full authority over the case. No other court could interfere. No appeals would be allowed. Anyone who tried to help Grandier would be fined five hundred livres, a fortune at the time.

Anyone brave enough to speak in Grandier's defence was threatened. Some were told they'd be declared traitors to France and that their property would be seized. A few nuns tried to retract their accusations. They were silenced, isolated, possibly tortured, though the records are carefully vague on that point. The trial was a foregone conclusion before it even started.

8th July 1634. Seventeen judges, all from Catholic territories surrounding Loudun, all owing their positions to Richelieu or men loyal to Richelieu. Not a single judge from Loudun itself. Not a single Protestant on the panel, despite Loudun being a mixed town where Catholics and Huguenots had lived peacefully for decades. The evidence presented was theatrical nonsense. The possessed nuns testified, writhing and screaming on cue. The pacts with demons were entered into evidence. The testimony of exorcists who swore they'd personally witnessed supernatural phenomena.

Grandier's defence was systematically dismantled. Witnesses for his character were threatened into silence. Evidence of his innocence was ruled inadmissible. Questions about the nuns' credibility, about the possibility of fraud or delusion or mass hysteria, were forbidden. The trial lasted eighteen days. Five thousand pages of testimony. None of it mattered. The verdict was written before the first witness took the stand.

From 15th August through 17th August, Grandier appeared before the judges. Maintained his innocence. Demanded to know who was really behind this persecution. Everyone in that courtroom knew the answer. Nobody said Cardinal Richelieu's name aloud. 18th August 1634, the sentence was pronounced. Guilty of magic, maleficia, causing demonic possession of several Ursuline nuns and other women of Loudun. Condemned to make public penance, then to be burned alive at the stake.

First, though, they'd torture him. The "extraordinary question" was a particular form of torture reserved for those about to be executed. Usually fatal or at least crippling. You only used it on people you were going to kill anyway, so it didn't matter what state their bodies were in afterwards. They brought out the Spanish boot. An iron vice filled with spikes, heated red-hot. Applied to Grandier's calves and ankles. The spikes shattered his leg bones. The heat cauterised and burned simultaneously. The pain must have been incomprehensible; the kind of agony that makes you wish for death.

They wanted a confession. Wanted him to admit to witchcraft, to making a pact with Satan, to sending demons to rape nuns. A confession would validate everything, prove the Church right, and justify the execution. Grandier never confessed. Through all the torture, he maintained his innocence. Screamed certainly, begged them to stop probably, but never said the words they wanted to hear.

That stubbornness, that refusal to give them satisfaction, made him a hero to Protestants and sceptics for centuries afterwards. Proof that the whole thing was a political assassination disguised as religious justice. Or if you believed the Church, proof that Satan had strengthened him against torture, a final service from his demonic master. Pick your interpretation.

They carried Grandier to the stake on a chair. He couldn't walk. His shattered legs wouldn't support him. The crowd numbered over six thousand. People from all over France had come to watch this. A priest burned for witchcraft, a servant of Satan, received his earthly punishment. Entertainment and a moral lesson combined. Father Grillau, a Capuchin friar, was supposed to give Grandier the last rites. Refused. Wouldn't perform the ritual for a sorcerer, he said. Wouldn't kiss him off, Peace either, the ancient Christian blessing reserved for the dying.

The Grandier went to his death unshriven. According to Catholic doctrine, that meant damnation. The Church wasn't just killing his body. They were consigning his soul to hell. They tied him to the stake and piled wood around him. Grandier looked out at the crowd. Some accounts say he spoke, proclaimed his innocence one final time, forgave his executioners, and asked God to have mercy on his enemies. Other accounts say he was too broken to speak, just hung there in his bonds waiting for the fire.

They lit the pyre. The flames caught quickly, wood properly stacked, everything arranged for maximum effect. This wasn't a quick death. Burning alive never is. The smoke might kill you first if you're lucky. Grandier wasn't lucky. He burned for an hour, they say, screaming at first, then silent. Whether from death or from his voice giving out, nobody could tell.

When it was over, they scattered his ashes. Didn't want any relics, no grave for his supporters to visit, no bones to venerate. Complete obliteration. Urbain Grandier was gone. Erased. A political inconvenience removed, a theological statement made, a warning issued to anyone who might challenge Cardinal Richelieu.

The possessed nuns, naturally, were cured. The demons driven out by Grandier's death, the evil ended, God's justice triumphant. Except that's not what happened at all.

The nuns were not cured. If anything, they got worse. Jeanne des Anges and the others kept convulsing, kept speaking in demonic voices, kept putting on their public spectacles. The crowds kept coming. The exorcisms continued. Month after month, year after year. Some of the exorcists started falling ill themselves. Father Tranquille, who'd been the most aggressive in accusing Grandier, developed strange symptoms. His body convulsed without pain, Laubardemont reported to Richelieu. By 1638, Tranquille was dead, convinced he'd been possessed by the demons he'd been fighting.

In December 1634, four months after Grandier's execution, a new exorcist arrived. Jean-Joseph Surin, a Jesuit mystic, was sent by the King and the Cardinal to address the ongoing possessions. Surin tried a different approach. No more public spectacles, no more theatrical interrogations of demons. Instead, he sat quietly with Jeanne des Anges, read her prayers, and talked to her about finding inner peace.

And he did something extraordinary. He prayed for her demons to possess him instead. Offered himself as a sacrifice, taking on her spiritual burden, suffering in her place. The kind of mystical theology that makes practical people uncomfortable but has a long tradition in Catholic practice. It worked, sort of. Jeanne's symptoms improved. The convulsions became less frequent. The demonic voices are quieter.

But Surin started manifesting symptoms himself. Headaches, breathing difficulties, trembling fits, and physical hallucinations. And then full possession, or something indistinguishable from it. Terrible pain in his stomach. Suicidal thoughts. Delusions. Eventually, he became catatonic, unable to speak for twenty years. He recovered near the end of his life, wrote memoirs describing the whole ordeal, and stood by his claim that Jeanne des Anges had been genuinely possessed and that he'd taken the demons into himself to save her.

Whether you believe that or think he had a psychological breakdown from the stress of the whole nightmare, from witnessing and participating in years of theatrical exorcisms and political manipulation disguised as spiritual warfare, is up to you.

In 1635, Jeanne des Anges claimed to be pregnant. By one of her demons, she said. Carried on loudly about how she'd rather die than birth a demon's child. The exorcists convinced the demonic father, through prayer and command, to abort the baby. Jeanne stopped being pregnant. Miracle or hysterical pregnancy that resolved when the attention shifted. Take your pick.

Sister Claire was caught using a crucifix to pleasure herself. The other nuns were made to strip and flagellate themselves as penance. The whole thing descended into something that looked less like spiritual warfare and more like sexual psychodrama played out in religious language, which is probably what it had been all along.

Finally, in 1637, three years after Grandier's death, the possessions ended. Jeanne des Anges had a vision. She'd be freed from the devil if she made a pilgrimage to the tomb of Saint Francis de Sales. She went to Annecy, then visited Cardinal Richelieu and King Louis XIII in Paris. Showed them her hand, where the names Jesus, Mary, Joseph, and Francis de Sales had miraculously appeared, written in red on her skin.

The demons were gone, she announced. God had triumphed. She'd been delivered. The crowds who came to see her numbered in the thousands. She became a celebrity, touring France, showing her miraculous hand like a living relic. Wrote an autobiography modelling herself after Saint Teresa of Avila. Died in 1665, having spent the last decades of her life basking in fame and religious veneration. Some scholars later annotated her autobiography with the subtitle "Autobiography of a Hysterical Possessed Woman." A bit harsh perhaps, but not entirely inaccurate.

So, what really happened in Loudun? The traditional Catholic narrative, at least the one that held for centuries, is straightforward. Urbain Grandier made a pact with Satan. He sent demons to possess the Ursuline nuns. The Church recognised the possession, performed exorcisms, tried the guilty party, and executed him according to law. Justice was served, evil was punished, God triumphed.

The Protestant narrative, pushed by Huguenots from Loudun living in exile because it wasn't safe to say these things in Catholic France, was different. Political assassination. Richelieu wanted Grandier dead for opposing him. The nuns were either coached, deluded, or both. The whole thing was a show trial, a demonstration of power, a warning to anyone else who might resist royal authority. Grandier died a martyr, a victim of Catholic oppression.

The Enlightenment narrative, developed over the next century as people began questioning supernatural explanations more systematically, focused on superstition and hysteria. The nuns were bored, frustrated, and sexually repressed. They developed collective psychosis, egged on by an ambitious confessor and manipulative exorcists who had their own agendas. Grandier was a convenient scapegoat. The whole affair shows the dangers of religious fanaticism and unchecked clerical power.

The modern psychological narrative focuses on mass hysteria in a closed female community, triggered by trauma from the plague, reinforced by social contagion, and exploited for political purposes. The nuns weren't faking, not exactly. They truly believed what they were experiencing. But belief and reality aren't always the same thing.

All of these narratives have evidence supporting them. All have problems.

The phenomena the nuns displayed were, by any standard, extraordinary. Convulsions that lasted hours. Voices that sounded nothing like their normal speech. Physical contortions that seemed impossible for the human body, though it can do remarkable things under the right conditions. Knowledge they shouldn't have possessed, though this claim is disputed and often relies on selective interpretation of what they said versus what witnesses remembered them saying.

Multiple exorcists, from different orders, with different theological perspectives, all concluded demonic possession was occurring. These weren't stupid men. They were educated, experienced, and trained to distinguish between possession and illness or fraud in accordance with the protocols of their time. The phenomena continued for five years under constant scrutiny from church officials, doctors, and sceptics. If it were entirely fraud, maintaining it for that long with that many witnesses would require extraordinary coordination and commitment, though smaller groups have certainly managed it.

Some of the physical manifestations, like the appearance of names on Jeanne's hand, have no obvious natural explanation. It could be self-induced through pressure and suggestion; dermatographia is real. It could be deliberately cut into the skin and hidden, to be revealed in a dramatic manner. Could be something else entirely.

Surin's experience is harder to dismiss as political theatre. His gradual descent into what looked exactly like possession after praying to take on Jeanne's demons, suffering for twenty years, writing about it when it comes to spiritual warfare rather than political manipulation, he truly believed. That doesn't make it supernatural; psychological contagion is real and well-documented, but it does complicate the simple fraud narrative.

But the evidence for fraud and manipulation is equally compelling. The demons couldn't speak Latin, failed the most basic test of genuine possession according to Church doctrine. When confronted with sceptical examiners, the phenomena often disappeared or diminished. The timeline is suspect. Visions of Grandier started after he rejected the convent, after Canon Mignon took over as spiritual director, and after political tensions in Loudun had reached a boiling point. Very convenient timing.

The evidence produced, the pacts with demons, the items vomited up, and the testimonies of the nuns all appeared exactly when needed to build the case against Grandier. Too perfect, too theatrical, too useful. Multiple nuns tried to retract their accusations, were threatened, silenced, and ignored. If they'd genuinely been possessed and Grandier genuinely guilty, why would they recant?

The possessions didn't end with Grandier's death. In fact, they intensified and became more elaborate. If he'd been the source, killing him should have stopped everything immediately. But it didn't, because the possessions served multiple purposes: maintaining attention, providing meaning, and creating structure in a community that thrived on drama.

The political context is damning. Richelieu needed Grandier gone for purely secular reasons. Laubardemont, his agent, orchestrated the entire investigation with extraordinary powers that prevented any genuine legal defence. The trial was a sham, the verdict predetermined, the execution a foregone conclusion. The possessions provided convenient cover for political murder.

Maybe it's not either or. Maybe multiple things were true simultaneously, which is usually how reality works. The nuns could have actually been experiencing psychological distress. Mass psychogenic illness is real, well-documented, particularly in closed communities of young women under stress. The plague had traumatised Loudun. The convent was isolated, boring, and sexually frustrating for women with no vocation beyond avoiding being unmarried burdens on their families.

Canon Mignon could have recognised an opportunity in their distress. Encouraged it, shaped it, directed it toward Grandier without the nuns fully understanding they were being manipulated. Not because he was evil, but because he truly believed Grandier was evil and this was God's way of exposing him.

Richelieu could have seized on the situation to eliminate a political opponent, turning a local religious drama into a state trial with national implications. The exorcists could have truly believed in possession whilst also being willing to embellish, to stage-manage, to make the phenomena more dramatic for public consumption.

Grandier could have been innocent of witchcraft, whilst still being guilty of enough sexual misconduct and political arrogance to make people willing to believe the worst about him. Truth is rarely simple. Usually, it's a mess of competing motivations, partial understandings, sincere beliefs, mixed with cynical exploitation.

The Loudun possessions became infamous and still are. Aldous Huxley wrote a book about it in 1952. John Whiting adapted it for the stage in 1961. Ken Russell made a film in 1971 with Oliver Reed and Vanessa Redgrave, notorious for its sexual content and graphic violence, which was banned in several countries. The case appears in every serious discussion of European witch trials, mass possession, and Church corruption in the 17th century.

The town of Loudun still carries it. Tourist attraction, local shame, historical footnote, depending on how you look at it. The church where they burned Grandier is gone now. No plaque marks the spot. The convent where the nuns writhed and screamed is a museum. You can visit if you want, stand in those rooms and imagine what happened there.

Jeanne des Anges's autobiography is still in print. Her hand, with its miraculous names, was preserved as a relic. Whether those inscriptions were divine intervention, self-mutilation, dermatographia or something else entirely, they lasted until she died in 1665. The case influenced Church policy on exorcism for centuries, making authorities more cautious, more willing to consider natural explanations before jumping to supernatural ones. Not cautious enough, obviously, given what happened to Anneliese Michel three hundred years later, but more than they had been.

John Locke visited France in 1679, studied the case, and reached his conclusion: "The story of the nuns of Loudun possessed was nothing but a contrivance of Cardinal Richelieu to destroy Grandier." But Locke didn't talk to the nuns. Didn't witness the exorcisms. Didn't experience what Surin experienced when he prayed to take on Jeanne's demons. He looked at the political situation, the timeline, and the outcomes, and reached a rational conclusion based on the evidence he had access to. Rationality doesn't always have access to the whole truth, but it's usually a better starting point than supernatural explanations that can never be verified.

We know Urbain Grandier was burned alive on 18th August 1634. We know seventeen Ursuline nuns claimed to be possessed by demons he'd sent. We know the possessions lasted five years, drew thousands of spectators, and influenced French politics and Church policy. We know Cardinal Richelieu used the case to consolidate power and eliminate an opponent. We know multiple exorcists ended up mentally ill or dead after dealing with the possessed nuns, though that could be guilt, stress, psychological contagion, or genuine spiritual attack, depending on your worldview.

What we don't know, what we'll never know for certain, is whether demons were ever really involved at all. Or whether the real devils were human all along, wearing the masks of priests and cardinals and devout nuns whilst pursuing very earthly agendas of power, revenge, attention, meaning in lives that otherwise felt trapped and purposeless.

That's what keeps me thinking about Loudun. Not the question of whether demons are real, but the question of what happens when people are absolutely convinced they're fighting evil. When that conviction gives them permission to torture and murder, to manipulate and lie, to destroy lives in the name of righteousness. The possession might have been fake, but the burning was real. The political machinations might have been calculated, but the psychological devastation was genuine. Surin's twenty years of suffering happened whether demons caused it or trauma did.

And that's the lesson of Loudun, if there is one. The explanation matters less than the outcome. Whether you believe in demons or mass hysteria, a man died screaming. Whether you believe in spiritual warfare or political assassination, a community was torn apart. Whether you believe Jeanne des Anges was delivered by God or recovered from psychosis through the power of ritual and attention, she spent decades of her life convinced she'd been possessed.

The mechanisms might be different. The suffering is the same.

CHAPTER VI

The Boy Who Became The Exorcist

COTTAGE CITY, MARYLAND. JANUARY 1949.

Ronald Edwin Hunkeler was thirteen years old when the scratching started. Decades later, after the book and the film had made him famous without anyone knowing his name, after he'd spent a successful career at NASA helping put men on the moon, after seventy-one years of looking over his shoulder wondering if this would be the year someone finally connected the dots, the woman who lived with him for twenty-nine years would say something that breaks my heart every time I think about it. "He had a terrible life from worry, worry, worry."

But in January 1949, Ronnie was a kid. Only child in a German Lutheran household. Father Edwin, mother Odell, and Grandmother Anna are living with them in a modest house on 40th Avenue. By all accounts, he was normal, maybe a bit lonely the way only children in houses full of adults can be. Maybe too attached to his Aunt Tillie because she was the one person who really paid attention to him.

Mathilda Hendricks. Everyone called her Tillie. She was a spiritualist, which wasn't unusual in the 1940s. Spiritualism was having a moment after the war. People wanted to believe in something beyond the horror they'd just lived through, beyond atomic weapons and Cold War paranoia settling in like fog. The spirit world seemed gentler than the real one, more hopeful, a place where the dead weren't really gone.

Tillie taught Ronnie things. How to read tarot cards, how to interpret signs, how to use a Ouija board to communicate with the dead. The family was Lutheran but not particularly strict about it. They let Tillie share her interests with the boy. Harmless fun, probably. What could it hurt?

Tillie died in early January 1949. Ronnie was devastated. The aunt who'd made him feel special, who'd shared her mysteries with him like he was worth confiding in, was gone. He'd lost his only real friend in that house full of distant, practical adults who didn't quite know what to do with a lonely teenage boy.

So he tried to contact her. Used the Ouija board she'd given him, sat alone in his room asking if she was there, if she could hear him, if she had a message for him from wherever she'd gone. And something answered. Whether it was Tillie or something else, or just his own grief and loneliness finding expression through the ideomotor effect, that unconscious muscle movement that makes the planchette slide across the board like invisible fingers are guiding it, something started responding to his questions.

Saturday evening, 15th January 1949. Ronnie and his grandmother, Anna, heard water dripping somewhere in the house. That maddening irregular plop, plop, plop that drives you mental when you can't find the source. They looked everywhere. Bathroom and kitchen:

checked all the taps and pipes. Nothing. No leak, no explanation, just that sound that wouldn't stop.

Whilst they were searching, something else caught their attention. A picture of Jesus hanging on the wall started shaking. Just that picture, nothing else. Vibrating against the plaster like someone was tapping it from behind. By the time Ronnie's parents got home, the dripping sound had changed. Turned into scratching. Like claws on wood, rhythmic and deliberate, coming from inside the walls.

Rats, Edwin Hunkeler said. Old house, bound to have rats. He called pest control the next day. They found nothing. No rats, no mice, no evidence of any infestation whatsoever. But the scratching continued anyway, night after night. Always when Ronnie was in the house. Always worse in his room.

Things escalated the way these situations do, gradually, then all at once. Furniture started moving. Ronnie's bed would shake violently whilst he was in it, not just trembling but moving across the floor. Chairs slid around. Objects flew through the air. The family heard footsteps in empty rooms and doors slamming when no one was near. The kind of phenomena that sound absurd when you write them down, but are genuinely terrifying when you're living through them.

The Hunkelers did what practical people do. They consulted doctors first. Had Ronnie been examined thoroughly? Physical health was fine. Mental health was fine too, as far as 1940s psychiatry could determine, which admittedly wasn't as sophisticated as what we have now, but they tried. No obvious explanation for any of it. Their Lutheran minister, Reverend Luther Miles Schulze, suggested they keep a record. Document everything. Schulze was interested in parapsychology and had contacts at Duke University's Parapsychology Laboratory.

Maybe this was genuine paranormal activity that could be studied scientifically, he thought.

On the night Ronnie stayed at Schulze's house, the phenomena followed him there. "Chairs moved with him, and one threw him out," Schulze wrote to Duke. The reverend's conclusion after witnessing it himself was simple and chilling. "Evil was at work." He attempted a Lutheran exorcism rite. It didn't work. Whatever was happening to Ronnie Hunkeler, Lutheran prayers couldn't stop it. The minister made a recommendation. Try the Catholics. They had more experience with this sort of thing.

Father Edward Albert Hughes was the priest at St James Catholic Church in Mount Rainier. When the Hunkelers came to him in February 1949, desperate and exhausted from weeks of phenomena they couldn't explain or control, he listened carefully. Catholics took possession seriously then and still do. The Church has protocols, procedures, and approval levels that must be met before performing the major exorcism rite. But the situation was escalating. Ronnie's behaviour was getting worse, the manifestations more violent.

Hughes obtained his superiors' permission to attempt an exorcism. He arranged to perform the ritual at the Hunkeler house in late February. They strapped Ronnie to his mattress because you can't have someone thrashing about during the prayers, hurting themselves or others. Hughes began the Latin recitations, those ancient formulas meant to drive out unclean spirits.

Ronnie went berserk. Started screaming, writhing against the restraints with strength that seemed impossible for a thirteen-year-old boy. Then somehow, he got a hand free. Ripped a piece of metal spring from the mattress. The thing was sharp, jagged. He slashed Father Hughes across the shoulders. Deep enough to draw blood, deep enough to send the priest stumbling backwards in shock and pain.

The exorcism stopped. Hughes left, shaken and bleeding and unsuccessful. A few days later, something strange appeared on Ronnie's body. Scratches form words. Deep red welts that spelt out a message: LOUIS.

Odell Hunkeler took this as a sign. Her deceased sister, Tillie, had been from St Louis. The family still had relatives there, cousins attending St Louis University. Maybe that's where they needed to go. Maybe that's where Ronnie could find help. They packed up and headed west.

Father Raymond Bishop was a professor at St Louis University. Scholar, intellectual, not typically the sort who dealt with alleged demonic possession. But when a family member approached him about young Ronnie Hunkeler's situation in early March 1949, Bishop agreed to investigate. He met Ronnie and witnessed phenomena that he later documented carefully in a detailed diary. Mattresses shaking. Objects moving without physical contact. The boy was entering trance states, speaking in voices that didn't sound like a thirteen-year-old from Maryland.

Bishop consulted with Father William Bowdern, a Jesuit priest who'd eventually become president of Campion High School. Together, they decided this warranted the full exorcism ritual according to the Rituale Romanum. They weren't alone in this. Forty-eight witnesses eventually observed parts of the exorcism process. Nine of them are Jesuits. Doctors, medical students, family members, and other clergy. This wasn't happening in secret. It was documented, observed, and recorded by educated people trying to understand what they were seeing.

Father Walter Halloran, who assisted in the exorcisms, was still alive decades later when researchers started investigating the case properly. His testimony never wavered. Whatever he'd seen in that house on Roanoke Drive in St Louis, it had convinced him absolutely that something beyond normal explanation was occurring.

Bishop's diary is the primary source for what happened during those weeks in spring 1949. Twenty-nine pages of careful, clinical observations. He used the initial "R" to protect Ronnie's identity. Described phenomena in precise, unemotional language. On 10th March 1949, he wrote: "Next, the Fathers began the Litany of the Saints, as indicated in the exorcism ritual. In the course of the Litany, the mattress began to shake."

The shaking stopped when they blessed the bed with holy water. Started up again when the prayers continued. R was seized violently so that he began to struggle with his pillow and the bedclothes. The arms, legs, and head of R had to be held by three men. The contortions revealed physical strength beyond the natural power of R."

Ronnie spat at the relics they held near him. Writhed under the sprinkling of holy water. Made guttural sounds that didn't match anything a boy his age should be able to produce. On one occasion, a relic of St Margaret Mary was thrown to the floor. The safety pin holding it closed had somehow opened. "No human hand had touched the relic," Bishop wrote. "R started up in fright when the relic was thrown down."

Words appeared on Ronnie's skin. Scratched in red welts that formed letters. HELL. EVIL. And that recurring message: LOUIS. Then, more specifically: SATURDAY. And later: 3 1/2 WEEKS, indicating how long they should stay in St Louis for the exorcisms to work. "It seems that whatever force was writing the words was in favour of making the trip to St Louis," Bowdern noted in his own records.

The scratching sounds were particularly unnerving, according to witnesses. Rhythmic noises like marching soldiers came from the walls and floors whenever the prayers intensified. During the day, Ronnie was perfectly normal. Calm, polite, cooperative. Seemed like any other teenager. But at night, after settling in for bed, the changes would begin. He'd enter trance states. His voice would drop. He'd speak in what the priests believed was Latin, though when tested, he couldn't actually conjugate verbs or demonstrate any real knowledge of the language. The guttural sounds, the violence, the superhuman strength, all of it emerged after dark in a pattern that was consistent enough to feel deliberate.

By late March, the Hunkelers had had enough of doing this at home. Weeks of their son tied to beds, priests praying over him for hours, phenomena that defied explanation but never seemed to end. They took Ronnie to Alexian Brothers Hospital in St Louis. Medical setting, controlled environment, trained staff. If this were psychological, the hospital could help. If it were physical, they'd find it. If it was something else, well, at least there'd be more witnesses and better documentation.

The exorcisms continued at the hospital. Over twenty sessions total, spread across three months. The priests kept meticulous records. Bishop's diary, Bowdern's notes, reports from the other Jesuits involved. On 21st March 1949, Ronnie entered the hospital, and the violent convulsions intensified. During one session, he broke a priest's nose. A thirteen-year-old boy, supposedly in a trance, generating enough force to shatter bone.

The priests reported that he was speaking Latin phrases he

shouldn't have known. Reacting violently to religious objects. Demonstrating knowledge of things he'd never been taught. Classic signs of demonic possession according to Catholic doctrine. Sceptics would later point out inconsistencies. The "Latin" was often just glossolalia, speaking in tongues, meaningless sounds that resembled language. The "unknown knowledge" was vague enough to be a coincidence or information Ronnie had picked up without realising. The superhuman strength could be explained by adrenaline and the mechanics of leverage when a frightened person is thrashing against restraints.

But the witnesses believed. Forty-eight people were watching, documenting, participating in the ritual. They saw something that convinced them this wasn't just a disturbed teenager acting out.

Easter Monday, 18th April 1949. Seven weeks of exorcisms. Ronnie's family was exhausted. The priests were nearing the end of their own endurance. That morning, Ronnie woke with violent seizures and started shouting and thrashing. According to witnesses, he screamed: "Satan! Satan! I am Saint Michael, and I command you, Satan, and the other evil spirits to leave the body now!"

The voice didn't sound like Ronnie. Deeper, more authoritative. Then: "Satan! I am Saint Michael, and I command you to leave this body NOW."

Then silence. Ronnie went still. Eyes closed, breathing slowed. The witnesses held their breath, not sure what they'd just seen, not sure if it was over or if this was another phase in whatever was happening.

Seven minutes later, Ronnie's eyes opened. Normal eyes, clear and focused. The boy they knew, not whatever had been speaking through him. "He's gone," Ronnie said simply. The exorcisms were over.

Ronnie Hunkeler went home. Back to Maryland, back to school, back to what should have been normal life. The Washington Post ran a story in August 1949. Bill Brinkley wrote it, though he used a pseudonym for the boy. "Roland Doe", they called him. "In what is perhaps one of the most remarkable experiences of its kind in recent religious history, a 14-year-old boy has been freed by a Catholic priest of possession by the devil."

The article described the exorcisms in general terms. The violent outbursts, the cursing, the Latin phrases. It mentioned that Catholic sources had confirmed the story. But it kept Ronnie's real identity hidden, which was exactly what Ronnie wanted. Desperately wanted.

He graduated from Gonzaga High School in 1954. Went to university, became a brilliant engineer, got a job at NASA in 1962, working in the spacecraft technology division at Goddard Space Flight Centre in Maryland. He was good at it, really good. Developed heat-resistant ceramic compounds for space shuttle panels. The technology that helped the Apollo missions succeed enabled the landing of men on the moon in 1969. Worked at NASA for nearly forty years. Respected colleague, valued employee, expert in his field.

And terrified every single day that someone would find out who he really was.

William Peter Blatty had read that Washington Post article in 1949 while studying at Georgetown. Years later, he wrote a novel loosely based on the case. Changed the boy to a girl, changed Maryland and St Louis to Georgetown, and added dramatic elements that never happened in real life. Published *The Exorcist* in 1971. The book was a massive success. William Friedkin directed the 1973 film adaptation. Even bigger success, one of the scariest films ever made, people said. Revolutionised horror cinema, made millions, became a cultural touchstone.

And Ronald Hunkeler watched it all happen, knowing his childhood was the inspiration, powerless to stop it, terrified of being exposed. The woman who lived with him for twenty-nine years spoke to the New York Post after his death. Wouldn't give her name but described what life had been like for him. "On Halloween, we always left the house because he figured someone would come to his residence and know where he lived and never let him have peace."

Hold that thought. A successful NASA engineer, a man who'd achieved remarkable things in his career, a brilliant mind, a respected professional. And every Halloween for decades, he'd flee his own house. Hide. Because he was afraid some enterprising horror fan would connect the dots and show up at his door wanting to see the real exorcist boy.

"He had a terrible life from worry, worry, worry."

His NASA colleagues didn't know. Twenty-nine years working with these people, and he never told them. Kept it locked away. The woman who lived with him knew, obviously. Maybe a few close friends. But mostly it stayed buried, this secret that shaped every decision he made, every risk he avoided, every moment he spent looking over his shoulder.

Then came his final days. May 2020. Ronnie suffered a stroke at his home in Marriottsville, Maryland. He was dying. And a priest arrived, unexpected, to administer last rites. Whether that was connected to his history, whether someone had tracked him down one final time, or whether it was a coincidence, nobody knows. Ronald Edwin Hunkeler died on 10th May 2020, one month before his eighty-sixth birthday.

In December 2021, investigator JD Sword published an article in *Sceptical Inquirer* identifying Roland Doe definitively and publicly as Ronald Edwin Hunkeler. Ronnie had been dead for over a year, couldn't be hurt by the revelation anymore, couldn't spend another Halloween hiding from his own past. Sword felt the truth could finally be told.

The media picked it up immediately. NASA confirmed Hunkeler's employment, his work on the Apollo missions, and his contributions to space exploration. Perfect story. The engineer who helped put men on the moon was the possessed boy from *The Exorcist*. Human interest gold.

What actually happened in 1949? Here's what the sceptics say, and it's convincing. Ronnie Hunkeler was a lonely, grieving thirteen-year-old who'd just lost his favourite aunt. He'd been using an Ouija board, a tool that produces what psychologists call the ideomotor effect, unconscious muscle movements that seem like messages from spirits. His mind was primed to believe in the supernatural through Tillie's teachings and his own desperate desire to contact her.

The scratching sounds, the moving furniture, and the physical phenomena are all explainable through natural causes combined with suggestion and expectation. Old houses make noises. Objects can seem to move when you're looking for proof of paranormal activity. Mass hysteria is real and well-documented, particularly when authority figures reinforce the belief that something supernatural is occurring.

The exorcism itself likely triggered psychogenic symptoms. When priests tell you you're possessed, strap you to a bed, throw holy water on you, and command demons to leave your body in dramatic rituals that go on for hours, your mind responds to those expectations. Trance states, personality changes, guttural voices, all within the range of what dissociative disorders or stress-induced psychosis can produce in vulnerable people.

The "superhuman strength" was adrenaline and leverage. A frightened, thrashing teenager can generate surprising force, especially when people are trying to hold him down, and he's fighting with everything he has. The broken priest's nose proves violence occurred, not that demons were involved. The scratches forming words on his skin could have been self-inflicted, consciously or unconsciously. Dermatographia is real; some people's skin easily welts under pressure. Words can be "written" that way deliberately or through unconscious scratching during sleep or trance states.

The Latin phrases he supposedly spoke were tested and found wanting. He couldn't speak Latin, just made sounds that resembled it. The "unknown knowledge" he demonstrated was vague enough to be a coincidence or information absorbed without conscious awareness. And critically, according to the woman who lived with him, Ronnie himself said it was all fake. "He said he wasn't possessed; it was all concocted."

Psychological crisis. Grief. Suggestion. Hysteria. Exploitation by well-meaning but misguided clergy who truly believed they were helping but were actually reinforcing delusions. That's the sceptical explanation, and it accounts for everything without requiring belief in demons.

But here's what the believers say, and it's not easily dismissed. Forty-eight witnesses. Medical professionals, university professors, and nine Jesuit priests with education and training. They weren't stupid. They weren't all deluded simultaneously. They witnessed phenomena they couldn't explain through natural causes, documented them carefully, and maintained their testimonies for decades.

The relic thrown across the room with its safety pin mysteriously opened. The mattress shakes during specific prayers, stopping when blessed with holy water. The scratching sounds heard by multiple people independently sounded like marching soldiers. Objects moving when Ronnie was nowhere near them, when he couldn't have physically manipulated them.

Father Halloran maintained until his death that what he'd witnessed was genuine demonic possession. He'd been there, seen it firsthand, and participated in the ritual. Never changed his story, never expressed doubt. Bishop's twenty-nine-page diary is clinical, detailed, and careful. These weren't hysterical accounts by superstitious peasants. They were precise observations by educated men trying to document what they were witnessing.

The cure came on Easter Monday. After seven weeks of escalating phenomena, after nothing else had worked, the exorcisms finally succeeded. Ronnie said, "He's gone", and the manifestations stopped. Completely. Immediately. That's not how psychological disorders typically resolve, they argue. They fade gradually, respond to treatment over time, and have relapses.

And Ronnie's later claim that it was "all concocted," if he said that, could have been his way of coping. Easier to believe you faked it all than to believe you were genuinely possessed by demons as a child. Less terrifying, more manageable, something you can control retrospectively, even if you couldn't control it at the time.

Or maybe he really was faking and lived with the guilt of deceiving forty-eight witnesses, multiple priests, and his own family for seventy years. Carried that deception to his grave, whilst living in fear that people would find out about the lie. Which is worse? Being possessed by demons or being a fraud who destroyed his own life, or maintaining a childhood deception? Either way, the burden was real, and it destroyed him.

In the picturesque Bel-Nor neighbourhood of St Louis, Missouri, sits a beautiful colonial-style house on Roanoke Drive. Brick exterior, white shutters, huge trees in the yard. Looks perfectly normal, unremarkable. That's where they performed the exorcisms. Where Ronnie Hunkeler spent those weeks in spring 1949 strapped to beds whilst priests commanded demons to leave his body. William Bowdern's great-niece won't set foot in that house. Says there's still a demonic force there, refuses to visit, refuses to discuss it. Whether that's genuine spiritual sensitivity or just family trauma passed down through stories, who can say?

The house on 40th Avenue in Cottage City still stands, too. Where it all started. Where Aunt Tillie's Ouija board opened something that maybe shouldn't have been opened. Where a lonely boy tried to contact his dead aunt and got something else instead. Or where a grieving teenager fell into a psychological spiral that was misinterpreted as possession and reinforced by well-meaning but misguided adults. Or where absolutely nothing supernatural happened at all, and a clever boy figured out he could get attention, avoid school, manipulate adults, and it all spiralled beyond his control until he couldn't stop it.

We'll never know for certain. Ronald Hunkeler is dead. The priests who performed the exorcisms are dead. The witnesses are mostly dead. What's left are documents, memories, and interpretations that fit whatever worldview you bring to the story.

But here's what we know without question. Whether Ronnie was possessed by demons, suffering from a psychological crisis or deliberately faking, the experience defined his entire life. Shaped every decision he made. Made him flee his own house every Halloween for decades. Made him live in constant fear that his secret would be exposed. "He had a terrible life from worry, worry, worry." That's real. Documentably real. The consequences haunted Ronald Hunkeler for seventy-one years.

The Exorcist made millions. William Peter Blatty became rich and famous. The film revolutionised horror cinema. People still watch it, still talk about it, still use it as the definitive portrayal of demonic possession. And the boy who inspired it all spent his life hiding. Accomplished brilliant things at NASA, helped humanity reach the moon, and developed technology that protected astronauts from extreme heat. Should have been celebrated for those achievements, should have been able to talk proudly about his contributions to space exploration.

Instead, he's remembered as the possessed boy. Roland Doe. The real Exorcist case. His engineering work is a footnote to the horror story, which seems unbearably unfair regardless of what actually happened in 1949.

In his final moments, a priest arrived to give him the last rites. Whether Ronnie wanted that, whether it brought him peace, whether he believed in God or demons or anything supernatural at all by the end, we don't know. What we know is this: On 18th April 1949, after seven weeks of exorcism, Ronnie Hunkeler opened his eyes and said, "He's gone."

Whether he meant a demon or something else, whether it was real or performance, whether he believed it himself or knew he was lying, that moment ended the possessions. But it didn't end the haunting. That followed him for seventy-one more years until 10th May 2020, when Ronald Edwin Hunkeler finally, truly, escaped.

And that's the tragedy of this case, regardless of what you believe.

If demons were real and he was genuinely possessed, he lived his entire life traumatised by an experience of evil that nobody could adequately explain or help him process. If it were a psychological crisis, he was failed by every adult around him who chose supernatural explanations over proper mental health treatment. If it was deliberate deception, he trapped himself in a lie so completely that it became his prison.

Any of those explanations means a thirteen-year-old boy needed help and instead got exorcisms. Strapped to a bed and prayed over, his suffering turned into a spectacle. Got his trauma or his crisis or his deception documented for posterity, published in newspapers, turned into the most famous horror story of the twentieth century. And spent the rest of his life running from it.

"He's gone," Ronnie said on Easter Monday, 1949. But he wasn't. Not really. The experience never left him. Whether demons are real or not, the fear was real. The worry was real. The terrible life of looking over your shoulder for seventy-one years was real.

That's what possession looks like from the outside, maybe. But this is what it looks like from the inside. A lifetime of fear. A brilliant career overshadowed by childhood abuse. Hiding on Halloween. Never feeling safe. Never feeling free. Until death finally releases you from whatever it was that took hold when you were thirteen and grieving and lonely and tried to contact your dead aunt with a Ouija board.

He's gone now. Really gone. And maybe that's the only deliverance Ronald Hunkeler ever truly found.

CHAPTER VII

The Church That's Killed To Save

VILLA EL CARMEN, NICARAGUA. WINTER 2017.

Vilma Trujillo García was twenty-five years old when members of her own church tied her up, starved her, beat her, and set her on fire. They did this, they said later, to save her soul. To drive out the demons that had taken hold of her. They watched her suffer for days, watched her beg for water, watched her body fail. And when she finally died, they buried her quickly in a shallow grave and told her family she'd gone away.

This didn't happen in medieval Europe. Not during the witch trials. Not in some distant historical period we can comfortably distance ourselves from. This happened in 2017. The same year, people were streaming Netflix, scrolling through Instagram, and arguing about politics on Twitter. The same year, we supposedly knew better.

But knowing better doesn't stop people from doing terrible things when they believe God wants them to.

El Cortezal doesn't appear on Google Maps. Barely appears on local maps either. It's a cluster of poor wooden houses scattered through the rainforests of northeastern Nicaragua, about 40 kilometres from the nearest town, Rosita. No electricity. No telephone. No police. No doctors. Not even a shop. To reach it, you travel four hours in a 4x4 on terrible roads, then walk three hours through rivers and jungle and rocky slopes, then ride two more hours on a mule. Mobile phone signal exists only in a few elevated spots. The kind of place where the outside world feels very far away, where community is everything, where the church provides the only structure in lives defined by isolation and poverty.

Vilma Trujillo García was born there in the early 1990s. Her father was Catalino López Trujillo. Her mother, whose name somehow got lost in the records, died of cancer discovered too late, leaving Vilma and her siblings to grow up in a house full of grief. Vilma made it to third grade before she had to leave school. Got pregnant young, had her first child, stayed in El Cortezal because where else would you go? Had a second child with Reynaldo Peralta Rodriguez. Worked hard. Loved her children. Tried to build a life in a place where options were limited and futures uncertain.

She could read and write, which mattered in a community where education was scarce. She was kind, according to her aunt Ángela García. Radiant, people said later. Full of life. The sort of person you noticed who made things feel brighter just by being there.

Until she started acting strangely.

"She was saying weird things," Ángela García remembered. "She told her sister, who was pregnant, that she wasn't going to have a baby but a snake." Vilma was seeing things, hearing voices, and talking to herself. She hallucinated, which terrified her family. Something was wrong, clearly wrong, but nobody in El Cortezal had the vocabulary to understand what.

The nearest doctor was almost a day's journey away. Even getting to Rosita, the closest town with any medical facilities, meant hours of difficult travel through terrain that becomes impassable in the rainy season. The family knew Vilma needed help. But help, in the way that matters, in the way that involves diagnosis and medication and proper medical care, was impossibly far away.

So, they called for the pastor instead.

Juan Gregorio Rocha Romero was twenty-three years old. He'd made it to fourth grade, the educational level typical of a ten-year-old child, before leaving school. But that was enough to give him authority in El Cortezal, where literacy itself was power. He'd joined the Assemblies of God congregation just eight months earlier, presented himself as a man of God, and started preaching. The church he led was called Iglesia Misión Celestial, the Celestial Vision Church. A modest wooden structure perched on a lonely corner of a hill, about an hour's walk from the main settlement. Dark wood walls covered with handwritten scripture, some with spelling mistakes, some clearly written by devoted followers. "I am the good shepherd. I know my sheep and my sheep know me." Another: "May God bless your work, Pastor Juan."

The Assemblies of God would later insist that Rocha wasn't a recognised pastor. Just a layperson who'd taken it upon himself to lead. But in El Cortezal, that distinction didn't matter. He preached, people listened, and when Vilma's family needed help, they turned to him. He told them he could help. He could heal her. Drive out whatever evil had taken hold.

On 15th February 2017, Pastor Juan Rocha came to see Vilma.

Said she needed deliverance. Not a doctor, not a psychiatrist, not medication or proper evaluation. An exorcism. He convinced the family that evil spirits had possessed this young woman, and the only way to save her was through spiritual warfare.

They took her to Iglesia Misión Celestial. She went willingly, as far as anyone knows. Why wouldn't she? These were people she trusted. Her church family. The community she'd known her whole life. The pastor who spoke with God's authority.

What happened over the next six days would shock Nicaragua and make international headlines. But in that isolated mountain community, cut off from the world, hidden in the rainforest where mobile signals don't reach, and roads wash out in the rain, nobody outside knew anything was wrong.

They tied her up immediately. Bound her hands and feet. Later, witnesses would describe seeing her tied to a hammock, unable to move, whilst Pastor Rocha and his closest followers, between ten and fifteen people total, began the ritual. Not a recognised Catholic exorcism with protocols and oversight. Not a careful process with medical evaluation and psychiatric consultation. Just prayer and fasting, and conviction that demons were real and could be driven out through faith.

"He told us not to feel any love for her," Vilma's cousin Roberto Trujillo testified later at trial, his voice breaking. "Because that was the devil. That she had to be burned until only her head was left."

Read that again. "She had to be burned until only her head was left." That's what the pastor told them. That's what they believed. And because Pastor Juan Rocha said it, because he had spiritual authority, because dissent in a tight-knit religious community is nearly impossible, nobody questioned him.

Vilma's sister, Marlene, tried to visit. They wouldn't let her near. "Pastor Juan Rocha told us not to pay any attention to her because she was possessed by a demon," Marlene testified, weeping. "They wouldn't let me near her." When family members came to check on Vilma, church members turned them away. Said she wasn't cured yet. Told them to come back later. The family accepted this because they trusted the pastor. Believed he was helping.

They stopped giving Vilma food. Then water. This wasn't an oversight or an act of neglect. This was deliberate, systematic starvation. The logic, presumably, was that demons don't need sustenance. That depriving the body would weaken evil spirits. Fasting has deep roots in Christian tradition, and if Jesus fasted for forty days in the wilderness, surely a few days without food and water would help drive out demons.

Except Vilma wasn't possessed by demons. She was a human being experiencing a psychiatric crisis, probably psychosis, possibly schizophrenia or bipolar disorder with psychotic features, conditions that are treatable with proper medication and medical care. But in El Cortezal, with no doctors and no mental health services and a community that filtered everything through a spiritual lens, her symptoms looked like demon possession. And once that label was applied, everything she did was interpreted as evidence confirming the diagnosis.

For six days, Vilma remained bound in that wooden church on the hill. No food. No water. The human body can survive about three days without water, maybe a week if conditions are perfect. By the sixth day, Vilma's organs would have been shutting down. Kidneys failing first, unable to filter toxins without adequate hydration. The heart is struggling to pump blood that is thickening. Brain swelling from electrolyte imbalances, confusion setting in, then delirium. She would have been begging for water, pleading for mercy, crying out in agony.

But her pleas were interpreted as demons speaking through her. Trying to manipulate them into stopping the ritual. The more she suffered, the more convinced they became that it was working. That the demons were being driven out. That victory was close.

On the morning of 21st February 2017, the sixth day of the exorcism, something shifted. One of the church members, a woman named Esneyda Orozco Téllez, announced that she'd received a divine revelation. God had told her, she said, that they needed to build a bonfire in the church courtyard. That they needed to throw Vilma into the fire to purify her. To burn the demons out completely.

Nobody questioned this. Nobody said, "Wait, that's madness. We can't burn a human being." The group dynamics, the spiritual certainty, the charismatic authority of the pastor, the six days of escalating commitment to this course of action, all of it combined to make the horrific seem holy.

They built the fire. Dragged Vilma outside. At 5:30 in the morning, whilst it was still dark, they tied her to a tree trunk near the bonfire. Franklin Hernández and Pedro Rocha, two of Pastor Juan's close followers, carried her to the flames.

Then they threw her, naked and bound, into the fire.

Vilma screamed. Thrashed against the ropes, holding her. Her skin blistered and blackened, second and third-degree burns spreading across her body as the flames consumed her. The smell of burning flesh filled the air. And Pastor Juan Rocha stood there watching, according to witnesses, saying with joy in his voice: "She's going to die and then resurrect! As soon as she dies, we'll bring her into the church and give her to God, and she'll be healthy, she won't have those burns anymore!"

He truly believed that. So convinced of his spiritual authority, so certain that God was working through him, that he thought Vilma would die and come back to life healed. Resurrection. Proof of divine power. Vindication of everything they'd done.

Vilma burned for five hours. Five hours tied to that tree trunk, exposed to flames reaching temperatures of 400 degrees Celsius, according to forensic analysis later. Five hours whilst her skin melted and her flesh charred and her screams eventually stopped, whether from death or from her voice giving out, nobody could tell.

Her fifteen-year-old sister found her at dawn. Ran through the predawn darkness, stumbling down muddy paths, sobbing so hard she could barely breathe, to reach their aunt Ángela's farm. The only place in El Cortezal with any connection to the outside world. When Ángela understood what had happened, they rushed back to the church.

Vilma was still alive. Barely. Burns covering 80 per cent of her body. Second and third-degree burns from her face to her legs, across her torso, her arms, everywhere the flames had touched. The kind of burns forensic pathologist Dr Ricardo Larios would later testify were "not compatible with life." The kind of injuries where survival is nearly impossible, even with immediate advanced medical care.

They untied her from the tree. Carried her down from that hill, through the rainforest paths, a journey that must have been excruciating beyond imagining. Every movement, every jostle, pain layered upon pain. Got her to Rosita eventually, to the small hospital there.

Dr David Saravia Flores, the hospital's director, did what he could. "We received the patient in critical condition," he said later. "Second and third-degree burns from the face, behind the ears, across the chest, abdomen, thighs, and legs. These burns are classified as not compatible with life. We performed surgical washing, all the examinations, and prepared her for air transport to Managua. Burns are the type of pain that humans tolerate least."

They airlifted Vilma to Managua on 23rd February. Hospital Lenín Fonseca, the capital's main facility. The doctors there tried everything. Surgical debridement to remove dead tissue. IV fluids to combat the massive dehydration. Pain medication, though nothing truly stops the agony of burns that severe. Antibiotics are necessary because infection is almost inevitable. But the damage was too extensive. Vilma's body couldn't recover.

She died on 28th February 2017. Seven days after she was thrown into the fire. Thirteen days after the exorcism began. Official cause of death: severe burns covering 80 per cent of her body, dehydration, starvation, and organ failure from prolonged trauma.

Back in El Cortezal, the congregation tried to hide what they'd done. Buried evidence. Told a story about Vilma throwing herself into the flames, possessed by a demon that lifted her spirit and dropped her into the fire. Pastor Juan Rocha insisted to the police, insisted to journalists, that he hadn't killed her. That the demon had done it. That evil was to blame.

But Vilma's husband, Reynaldo Peralta Rodriguez, who'd been away travelling when it happened, knew better. "It's unforgivable what they did to us," he told La Prensa newspaper. "They killed my wife, the mother of my two little ones."

The police investigation was swift. Nicaragua's vice president and first lady, Rosario Murillo, called the crime "deplorable and to be condemned" on state media. Called it evidence of "backwardness" that needed to be rooted out. Fifteen people were arrested. Pastor Juan Gregorio Rocha Romero, twenty-three years old. Pedro Rocha, Tomasa Rocha, Franklin Jarquín Hernández, and Esneyda Orozco Téllez, the woman who'd claimed divine revelation told her to build the fire.

The trial began in April 2017. Broadcast live on Nicaraguan television. The entire country was watching as Vilma's relatives took the stand, weeping as they described what they'd witnessed. Roberto Trujillo repeated what Pastor Juan had told him about burning her until only her head was left. Marlene sobbed as she described seeing her sister tied up, unable to help. The fifteen-year-old sister who'd found Vilma burning, traumatised beyond words, struggling to testify.

Ángela García, Vilma's aunt, gave testimony but seemed restrained. Careful. Later, she admitted why. "They told me if I testified at trial, they'd burn my house down," she said. "Here, death threats aren't just words." The family was afraid. Still living in that community. Still surrounded by people loyal to Pastor Juan, people who believed he'd done nothing wrong.

Because that's the other horrifying aspect of this case. The community supported him. In El Cortezal, when journalists came asking questions, nobody wanted to talk. People whispered about "that woman" and echoed the pastor's story that Vilma had thrown herself into the flames. Their loyalty to Pastor Juan was complete. They expressed hope he'd be freed and return to lead them. The church remained an anchor for the community, even after the murder that happened there.

The accused maintained their innocence throughout the trial. "I'm innocent of what they're accusing me of," Esneyda Orozco insisted, pregnant at the time, later raising her child in prison. All five defendants claimed they'd been trying to help. That Vilma was possessed. That they'd been doing God's work.

The jury didn't agree. On 9th May 2017, Judge Alfredo Silva Chamorro handed down the verdicts. Guilty. All five were convicted of murder. Four were also convicted of kidnapping. "The suffering that Trujillo was subjected to is something no human being should go through," Judge Silva said, his voice heavy.

Pastor Juan Gregorio Rocha Romero: thirty years in prison, the maximum sentence under Nicaraguan law. Pedro Rocha, Tomasa Rocha, Franklin Jarquín Hernández, and Esneyda Orozco Téllez: sentences ranging from fifteen to thirty years depending on their level of involvement. Ten more people received shorter sentences, ranging from 12 to 15 years, for participating in or failing to stop the exorcism.

Nicaragua doesn't have the death penalty. Thirty years was all the court could give. The judge noted aggravating circumstances: Vilma had been tied to a tree trunk and left in the fire for five hours. The cruelty was deliberate, systematic, and prolonged.

But here's what haunts me about this case. Those fifteen people truly believed they were helping. They weren't sadists who enjoyed watching someone suffer. They were ordinary people. Churchgoers. Neighbours. Someone's mother, brother or friend. They believed in demons, deliverance, and the power of faith to overcome evil. And that belief, combined with group psychology and a charismatic leader and complete absence of medical oversight, led directly to a young woman's agonising death.

Let's talk about what actually happened to Vilma, not the spiritual interpretation but the psychological and physiological reality. A young woman experiencing acute psychosis, the exact nature of which we'll never know because she never received a proper evaluation, was

identified by her community as possessed. This label changed everything about how people interacted with her. She went from being
Vilma, who needs help, to Vilma, who has demons. And once that
label was applied, once the community agreed this was a spiritual
rather than medical problem, every behaviour she exhibited got filtered through that lens.

Her hallucinations about her sister giving birth to a snake? Classic
psychotic delusion, often religious or supernatural in content. Is she
talking to herself? Responding to auditory hallucinations, hearing
voices that weren't there. Her apparent agitation and fear? Symptoms
of untreated psychosis are terrifying for the person experiencing it. All
of it is treatable with antipsychotic medication and medical care.

But in El Cortezal, these symptoms looked like demon possession.
And once Pastor Juan decided that's what it was, everything Vilma did
confirmed the diagnosis. If she cried, it was demons causing distress. If
she screamed, demons were fighting back. If she begged for water,
demons were trying to manipulate them into stopping. There was no
behaviour, no matter how obviously human, that couldn't be reinterpreted as evidence of possession. This is confirmation bias at its most
lethal.

The group dynamics here are crucial. Fifteen people, all reinforcing each other's beliefs, all witnessing the same events and interpreting
them the same way. When you're in a group, especially a tight-knit religious community with a respected leader, dissent becomes nearly impossible. The pressure to conform, to agree with the group consensus,
is overwhelming. Social psychologists call this groupthink, the phenomenon where the desire for harmony results in irrational decision-
making.

Nobody wanted to be the one to say, "Maybe we should stop.

Maybe we should call a doctor. Maybe she's not possessed, maybe she's just ill." To question the pastor was to question God. To suggest stopping the exorcism was to side with the demons. The psychological pressure to conform and maintain group unity was immense.

And Pastor Juan Rocha, the authority figure, was certain he was right. He had spiritual authority in this community. People trusted his judgment, believed in his connection to God, and deferred to his interpretation of reality. When a charismatic leader speaks with absolute certainty and frames dissent as spiritual weakness or demonic influence, followers find it nearly impossible to question them. This is how cults operate. This is how good people do terrible things whilst believing they're doing good.

As the days passed and Vilma's condition worsened, the group faced a choice. They could admit they were wrong, that this wasn't possession but a medical emergency, that they needed to stop immediately and get her help. Or they could double down, convince themselves that her suffering meant the ritual was working, that they needed to push through to victory.

They chose the latter. Because admitting you're wrong when you've already caused someone immense suffering is psychologically devastating. It's easier to believe you're fighting demons than to accept you're torturing an innocent person. So they escalated. Six days of starvation and dehydration became burning her alive, because once you're that committed to a course of action, once you've invested that much suffering, retreat feels impossible.

Nicaragua is a deeply religious country. Catholicism traditionally dominated, but Evangelical and Pentecostal churches have grown explosively in recent decades, particularly in rural and working-class communities. The Assemblies of God alone has 600,000 members in

Nicaragua. These churches often emphasise spiritual warfare, the reality of demons, the power of faith healing and exorcism. For many people, this isn't a metaphor. It's a literal reality. Demons are real. Possession happens. Deliverance is necessary.

In contexts where mental health services are limited or non-existent, where poverty means people can't afford proper medical care, and where education about mental health conditions is minimal, spiritual explanations fill the gap. If you don't have the vocabulary or framework to understand schizophrenia or bipolar disorder or psychotic episodes, if you've been taught that the spiritual realm is more real than the material one, then possession becomes the obvious explanation for disturbing behaviour.

This doesn't excuse what happened to Vilma. Nothing excuses that. But it helps explain how a community of otherwise decent people convinced themselves that torturing a young woman was an act of love.

After the convictions, there was discussion in Nicaragua about regulating religious practices. About requiring oversight for exorcisms, establishing clearer boundaries between spiritual care and medical neglect. Pablo Cuevas, spokesman for Nicaragua's Human Rights Commission, said: "It is incredible that these things can happen today. There has to be a review by the authorities into all the different denominations and religions. We can't have things like this happening."

But these conversations are complicated. Religious freedom is protected. The government can't tell churches what to believe or how to worship. Where do you draw the line between legitimate religious practice and criminal abuse?

The Assemblies of God leadership tried to distance itself from what happened. Rafael Arista, the superintendent, told reporters wearily that Pastor Juan wasn't a recognised leader. "Unfortunately, it was the press that started using the word 'pastor,'" he sighed. The church has 600,000 members, he said, and this was an isolated incident that didn't represent their beliefs or practices.

But when asked directly about the incident, Arista said something revealing. "In my opinion, this young woman may have thrown herself into the fire." Suggesting she was responsible for her own death. Later, he added, "They fasted for six days seeking liberation for this girl. The intention was good: they sought liberation, but by following a strange voice, they ended up in death. It's possible that a spirit or strange being can take over a human being, but that's no basis for literally throwing them into fire."

The intention was good. That phrase keeps appearing. The road to hell is paved with good intentions.

Vilma's mother, who'd trusted the church to help her daughter, was left with unbearable grief and guilt. She'd allowed the exorcism to happen. She'd believed, along with everyone else, that Vilma was possessed. She'd trusted the pastor's judgment over her own maternal instincts. How do you live with that? How do you reconcile your faith in God with the fact that people acting in God's name murdered your child?

Vilma's two children were split up. The two-year-old daughter went with Reynaldo, who moved away from El Cortezal, and couldn't stay in the place where his wife was murdered. Vilma's older son from a previous relationship moved in with her brother. Aunt Ángela took them under her care as best she could, always carrying the memory of her niece. The fifteen-year-old sister who found Vilma burning struggled with trauma, haunted by the loss, by the guilt of not being able to stop it. "The image that's burned into her mind is her sister being burned alive," said Miuriel Gutiérrez, a women's rights activist who worked with the family. "She says she's okay, but she doesn't want to go back to church."

Pastor Juan Rocha and his co-defendants left ten children behind when they went to prison. All are now being raised by grandparents. Esnayda Orozco Téllez, pregnant at trial, gave birth in prison. The children of both victims and perpetrators are paying the price for adults' decisions.

El Cortezal was torn apart. The Iglesia Misión Celestial still stands, that wooden structure on the hill, but it's largely abandoned now. Some people still gather there, but the shadow of what happened lingers. The spot where they built the bonfire is overgrown now with grass and undergrowth, watered by a rainy season that lasts more than six months. Only a scorched branch and a few inches of frayed rope remain as evidence of the horror that happened there.

The case made national headlines. Dominated newspapers and television news for weeks. When the Nicaraguan portal El 19 Digital made a list of "regrettable events that marked Nicaragua's history in 2017," Vilma's death featured prominently. "Put thousands of Nicaraguans on alert, who, disconcerted by what occurred, joined in the pain of the deceased's mother and children."

But international attention was brief. A few stories in major outlets, then silence. There are no Hollywood films about Vilma Trujillo. No Netflix documentaries. It's too recent, too raw, too uncomfortable. We prefer our possession stories to be historical or at least somewhat distant. Contemporary cases force us to confront that this still happens.

Miuriel Gutiérrez, who works for a women's rights organisation in Rosita, has returned to El Cortezal multiple times over the past years to visit Vilma's family and offer support. She says the murder has had profound effects on surrounding communities. "People started saying, 'Be careful. Don't let what happened to Vilma happen to you," she explained. "Now we pay more attention to how religion is practised."

María López Vigil, a journalist and theologian in Managua, put it this way: "What happened with Trujillo is not a daily occurrence. But priests and pastors preach that the world is divided into light and forces of darkness, and that people need to search for the light through religion to escape the power of the devil." That worldview, that binary division of reality into spiritual warfare, creates conditions where tragedies like Vilma's become possible.

Legal activist Miuriel Gutiérrez had a more direct explanation: "This was a case of misogyny, where there is an explosive mix of religious fundamentalism and abuse of power."

I've thought a lot about what I would say to the people who killed Vilma, if I could. The easy thing would be to call them monsters. To place them in a category separate from normal humanity, to reassure ourselves that we could never do something like that. But I don't think they were monsters. I think they were ordinary people who believed something dangerous and acted on that belief with catastrophic consequences.

They loved God. They wanted to help. They honestly thought they were saving Vilma's soul. And those good intentions led directly to her death. Because good intentions without wisdom, without medical knowledge, without the humility to admit you might be wrong, without the willingness to seek help from people with actual expertise, aren't enough. Sometimes they're actively harmful.

If Vilma had been taken to a psychiatrist instead of a pastor, she'd probably still be alive. If her community had understood mental illness as a medical condition rather than a spiritual one, she'd have received treatment instead of torture. If even one person in that group of fifteen had said, "This isn't right. We need to stop. We need to call for help," she might have survived.

But nobody did. And now Vilma Trujillo García is dead, buried in the ground at twenty-five years old, and fifteen people are in prison trying to understand how their faith led them to commit murder.

The theological questions here are profound and, for believers, deeply troubling. If God is good, if prayer works, if faith can move mountains, why didn't the exorcism heal Vilma? Why did she suffer? Why did she die? The believers would answer that they hadn't completed the ritual properly; that if they'd been stronger in their faith, Vilma would have been delivered. This is the same logic that kept the exorcism going even as she was dying. The ritual can't fail. Only the participants can fail.

But there's another possibility. That the entire belief system is wrong. That Vilma wasn't possessed. Those demons, if they exist, don't operate the way Pastor Juan believed. That God doesn't require us to torture people in His name. That faith, when it contradicts basic human decency and medical reality, has gone badly wrong.

What strikes me most is how preventable this was. At every stage, there were off-ramps. Moments where different choices could have led to a different outcome. When Vilma first showed signs of mental distress, she could have been taken to a doctor in Rosita. When the exorcism began, and she started suffering, someone could have stopped it. When she begged for water, someone could have given it to her. When Esneyda claimed divine revelation to burn her, someone could have said that's madness. At any point during those six days, one person speaking up, one person breaking from group consensus, one person choosing compassion over theology, could have saved her life.

But nobody did. The group dynamics, the spiritual certainty, the charismatic authority of the pastor, the shared belief in demons and deliverance, all of it combined to create a situation where fifteen people watched a young woman die and convinced themselves it was God's will.

I don't know how to end this chapter. There's no redemption here, no silver lining, no lesson that makes Vilma's death feel meaningful. She died horribly, unnecessarily, at the hands of people who thought they were saving her. Her mother lost a daughter. Fifteen people destroyed their own lives and took someone else's. Two small children lost their mother. A community was shattered.

And for what? For a belief. For an interpretation of reality that placed spiritual warfare above human welfare. For a version of faith that values doctrine over compassion, certainty over doubt, and religious authority over medical expertise.

Vilma Trujillo García should be alive. She should be thirty-two years old now, living her life, loving and being loved, watching her children grow up. Instead, she's a name in court records, a victim of religious violence, another person killed by an exorcism that was supposed to save her.

The believers would say I'm wrong. That demons are real, that possession happens, and that deliverance is necessary. That the problem wasn't the exorcism itself but how it was performed. That, with better training, more oversight, and stronger faith, it could have worked.

I look at Vilma's case and see something simpler. I see a young woman who needed help, who trusted her community to provide it, and who died because they gave her religion instead of medicine. I see fifteen people so convinced of their spiritual authority that they couldn't see they were committing murder. I see the catastrophic result of believing faith can substitute for expertise, that prayer can replace medical care, that spiritual intuition trumps objective reality.

And I see how easily it could happen again. Because people still believe in demons. Pastors still perform exorcisms. Communities still interpret mental illness as spiritual warfare. And somewhere, right now, another Vilma might be suffering whilst people who love her watch and pray and convince themselves they're helping.

That's what keeps me up at night. Not the historical cases, not the stories from decades past, but knowing that this isn't over. That faith without wisdom is still killing people. Good intentions without expertise are still causing immense harm. That the next Vilma Trujillo might be dying right now, whilst her community prays over her instead of calling for help.

Vilma Trujillo García died on 28th February 2017. She was twenty-five years old. She deserved better than what her community gave her. She deserved medical care, medical treatment, compassion, and respect for her humanity. She deserved to live.

Instead, she got six days of starvation and five hours of burning alive, all disguised as salvation. And fifteen people who loved God more than they loved her are now in prison, trying to understand where it all went wrong.

The answer is: from the very beginning. The moment they decided she was possessed rather than ill. The moment they chose exorcism over medicine. The moment they prioritised their beliefs over her suffering. That's when it went wrong. Everything that followed was the inevitable consequence of that initial, fatal mistake

CHAPTER VIII

The Demon That Wasn't There

NEW YORK CITY. SUMMER 1977.

David Berkowitz shot thirteen people over the course of a year, killed six of them, and when the police finally caught him in August 1977, he told them a demon living in his neighbour's dog had commanded him to do it. The dog's name was Harvey. He belonged to Sam Carr, which is where the "Son of Sam" name came from. Berkowitz said Harvey was possessed by an ancient demon, that the dog spoke to him in a human voice, gave him orders, told him to kill young women with long dark hair.

The story was bizarre enough to make headlines immediately. Demon dog commands lonely postal worker to murder. Perfect tabloid material. Psychiatrists examined him, debated his sanity, and argued about whether he was psychotic or malingering. The prosecution wanted him to be competent to stand trial. The defence wanted him declared insane. Everyone had an opinion about whether David Berkowitz was hearing demonic voices or just making it all up.

Decades later, in prison, Berkowitz admitted the truth. There was no demon. Harvey the dog never spoke to him. The whole thing was a fabrication, a story he'd constructed because it seemed better than admitting the real reason he'd spent a year hunting young couples in parked cars and shooting them with a .44 calibre revolver.

The real reason, he said, was simpler and somehow worse. He was lonely. Angry. Sexually frustrated. Hated seeing happy couples whilst he sat alone in his apartment with nothing and nobody. So he killed them. That's it. No supernatural compulsion, no demonic possession, no dog whispering murder commands in the night. A man who decided that if he couldn't have what other people had, he'd take it away from them permanently.

But first, that confession, before the decades of recantation and born-again Christianity and admissions that he'd lied about the whole demon thing, we need to understand who David Berkowitz was in 1976 when the killings started. Because the question isn't really whether a demon made him do it. The question is why he thought saying a demon made him do it was preferable to telling the truth about himself.

David Berkowitz was born Richard David Falco on 1st June 1953. His mother, Betty Broder, was married to Tony Falco at the time but was having an affair with a married real estate agent named Joseph Kleinman. When she got pregnant, she couldn't keep the baby without destroying her marriage and exposing the affair. She gave him up for adoption. He was adopted days after birth by Nathan and Pearl Berkowitz, a Jewish couple from the Bronx who couldn't have children of their own. They renamed him David Richard Berkowitz, loved him, and gave him a stable middle-class upbringing.

By all accounts, his childhood was relatively normal until Pearl died of breast cancer when David was fourteen. That loss hit him hard, the way losing a parent in adolescence does. He became withdrawn, difficult, and started getting into trouble. Nathan eventually remarried to a woman David didn't particularly like, which made him feel even more displaced and alone. He was an only child who'd already felt like an outsider, and now his father had a new wife and a new life that didn't seem to have much room for an angry teenage boy.

He joined the Army in 1971, served in South Korea, and got an honourable discharge in 1974. Came back to New York, got a job as a postal worker. Lived alone in various apartments in the Bronx and Yonkers. By his own later admission, he was profoundly lonely. No friends, no girlfriend, no real connections to anyone. Work and home, and long, empty evenings by himself.

He tried to find his birth mother in 1975. Tracked her down, discovered she'd died of cancer in 1967. Never got to meet her, never got answers to the questions he had about why she'd given him up, whether she'd thought about him over the years, whether she'd regretted it. That search ending in another dead mother, another rejection, even if it wasn't intentional, seemed to push something in him over an edge he'd been walking for years.

In his apartment, isolated and angry, David Berkowitz started building a fantasy life that made sense of his isolation. He wasn't alone because he was awkward, difficult, or unable to connect with people. He was alone because he was special, chosen, part of something bigger and darker than ordinary human relationships. The isolation wasn't his fault. It was fate. Destiny. A calling from forces beyond normal human understanding.

This is where the demon story started, in his head, months before he ever mentioned it to the police. Not as a legal defence strategy but as a personal mythology that gave meaning to his loneliness. He moved to an apartment at 35 Pine Street in Yonkers in 1976. His neighbour was Sam Carr, a man in his sixties who owned a black Labrador named Harvey. Berkowitz claimed he started receiving messages through Harvey. That supernatural forces were communicating with him. That Sam Carr's dog was a demon in disguise, speaking to him in a voice only he could hear.

It's worth pausing here to think about what that kind of delusion does psychologically. When you're profoundly isolated, when you feel disconnected from everyone around you, when you look at other people's lives and feel like you're on the outside looking in at something you'll never have, creating a secret spiritual reality can be a way of making that isolation feel chosen rather than inflicted. If demons are talking to you, you're not alone. If you're receiving commands from supernatural forces, you're not powerless. If you're part of some cosmic battle between good and evil, your life has meaning beyond just being a lonely postal worker nobody notices.

The first shooting happened on 29th July 1976, just after 1 am. Jody Valenti, nineteen, and Donna Lauria, eighteen, were sitting in Donna's father's Oldsmobile outside her apartment building at 2860 Buhre Avenue in the Bronx. Just talking, two young women at the end of an evening out. Berkowitz approached the passenger side, pulled out a .44 calibre Bulldog revolver, and fired five shots through the window. Donna died instantly, a bullet to the neck and head. Jody survived, wounded in the thigh.

Berkowitz walked away. Nobody saw him clearly; nobody connected him to the shooting. He'd gotten away with murder. And that success, that rush of power after months of feeling powerless, was apparently intoxicating.

Over the next year, he did it again and again. Always the same pattern. Young couples or young women, sitting in parked cars, usually late at night. He'd approach, fire multiple shots, and disappear into the darkness before anyone could react.

23rd October 1976. Carl Denaro, twenty, and Rosemary Keenan were sitting in a car in Flushing, Queens. Berkowitz fired through the rear window. The bullet grazed Carl's skull and nearly killed him, but he survived. Rosemary was uninjured.

27th November 1976. Joanne Lomino, eighteen, and Donna DeMasi, sixteen, were sitting on Joanne's front porch in Bellerose, Queens, just after midnight. Berkowitz approached, asked for directions, then pulled out the gun. Shot them both. Donna survived relatively unscathed. Joanne was paralysed from the waist down, confined to a wheelchair for the rest of her life.

30th January 1977. Christine Freund, twenty-six, and her fiancé, John Diel, were sitting in a car in Ridgewood, Queens, after seeing a film. Two shots through the window. Christine died hours later from gunshot wounds to the head. John survived.

8th March 1977. Virginia Voskerichian, twenty-one, a student at Barnard College, was walking home from school in Forest Hills. Berkowitz shot her in the face at close range. She raised her textbooks to shield herself, but the bullet went straight through. She died instantly.

The city was terrified. The tabloids screamed about a killer targeting young women. Women with long dark hair started cutting it short or dyeing it blonde because that seemed to be his type, though that pattern wasn't as clear as people believed. Couples stopped parking in secluded spots. Police had almost nothing. Just a .44 calibre revolver, ballistics matching across the shootings, and a pattern of seemingly random violence.

17th April 1977. Valentina Suriani, eighteen, and Alexander Esau, twenty, were sitting in a car near the Hutchinson River Parkway in the Bronx. Multiple shots. Both killed. This time, Berkowitz left something behind. A letter addressed to Captain Joseph Borrelli of the NYPD was placed near the bodies.

The letter was rambling, misspelt, and strange. "I am deeply hurt by your calling me a woman hater," he wrote. "I am not. But I am a monster. I am the 'Son of Sam.' I am a little 'brat.'" He talked about his bloodlust, about being programmed to kill. "I love to hunt. Prowling the streets looking for fair game, tasty meat." He signed it "Mr Monster."

In May, he sent another letter, this time to columnist Jimmy Breslin at the New York Daily News. "Hello from the gutters of N.Y.C., which are filled with dog manure, vomit, stale wine, urine and blood." He mentioned "Sam" and being controlled, gave cryptic hints about future attacks. The Daily News published it on 5th June. "Son of Sam" became headline news. Everyone in New York knew about him, feared him, speculated about who he was.

26th June 1977. Judy Placido, seventeen, and Sal Lupo, twenty, were in a car outside a disco in Bayside, Queens. Three shots. Both were wounded but survived.

31st July 1977. Stacy Moskowitz, twenty, and Robert Violante, twenty, were parked near the Shore Parkway in Brooklyn. Four shots. Stacy died from head wounds. Robert survived but was blinded in one eye, his sight in the other severely damaged.

But this time, witnesses had seen something. A man walking away from the scene, getting into a car parked near a fire hydrant. The car, a cream-coloured Ford Galaxie, had received a parking ticket that night. Police traced the ticket to David Berkowitz, 35 Pine Street, Yonkers.

On 10th August 1977, detectives John Falotico and Ed Zigo drove to Yonkers. Found Berkowitz's car parked on the street. Looked through the window. Saw a duffel bag on the back seat. Inside the bag, visible through the car's window, was the handle of what appeared to be a rifle.

They waited. At 10 pm, Berkowitz came out of his apartment building and got in his car. Detectives surrounded him. Detective John Falotico approached. "Police. Don't move."

Berkowitz smiled. "Well, you got me. What took you so long?"

In the car, they found a .44 calibre Bulldog revolver loaded with bullets. In his apartment, they found a journal documenting his stalking patterns, maps with locations circled, letters about demons and Sam and Harvey. On his walls, bizarre writings about destruction and fire.

He confessed immediately. Seemed almost relieved. Started telling them about the demons, about Sam Carr's dog Harvey, about voices that commanded him to kill. "Sam is the Devil," he said. "I am Sam's slave." Harvey was six thousand years old, he claimed. An ancient demon who'd been commanding him through Sam Carr. There were other demons too, operating through neighbourhood dogs, part of an ancient network of evil.

The confession was detailed, elaborate, and completely insane sounding. Dr David Abrahamsen, examining him for the prosecution, concluded he was psychotic. "His thinking was so abnormal, so primitive, that he believed he was following the instructions of a demon who lived inside a dog." But Abrahamsen also concluded that Berkowitz was legally sane, capable of knowing right from wrong, and capable of conforming his behaviour to the law, even if he'd chosen not to.

Dr Martin Lubin, examining him for the defence, concluded he was paranoid schizophrenic, that the demons were real to him, genuine delusions driving his behaviour.

Judge Joseph Corso ordered a medical evaluation. A panel of psychiatrists spent thirty days examining Berkowitz. Their conclusion: competent to stand trial. He understood the charges against him, could assist in his own defence, and knew the difference between right and wrong.

On 23rd May 1978, Berkowitz appeared before Judge Corso in the Brooklyn Supreme Court. Pleaded guilty to six counts of second-degree murder, seven counts of attempted murder, and numerous assault charges. He waived his right to an appeal. "I'm guilty," he said simply. "I'll plead guilty. I'll go to prison forever."

Judge Corso sentenced him to 365 years. Six consecutive life sentences of twenty-five years to life for each murder. No possibility of parole. David Berkowitz would die in prison.

And then, years later, in Attica, Sullivan, and later Clinton Correctional Facility, he started telling a different story.

In the late 1970s and early 1980s, whilst in prison, Berkowitz became a born-again Christian. Started reading the Bible, attending chapel services, and talking about finding redemption and forgiveness. And as part of that transformation, he began admitting that the demon-dog story was a lie.

No, Harvey wasn't speaking to him in demonic voices. No ancient evil commanding him to kill. No supernatural compulsion at all. He'd made it all up because it seemed like a better story than the truth. Claiming demon possession might get him declared insane. Saying he was following orders made him feel less responsible for what he'd done.

The real reason he'd killed those people, he said in various interviews over the years, was anger and sexual frustration and profound loneliness. He'd see couples kissing in parked cars and feel such rage at his own isolation that he wanted to destroy what he couldn't have. The murders weren't random. They were targeted at a specific kind of happiness he felt excluded from. Young people in love, couples enjoying each other's company, intimacy he'd never experienced and didn't think he ever would.

"The demons were an elaborate fantasy," he told journalist Maury Terry in the 1990s. "I created them to shift the blame. I didn't want to take responsibility for the terrible things I'd done, so I invented this story about being controlled by forces beyond my power."

In a 1999 interview from prison, he was even more explicit. "I just wanted to hurt people because I was hurting. I saw people being happy, and I hated them for it. So, I shot them. That's the truth. Not demons, not voices, not possession. Just me, being angry and alone and taking it out on innocent people."

But there's another complication. Some investigators, particularly journalist Maury Terry, believed Berkowitz wasn't acting alone. That he was part of a satanic cult, that some of the shootings were committed by other members, that the demon story was partly true in the sense that he was involved with people who believed in demons and practised ritual magic. Terry spent decades investigating these claims and published "The Ultimate Evil" in 1987, laying out the cult theory.

Berkowitz himself gave inconsistent statements about this. Sometimes he hinted that others were involved. Sometimes he insisted he acted alone. Sometimes he said he was protecting cult members. Sometimes he said the cult theory was nonsense. The NYPD investigated, found no credible evidence of accomplices, and concluded Berkowitz acted alone.

So which version is true? Was David Berkowitz experiencing genuine psychotic delusions when he killed six people, or was he a lonely, angry man who invented the demon story to avoid responsibility? Was he part of a satanic cult, or was that another fabrication? Did he hear voices commanding him to kill, or did he pretend to hear voices because it was easier than admitting he'd made a conscious choice to murder strangers?

The psychiatric evidence is contradictory. Some experts genuinely believed he was psychotic. Others thought he was malingering. His own testimony changed over time, from insisting the demons were real to admitting they were fabricated to sometimes hinting that maybe there was some truth to multiple versions.

Here's what we know for certain. David Berkowitz was profoundly isolated and lonely in the months leading up to the first murder. He'd lost his adoptive mother at fourteen and discovered his birth mother was dead when he tried to find her at twenty-two. He had no close relationships, no romantic connections, no real friends. He worked a job that required minimal human interaction and lived alone in increasingly shabby apartments.

Social isolation combined with loss and rejection can trigger or exacerbate mental illness in vulnerable people. Loneliness isn't just unpleasant; it's physiologically stressful. Chronic isolation affects brain chemistry, increases inflammation, disrupts sleep, and impairs cognitive function. In someone already predisposed to psychiatric problems, that kind of sustained stress can push them into psychosis.

But we also know that Berkowitz was intelligent and calculating enough to plan these murders, to avoid capture for over a year, to taunt police with letters that demonstrated clear awareness of what he was doing and how it would be perceived. That argues against severe psychosis impairing his judgement. A truly delusional person doesn't usually have that level of organised planning ability.

The demon dog story could have been a genuine delusion. Command hallucinations are a real symptom of schizophrenia and other psychotic disorders. People hear voices telling them to do things, often violent things, and those voices can seem completely real and external and impossible to resist. The voices might be attributed to demons, gods, aliens, government mind control, whatever cultural framework the person has available to explain the inexplicable experience of hearing voices that aren't there.

But the demon dog story could also have been exactly what Berkowitz later said it was: a fabrication designed to make him seem crazy and, by extension, less responsible. Malingering mental illness is well-documented. People constantly fake symptoms to avoid legal consequences. If you're facing 365 years in prison, claiming demonic possession might seem like a reasonable strategy even if you know it's a lie.

Or, and this is the possibility that interests me most, it could have been both. Berkowitz might have genuinely experienced some form of dissociation or delusional thinking whilst also consciously elaborating and exaggerating those experiences into a more coherent narrative for legal purposes. The line between delusion and fabrication isn't always clear. Sometimes people half-believe their own lies, especially when those lies serve an important psychological function.

Think about what the demon story did for Berkowitz psychologically. It explained his behaviour in a way that preserved some sense of himself as not fundamentally evil. He wasn't a man who chose to murder innocent people out of petty jealousy. He was a victim himself, controlled by forces beyond his understanding, compelled to do terrible things against his will. That narrative is much easier to live with than the alternative.

The born-again Christian conversion adds another layer of complication. When Berkowitz recanted the demon story in the 1980s and 1990s, he was in the middle of a religious transformation that required him to take full responsibility for his sins to be forgiven. The Christian framework he'd adopted didn't allow for "the devil made me do it" as an excuse. He needed to confess his own guilt, his own choices, his own evil to access redemption. So the recantation served that spiritual narrative as much as the original demon story had served his legal defence.

Which means we still don't know the truth. We have a man who told one story at arrest, a different story decades later after religious conversion, whose medical evaluations were contradictory. We have evidence that he was isolated and damaged and angry, which could explain the murders without requiring supernatural intervention. We also have evidence that loneliness and loss can trigger genuine psychosis in vulnerable people, which means the voices might have been real even if the demon interpretation was a cultural overlay on an internal psychiatric experience.

The families of his victims have never found peace in any of these explanations. Neysa Moskowitz, Stacy's mother, has been to every parole hearing, fighting to keep Berkowitz in prison. "He's a liar and a manipulator," she's said repeatedly. "Whether it was demons or not, he made a choice. He took my daughter from me." Donna Lauria's parents, Mike and Rose, never recovered. Rose died in 2007, still grieving her daughter. Mike survived until 2010, carrying that grief for thirty-three years.

Joanne Lomino, paralysed at eighteen by Berkowitz's bullets, has spent decades in a wheelchair. "I don't care about his demons or his excuses," she told reporters. "What he did to me was real. The wheelchair is real. Everything he took from me is real."

David Berkowitz is still in prison. He's been denied parole repeatedly, most recently in 2022, and will likely die there. He now works in prison ministry, counsels other inmates, and claims to have found redemption through Christianity. He's written letters of apology to victims' families. Most haven't responded. Some have told him his apologies mean nothing.

In a 2017 interview, he said: "The media made me out to be a terrible monster, and I was a pretty terrible monster. But the truth is I was just a very confused and angry young man." Then added: "There are no demons. I made the whole thing up. I take full responsibility for what I did."

But in that same interview, when pressed about the voices, about what he experienced in 1976 and 1977, he became vague. "I was hearing things, yes. Whether that was mental illness or something else, I don't know. All I know is I'm responsible for my actions regardless of what I was hearing."

That ambiguity feels deliberate. Leaving room for multiple interpretations. Maintaining the mystery because the mystery is all he has left. If the demon story is completely false, he's just a murderer who invented an elaborate lie. If it's completely true, he's a victim of forces beyond his control. The uncertain space between those extremes is where David Berkowitz lives now, decades into a sentence that will end only when he dies.

The Son of Sam case isn't about whether demons are real or whether David Berkowitz was genuinely possessed. It's about the stories we tell ourselves to make sense of our own worst impulses, the narratives we construct to preserve some sense of ourselves as not fundamentally monstrous.

David Berkowitz killed six people and wounded seven more. That's indisputable. Whether he did it because a demon dog commanded him, or because he was psychotic and heard voices he interpreted as demonic, or because he was lonely and angry and made a conscious choice to destroy what he couldn't have, the outcome is the same. Six people are dead. Families were destroyed. A city lived in terror for over a year.

The demon story, whether true or fabricated, ultimately doesn't change those facts. It doesn't bring anyone back. It doesn't undo the trauma inflicted on the survivors. It doesn't make Berkowitz any less responsible under the law.

But it does tell us something important about how we understand violence and evil. We want there to be a reason. A cause we can point to and say, "That's why this happened, that's the explanation." Demons are a reason. Psychosis is a reason. Loneliness and sexual frustration are reasons. They're all ways of making the incomprehensible slightly more comprehensible.

The truth might be that some acts of violence don't have satisfying explanations. Sometimes people just break, whether from psychosis or isolation or their own worst impulses overwhelming whatever better angels they might have had. Sometimes the demon is internal, the voice is your own worst thoughts amplified, the command to kill comes from yourself, even if it doesn't feel like it at the time.

In the end, here's what I think happened. I think David Berkowitz was profoundly damaged by isolation and loss. I think he probably did experience some form of psychiatric disturbance, whether full psychosis or something milder like severe dissociation or intrusive thoughts he couldn't control. I think he constructed the demon narrative partly because it felt true to his internal experience and partly because it served his legal and psychological needs. I think he later recanted because a different narrative, one of personal responsibility and redemption, better served his new identity as a born-again Christian.

I think all of those stories are partial truths, and none of them fully explain why a postal worker from the Bronx spent a year shooting young couples in parked cars. Because humans are complicated and our motivations are rarely pure or simple. We contain multitudes, contradictions, competing narratives about who we are and why we do what we do.

The demon didn't make David Berkowitz kill six people. But neither did simple loneliness nor calculated evil. It was probably all of those things at once, tangled together in ways even Berkowitz himself doesn't fully understand. The demon was real in the sense that something drove him to commit those murders, something he experienced as external to his conscious will, even if it originated in his own damaged psyche. The demon was fake in the sense that no supernatural entity was involved, no ancient evil spoke through a neighbour's dog.

What's left is a man who killed people and then tried to explain why. And like most explanations for inexplicable violence, it satisfies no one.

The dog didn't make him do it. Neither did demons. He did it himself, for reasons that probably made sense to him at the time but later stopped making sense, for motivations that shifted and changed as his own narrative about himself evolved. That's the uncomfortable truth. We're responsible for our actions even when we don't fully understand them ourselves, even when they seem to come from somewhere outside our conscious control, even when we construct elaborate mythologies to explain away our own capacity for evil.

David Berkowitz is where he belongs, in prison, regardless of whether demons were involved. The question of possession, genuine or fabricated, is ultimately irrelevant to justice. But it's not irrelevant to understanding how ordinary people commit extraordinary violence, how we make sense of our worst impulses, how we live with ourselves after we've done terrible things.

Sometimes the demon is us, looking back at ourselves in the mirror and not recognising what we've become.

CHAPTER IX

A Demon Named Ezurate

OKLAHOMA CITY, OKLAHOMA. SPRING 1986.

Sean Sellers was sixteen years old when he shot his mother and stepfather while they slept. Walked into their bedroom just after midnight, dressed only in black underwear to limit blood spatter, stood over them in the darkness, and fired a .44 Magnum revolver point-blank into their heads. Paul Lee Bellofatto, forty-three, died first. The shot woke Vonda Bellofatto, thirty-two. She rose, confused and terrified. Sean shot her in the face. Then he went back to his own room, arranged the crime scene to look like an intruder had broken in, hid the gun, and went to sleep.

When questioned by police the next day, Sean seemed genuinely shocked by what had happened. Confused. Like he couldn't quite remember doing it, or couldn't connect the memory to himself. "I didn't do it," he kept saying. Not defensively, not like someone caught in a lie. More like someone trying to understand something that didn't make sense. "I couldn't have done it. That's not me."

Except it was him. The evidence was overwhelming. His finger-prints are on the gun. Gunshot residue on his hands. No sign of forced entry, no evidence anyone else had been in the house. Sean had killed his parents. There was no question about that. The only real questions were why and whether the person who pulled that trigger was really Sean Sellers at all.

Six months earlier, on 8th September 1985, a convenience store clerk named Robert Paul Bower had been shot and killed during what looked like a robbery. Bower was thirty-six years old, working the night shift at a Circle K in northwest Oklahoma City. The case went cold almost immediately. No witnesses, no clear suspect, no obvious motive beyond the small amount of cash taken from the register. Another unsolved murder in Oklahoma City, another family destroyed by random violence.

After Sean was arrested for killing his parents, he eventually confessed to killing Robert Bower, too. Said he'd done it because Bower refused to sell him beer. Or because he wanted to know what it felt like to kill someone. Or because of a Satanic ritual. The story kept changing. Sometimes he remembered it clearly. Sometimes he claimed it was someone else, someone who looked like him but wasn't him. Someone named Ezurate.

Ezurate was a demon, Sean said. Or maybe Ezurate was an alternate personality. Or maybe Ezurate was just Sean himself when he stopped being Sean, when something else took over and did things Sean would never do. The explanation shifted depending on who was asking and when, but the core claim remained consistent. Sean Sellers didn't kill those people. Someone else did, someone who lived inside him, someone he couldn't control.

The prosecution called it an act. A disturbed teenager trying to avoid responsibility for murder by claiming demonic possession or multiple personalities or whatever story seemed most likely to get him off. The defence called it a genuine psychiatric illness, dissociative identity disorder caused by severe childhood abuse, a fractured psyche that had created alternate identities to cope with abuse Sean couldn't otherwise process.

Both sides had evidence. Both sides had expert witnesses. Neither side could prove definitively what had happened inside Sean Sellers' head when he pulled those triggers. And that uncertainty, that fundamental unknowability of another person's internal experience, would follow Sean all the way to the execution chamber thirteen years later.

But first, the execution, before the legal battles and the international protests and the questions about whether it's right to kill a child even if that child committed murder, we need to understand who Sean Sellers was before he became Ezurate. Or before he claimed to become Ezurate. Or before something broke inside him that he could only explain through the language of possession and alternate identities.

Sean Richard Sellers was born on 18th May 1969 in California. His early childhood was unstable in a way that leaves marks. His biological father wasn't in the picture. His mother, Vonda, was young, struggling, and constantly on the move. Sean's early years were a series of different homes, different men in his mother's life, and different schools where he was always the new kid trying to fit in.

When Sean was about five, Vonda married a man who would become, by Sean's later account, his primary abuser. The details are hard to verify because they come mainly from Sean's own testimony years later, when he had every reason to make his childhood sound worse than it was to support an insanity defence. But multiple sources, including family members who had no reason to lie for him, confirmed that Sean's stepfather during those years was violent, unpredictable, and cruel in ways that went beyond normal discipline.

Physical abuse was part of it. Being hit, being locked in closets, and being punished harshly for minor infractions. But emotional abuse was worse in some ways. Being told he was worthless, a burden, that nobody wanted him. The kind of systematic psychological destruction that teaches a child they're fundamentally unlovable and wrong.

That marriage ended when Sean was about ten. Vonda divorced the abusive stepfather, moved to Oklahoma, and eventually married Paul Lee Bellofatto. By all accounts, Lee was decent to Sean, tried to be a good stepfather, and gave the family some stability they hadn't had before. But by then the damage was done. Sean was already struggling with depression, rage, and a sense of himself as fundamentally broken.

He was a bright kid. That's what everyone said. Smart, articulate, good at school when he bothered to engage. But he was also weird in ways that made other kids avoid him. Too intense, too interested in dark things, too willing to say shocking things to get attention. He didn't have many friends. The friends he did have were other outsiders, other kids who didn't quite fit, who were drawn to the same dark interests Sean was developing.

As a sophomore at Putnam City North High School in Oklahoma City, Sean got into heavy metal music. Not unusual for a teenage boy in the 1980s. But he went deeper than most kids did, past the mainstream bands into more extreme stuff. Death metal, black metal, and bands that explicitly incorporated Satanic imagery and anti-Christian themes. Again, not that unusual. Lots of teenagers go through a phase of fascination with transgressive content, pushing boundaries and shocking adults.

But Sean didn't just listen to the music. He started reading about Satanism. Not the Church of Satan's essentially atheistic philosophy, but darker traditions. Demonology texts. Grimoires. Instructions for summoning entities. And he started practising what he read. Rituals in his bedroom. Attempts to contact demons. Offerings and incantations and all the theatrical trappings of teenage occultism.

He read The Satanic Bible by Anton LaVey "hundreds of times" between the ages of fifteen and sixteen, he later wrote. In his own blood, he wrote: "I renounce God. I renounce Christ. I will serve only Satan. To my enemies, death." He drank his own blood at satanic rituals, took a Satanic Bible to classes, and talked of demons flying and influencing him. This wasn't casual interest. This was immersion.

In a confession letter written from prison years later, he reflected on this period: "I got very involved in Satanism. I truly thought it was an honest way to live, and the rituals of it would enable me to control my life."

Control. That word is important. For a child who'd been systematically abused, who'd been told repeatedly he was powerless and worthless, Satanism offered a lens for reclaiming power. The rituals, the transgression, the deliberate embrace of what society feared, all of it was about taking control in a life that had always been controlled by others.

His mother and stepfather knew something was wrong, but didn't know how to address it. They took him to counselling. The therapist diagnosed depression, prescribed medication, and suggested family therapy. Sean went a few times, said what he thought the therapist wanted to hear, and stopped going. The medication helped for a while, then stopped helping. The darkness he was carrying inside kept growing.

In the year before the murders, Sean's behaviour escalated. He was staying out late, possibly using drugs, though the evidence on that is unclear. He was becoming more hostile at home, more withdrawn, more obsessed with his Satanic interests. His grades were dropping. He was getting into fights at school. All the classic warning signs of a teenager in a serious crisis.

And he was hearing voices. Or he claimed he was hearing voices. Or something was happening in his head that he interpreted as voices, that he experienced as external to himself, even though they were coming from inside. A voice that called itself Ezurate. A voice that told him he was special, powerful, chosen for something important. A voice that told him he didn't have to take abuse from anyone anymore, that he could fight back, that violence was not only acceptable but necessary.

Whether that voice was a genuine auditory hallucination from psychosis, or an alternate personality from dissociative identity disorder, or just Sean's own dark thoughts that he projected outward to avoid taking responsibility for them, we'll never know for certain. What we know is that by September 1985, Sean Sellers believed he was sharing his body with a demonic entity named Ezurate. And Ezurate wanted blood.

The night Robert Bower died, 8th September 1985, Sean and his friend Richard Howard went to the Circle K convenience store around midnight. Sean was carrying a .357 Magnum revolver borrowed from Richard's grandfather. They'd been talking about Satanic rituals, about needing to make a sacrifice, about proving their commitment to dark forces. According to Sean's later confession, he wanted to know what it felt like to kill someone.

Robert Bower was working the night shift. Thirty-six years old, married, father of two. Working overnight at a convenience store to make ends meet, doing a job that's statistically one of the most dangerous in America because you're alone with a cash register and whoever walks through that door after midnight.

Sean walked in. Asked for cigarettes. When Bower turned to get them, Sean pulled out the gun and shot him three times. Bower fell. Sean grabbed some cash from the register, not much, maybe thirty or forty dollars. Then he left. The whole thing took less than a minute.

He and Richard drove around for a while. According to Richard's later testimony, they'd performed a Satanic ritual beforehand. Whether they were celebrating a successful sacrifice or panicking about having just committed murder, the accounts differ. Sean went home. Hid the gun. Went to sleep. Woke up the next morning and went to school as if nothing had happened.

For six months, he got away with it. The police had no leads. Bower's murder was tragic but not unusual enough to warrant extensive resources. Life went on. Sean kept going to school, kept living at home with his mother and stepfather, kept hearing Ezurate's voice telling him he'd done well, he'd proven himself, he was ready for the next step.

The next step, apparently, was killing his parents.

Sean's relationship with his mother and Lee had deteriorated badly by early 1986. They were trying to set boundaries, enforce curfews, and get him away from the friends who were clearly bad influences. They interfered in his relationship with his girlfriend, a high school dropout. Normal parenting stuff, but Sean experienced it as persecution. Ezurate told him they were trying to control him, suppress his power, keep him weak. Ezurate told him he needed to be free of their interference.

Or that's what Sean said later. What we know objectively is that on the night of 5th March 1986, Sean went days without sleep, taking speed and smoking marijuana according to later testimony. He performed an occult ritual beforehand. "There was nothing but cold hatred in me," he said later.

After his parents had gone to bed, Sean dressed in only black underwear to limit blood spatter. Loaded a .44 Magnum revolver. Walked into their bedroom. Stood over them in the darkness. Shot Paul Lee first in the head whilst he slept. The shot woke Vonda. She rose, trying to understand what was happening. Sean shot her in the face.

Then Sean went back to his room. Arranged the crime scene to look like an intruder had broken in. Cleaned the gun. Hid it. Got into bed. When police arrived the next morning, responding to a call from Sean saying he'd found his parents dead, he seemed visibly distressed. Crying, shaking, asking what happened, who could have done this. The performance was convincing enough that initially, police treated him as a witness, not a suspect.

But the evidence didn't support the presence of an intruder. No forced entry. No signs of struggle. Nothing stolen. Just two people were shot at close range in their bed, and their teenage son, who claimed to have slept through gunshots fired fifteen feet from his bedroom. When police tested Sean's hands for gunshot residue, it came back positive. When they searched his room, they found the gun.

Confronted with the evidence, Sean's story fell apart. Sort of. He admitted he'd been in the room when they died. He admitted he'd been holding the gun. But he maintained he didn't do it, not really.

Ezurate did it. Ezurate took control. Ezurate pulled the trigger whilst Sean watched from somewhere inside his own head, helpless to stop it.

The confession to Robert Bower's murder came later, after weeks of interrogation, after Sean's lawyers had already started building an insanity defence. Some investigators thought Sean confessed to Bower's murder to establish a pattern of demonic possession, to strengthen his claim that he wasn't in control of his actions. Others thought the confession was genuine, a breakthrough moment where Sean finally admitted the full extent of what Ezurate had made him do.

The trial began in September 1986. Sean was sixteen but would be tried as an adult because of the severity of the crimes. Oklahoma law allowed juveniles to be tried and sentenced as adults for capital murder. The question before the jury wasn't whether Sean had killed three people. That was established. The question was whether he was legally sane at the time, whether he could tell right from wrong, whether he should be held fully responsible or sent to a psychiatric facility instead.

The prosecution's case was straightforward. Sean Sellers was a disturbed, angry teenager who had gotten involved in Satanism, who'd confused fiction with reality, who had decided to kill for the thrill of it and then claimed demonic possession to avoid consequences. They brought in witnesses who testified about Sean's behaviour in the months before the murders. The Satanic interests, the violent fantasies, and the deteriorating relationship with his parents.

His attorneys also argued that Sellers was addicted to Dungeons & Dragons. Sellers would later write that the game had no part in his crimes and that "using my past as a common example of the effects of the game is either irrational or fanatical." This was the height of the Satanic Panic of the 1980s, when parents and prosecutors blamed everything from heavy metal music to role-playing games for teen violence.

They argued that his claim of demonic possession was internally contradictory. Sometimes he said Ezurate was a demon who possessed him. Sometimes he said Ezurate was an alternate personality. Sometimes he described it as a voice giving commands, other times as full blackouts where he couldn't remember what Ezurate did. The story kept changing, which suggested fabrication rather than a genuine psychiatric disorder.

Most damningly, they pointed out that Sean had tried to cover up both murders. He'd hidden the gun after shooting Bower. He'd arranged the crime scene and acted shocked when police arrived after his parents' deaths. Someone genuinely possessed, someone truly not in control of their actions, wouldn't have the presence of mind to hide evidence and feign innocence. The cover-up proved consciousness of guilt and showed he knew what he'd done was wrong.

The defence's case was more complicated. They brought in psychiatrists who'd examined Sean extensively. Dr Dorothy Lewis, a renowned neuropsychiatrist from New York who specialised in violent youth, testified that Sean suffered from dissociative identity disorder. She'd documented multiple personalities, she said. Ezurate was one of them, but there were others, too. Different ages, different characteristics, different memories.

According to Lewis, Sean's childhood abuse had been so severe and sustained that his psyche had fragmented as a survival mechanism. When the abuse got too bad to bear, his mind created other identities to take the suffering. Those identities continued into adolescence, and when Sean needed to do something his core personality couldn't handle, like committing murder, one of the alters would take over.

The Satanism, in Lewis's interpretation, wasn't the cause of the murders. Sean attempted to make sense of what was happening to him. He experienced himself as having multiple identities, as sometimes being controlled by something that wasn't him. The cultural framework available to a teenager in 1980s Oklahoma for understanding that experience was demonic possession. So he read about demons, practised Satanic rituals, named his alter identity Ezurate, and built a mythology that explained his fractured sense of self.

Other defence psychiatrists testified about Sean's brain scans showing abnormalities in the frontal lobe, about his family history of mental illness, and about the documented abuse. They argued this was a genuinely sick kid who needed treatment, not execution. Punishing Sean for what Ezurate did was like punishing someone for crimes committed while sleepwalking or in a psychotic fugue state.

The jury didn't buy it. In October 1986, after deliberating for several hours, they found Sean Sellers guilty of three counts of first-degree murder. In the penalty phase, they sentenced him to death. Three death sentences, one for each victim. The judge confirmed the sentences. Sean would be sent to death row at the Oklahoma State Penitentiary in McAlester to await execution.

He was sixteen years old.

Over the next thirteen years, Sean's case went through multiple appeals. His lawyers argued that executing someone for crimes committed as a juvenile violated international human rights standards, that new evidence of mental illness warranted a new trial, and that the original defence had been inadequate. The appeals were all denied.

During those thirteen years on death row, something changed in Sean. Or he claimed something changed. He became a born-again Christian. Renounced Satanism completely, said he'd been deceived by evil, that he'd opened himself to demonic influence through his occult practices.

He said he had become a Christian even before his 1986 trial. He later began a religious ministry from prison, even though his critics considered the change an act. "It's not some title I put upon myself, or display as a label on my shirt. It is the heart of WHO I AM and ALL I WANT TO BE. Christian. Christlike," he wrote in his Internet journal. "I dream of heaven."

He wrote books about his conversion, did interviews, appeared on The Oprah Winfrey Show, and appeared on Geraldo to discuss the dangers of devil-worshipping. A Christian book publisher issued his autobiography, Web of Darkness, in 1990. He also authored a book of love stories and poems titled Shuladore, self-published and sold via his website. Under Oklahoma law, a defendant cannot profit from crime, and a grand jury investigated whether Sellers profited from the book, but no indictment resulted.

The demonic possession narrative evolved. In his Christian period, Sean didn't deny that he'd committed the murders anymore. He took responsibility for the actions, said Ezurate wasn't an alter personality but an actual demon he'd invited in through Satanic rituals. He said becoming a Christian had driven the demon out, that he was no longer possessed, that he was genuinely remorseful for what he'd done.

Some people saw this as proof that the whole thing had been a performance. First, he'd claimed possession to avoid legal responsibility, then he'd claimed Christian redemption to gain sympathy and support for his appeals. Another manipulation by someone who'd been manipulating people since he was a teenager.

Others saw it as a genuine transformation. Bill Mason, a minister who prayed with Sellers and protested the execution, said Sean Sellers was being honest. "He wants to make up for what he's done," said Mason, who wore a picture of a young Sellers with the slogan, "Stop Killing Kids."

They pointed to his work in prison, his ministry to other inmates, and his consistent message about the dangers of occult involvement. They argued that whatever had been wrong with him as a teenager, whether possession or mental illness or both, had been healed through faith.

The psychiatric community remained divided. Some experts who'd examined Sean maintained he had genuine dissociative identity disorder that had never been adequately treated. Others thought he had antisocial personality disorder, that he was essentially a psychopath who'd learned to mimic whatever emotional responses got him what he wanted. A few thoughts, both diagnoses could be true simultaneously, that someone with dissociative disorder could also develop psychopathic traits as a result of severe early trauma.

As his execution date approached, international pressure mounted. Amnesty International called it a human rights violation to execute someone for crimes committed as a juvenile. The United Nations condemned it. Even prosecutors in other countries wrote letters to Oklahoma's governor asking for clemency, pointing out that most developed nations had abolished the death penalty entirely, and those that hadn't at least didn't execute people for crimes committed when they were children.

The argument wasn't that Sean was innocent. Everyone agreed he'd killed three people. The argument was about culpability. Can a sixteen-year-old with documented mental illness and serious psychological damage truly understand the finality of death, truly appreciate the consequences of murder, and truly be held to the same standard as an adult? And even if they can, is it right to kill them for it?

Oklahoma Governor Frank Keating denied clemency. Said Sean had been tried fairly, convicted properly, and sentenced in accordance with the law. The murders had been brutal and calculated, he said. Bower had been shot for no reason beyond Sean wanting to know what it felt like to kill someone. Vonda and Paul Lee had been executed in their sleep by the child they'd tried to help. Justice demanded that the sentence be carried out.

Oklahoma Attorney General Drew Edmondson defended the decision: "Sean Sellers' case is an aberration because Sean Sellers is an aberration. He committed multiple murders, the first one out of some sort of curiosity." The attorney general complained that the world media didn't appreciate that hundreds of juvenile killers in Oklahoma never faced the death penalty and many of their cases never left juvenile court.

Sean Sellers spent his final day in a holding cell next to the room where he was to die by lethal injection. He dined on Chinese food as his last meal: eggrolls, sweet-and-sour shrimp, batter-fried shrimp. He spent most of the day visiting with about ten friends he'd met since entering prison in 1986. His last appeal to the U.S. Supreme Court was rejected about 7 pm on 3rd February 1999.

On 4th February 1999, just after midnight, Sean Sellers was led into the execution chamber at the Oklahoma State Penitentiary. He was twenty-nine years old. He'd spent thirteen years on death row, nearly half his life.

His final statement addressed his stepsiblings: "All the people that are hating me right now and are here waiting to see me die, when you wake up in the morning, you're not going to feel any different. You're going to hate me as much tomorrow as tonight. When you wake up and nothing has changed inside, reach out to God, and He will be there for you. Reach out to God, and He will heal you. Let Him touch your hearts. Don't hate all your lives. I love you all."

In the final minutes before injection, Sellers sang modern Christian music. Then he said loudly, "Here I come, Father; I'm coming home."

They administered the drugs. Sodium thiopental to induce unconsciousness. Pancuronium bromide to paralyse the respiratory system. Potassium chloride to stop the heart. Sean Sellers died at 12:17 am, five minutes after the lethal drugs were injected.

He became the first person executed in the United States since 1959 for crimes committed at age sixteen. The last inmate executed for a murder committed at sixteen had been Leonard Shockley, who died in Maryland on 10th April 1959. Sean Sellers became the 512th person executed nationwide since the U.S. Supreme Court reinstated the death penalty in 1977. Of those, only 12 were juveniles at the time of their crimes, and all were 17 years old. Sean was unique in being only sixteen.

His execution was condemned by human rights organisations around the world. It didn't bring back Robert Bower, Vonda Bellofatto, or Paul Lee Bellofatto. Didn't heal the trauma inflicted on their families. Didn't answer the fundamental questions about what had actually happened inside Sean's head when he pulled those triggers.

Six years later, in 2005, the U.S. Supreme Court would rule in Roper v. Simmons that executing people for crimes committed under the age of eighteen was unconstitutional. The ruling came too late for Sean Sellers.

So, what's the truth? Was Sean Sellers possessed by a demon named Ezurate, or was Ezurate an alternate personality created by a fractured psyche, or was the whole thing a fabrication by a disturbed teenager who wanted attention and an excuse for violence?

Here's what we know for certain. Sean experienced severe abuse as a young child. That's documented by multiple sources, not just his own testimony. We know that severe early childhood abuse, especially when combined with neglect and emotional trauma, can cause lasting changes in brain development and increase the risk of psychiatric disorders.

We know that dissociative identity disorder, whilst controversial and rare, is a recognised condition that primarily develops in response to severe early abuse. The mechanism is straightforward: when a child experiences abuse, they can't escape; their mind escapes instead. Creates separate identities that can take the pain, hold the memories, and do things the core personality can't handle. It's a survival mechanism that becomes a disorder when it persists into adulthood.

We also know that some people fake dissociative identity disorder, either for attention or to avoid legal responsibility. The symptoms are easily mimicked if you've read about them. The dramatic personality switches, the different voices and mannerisms, the claimed amnesia for what the alters did. It's not hard to fake, which makes it extremely difficult to diagnose with certainty.

The brain scans showing frontal lobe abnormalities are interesting but not conclusive. Lots of people have similar abnormalities who never commit violence. And we don't know if the abnormalities were present before the abuse or caused by it, whether they contributed to Sean's behaviour or were just coincidental.

The Satanism piece is complicated. On one hand, teenage involvement in occult practices is strongly associated with other risk factors like depression, social isolation, and family problems. Kids who get into Satanism are usually already struggling. The occult interest is a symptom, not a cause. On the other hand, intensive involvement in violent imagery and ritualistic practice, especially when combined with a vulnerable mental state, can absolutely reinforce destructive thought patterns. You become what you rehearse, mentally and emotionally.

Whether Sean believed he was possessed by a demon or just used that cultural framework to explain his own fractured sense of self, the practical outcome is similar. He experienced himself as sometimes not being himself, as being controlled by something other than his conscious will. Whether that other thing was a demon named Ezurate or an alter personality created by early abuse or his own shadow self that he'd projected outward, he acted on impulses he later couldn't fully own or explain.

The religious conversion adds another layer. Lots of people find genuine transformation through faith, especially in prison, where there's time for reflection and limited alternatives for meaning-making. But religious conversion can also be a way of maintaining the same basic narrative whilst swapping out the supernatural agent. Instead of "the demon made me do it," it becomes "the demon deceived me, but now Jesus has saved me." The underlying structure is the same: Sean isn't fundamentally evil; he was influenced by external forces, and he's not the same person now who did those things then.

Which might be true. People do change, especially between sixteen and twenty-nine. The brain continues to develop through the early twenties. Someone who commits murder as a teenager might genuinely become a different person by their late twenties, might develop empathy and impulse control they didn't have before, might be genuinely horrified by what they did in adolescence.

But that doesn't answer the question of culpability. If Sean was genuinely mentally ill at sixteen, genuinely suffering from dissociative disorder caused by childhood abuse, should he have been executed for actions taken during a dissociative state? Most mental health professionals and human rights advocates would say no. Treatment, not execution. The possibility of rehabilitation, not the certainty of death.

If Sean was faking mental illness, using the demon story to manipulate the system, does that change anything? He still committed three murders at age sixteen. He was still a child, legally and developmentally, when he made those choices. The brain's prefrontal cortex, responsible for impulse control and understanding consequences, doesn't fully develop until the mid-twenties. That's not an excuse for murder, but it's a reason to question whether executing juveniles serves any purpose beyond revenge.

And if the truth is somewhere in between, if Sean had genuine psychiatric problems that were less severe than full dissociative disorder but more serious than just being a troubled teen, if he experienced some altered states whilst also consciously choosing violence, does that make him culpable? Can you be partially possessed? Partially dissociated? Partially responsible?

These questions don't have clean answers. The psychiatric evidence was contradictory because human psychology is messy. The legal system had to make a binary choice: guilty or not guilty, mentally ill or sane, death or life. But Sean's actual mental state probably didn't fit neatly into either category.

What we're left with is tragedy on multiple levels. Three people dead who shouldn't be. A fourth person, who was once a child, was killed by the state after spending half his life in a cage. The families of all the victims, including Sean's surviving family members, carry trauma that will never fully heal. The questions about possession, mental illness, and culpability remain unresolved.

I think Sean Sellers was genuinely damaged by childhood abuse. I think he probably experienced some form of dissociation or altered states, whether that rose to the level of full dissociative identity disorder or was something less severe. I think his involvement in Satanism gave him a language to understand his experiences that made sense within his cultural context. I think he probably did believe, at least some of the time, that he was possessed or influenced by something external to himself.

I also think he made choices. Even if Ezurate was real as a psychological construct, even if Sean experienced himself as sometimes being controlled by an alter personality, there were moments of decision along the way. The choice to get involved in Satanism rather than seeking help. The choice to borrow a gun. The choice to walk into that convenience store. The choice to enter his parents' bedroom. Dissociation doesn't eliminate agency; it fragments it.

But I don't think executing him was justice. I think it was revenge dressed up as a legal process. I think it served no purpose beyond satisfying a societal need to punish evil, to draw a line between them, to reassure ourselves that we'd never do something like that, so there must be something fundamentally different about people who do.

Sean Sellers became someone else, whether you interpret that as psychological or supernatural. We'll never know whether he could have become someone better. Whether the transformation he claimed to experience through Christianity was genuine. Whether the sixteen-year-old who pulled those triggers and the twenty-nine-year-old who died on a gurney were really the same person in any meaningful sense.

The demon of murder, if there is such a thing, doesn't need supernatural intervention to do its work. Childhood abuse creates it. Social isolation feeds it. Mental illness amplifies it. Violent imagery rehearses it. And when a damaged teenager picks up a gun and decides he's tired of being powerless, tired of being hurt, tired of being nobody, the demon finds a willing host, whether or not it's real.

Sean Sellers died, claiming Jesus had saved him from that demon. The families of his victims died a little more that day, watching their loved ones' killer elevated to martyr status by people who opposed the death penalty. Oklahoma claimed justice had been served. International observers claimed a human rights violation had been committed.

Everyone was probably a little bit right. That's what makes it tragic rather than just sad. There are no clean answers here, no clear villains except maybe the person who abused Sean as a child and started this whole cascade of damage. Just broken people breaking other people until the state steps in and breaks someone permanently in the name of making it right.

The demon didn't make Sean Sellers kill three people. But something did make a child into a murderer. Whether we call that something trauma, mental illness, evil, possession, or just the inevitable outcome of abandoning damaged kids to figure out their demons alone, it comes to the same thing in the end.

Three innocent people are dead. One damaged child executed. The rest of us are left trying to make sense of violence that refuses to make sense. Trying to assign blame when everyone involved was probably at least partly a victim. Trying to draw lessons from a tragedy that mostly just teaches us how little we understand about the darkness humans carry inside them.

Ezurate might not have been real. But the murder was. And killing Sean Sellers didn't make anyone safer, didn't heal anyone's trauma, didn't answer the questions we most need answered about how to prevent the next damaged child from becoming the next murderer.

It made us one more killer in a story already full of them.

CHAPTER X

When Faith Becomes Fatal

LONDON, ENGLAND. 25TH WINTER 2000.

Victoria Climbié died at 3:15 pm in the intensive care unit at St Mary's Hospital, Paddington. She was eight years old. Her body temperature, when paramedics found her the previous evening, had been 27 degrees Celsius, far below anything compatible with survival for long. She weighed just 52 pounds, skeletal from months of starvation. Dr Nathaniel Carey, the Home Office pathologist who examined her body, found 128 separate injuries and scars. Burns from cigarettes. Scalding marks from boiling water. Cuts from beatings with bicycle chains, hammers, and coat hangers. Scars where her skin had broken down from being tied up, night after night, in a black bin liner filled with her own excrement in an unheated bathroom.

"The worst case of child abuse I've encountered," Dr Carey said later. And he'd seen plenty.

Marie-Thérèse Kouao, Victoria's great-aunt, and Carl Manning, Kouao's boyfriend, were arrested immediately. Both were charged with murder. The evidence was overwhelming. Bloodstains on Manning's boots. Marks on the bathroom walls where Victoria had been kept prisoner. The bin liner itself is stiff with dried urine and faeces. The instruments of torture: bicycle chain, hammer, belt, wooden spoon. All documented. All photographed. All were presented to a jury that took less than a day to convict both defendants.

On 12th January 2001, Judge Richard Hawkins sentenced Marie-Thérèse Kouao and Carl Manning to life imprisonment. "What Anna endured was truly unimaginable," he said, using the false name Kouao had given Victoria on the forged passport that brought her to England. The judge called it "a gross violation of the trust placed in you by Victoria's parents," noted the suffering had been "beyond comprehension."

But the case didn't end there. It couldn't. Because Victoria hadn't died in secret. She'd been seen by social workers, doctors, nurses, housing officers, police, and church members. She'd been to the hospital multiple times. People had noticed something was wrong, filed reports, and raised concerns. Four local authorities had contact with her. Two child protection police teams. Two hospitals. An NSPCC centre. Several churches. Known to the system, visible to professionals, documented in files across multiple agencies.

And somehow, through all of that, nobody had saved her.

The public inquiry that followed, chaired by Lord Laming, identified catastrophic failures across every agency that had contact with Victoria. Social services that didn't follow up properly. Hospitals that discharged her back to her abusers. Police who didn't investigate adequately. Housing officers who saw and didn't report. A child protection system that was supposed to keep children safe had instead watched whilst Victoria was tortured to death over nine months. The

Laming Report produced 108 recommendations, became a watershed moment in British child protection policy, and led to the Children Act 2004 and Every Child Matters initiative.

But there was another thread running through the case, one that got less attention in the official inquiries, though it was there in the testimony, in the witness statements, in the accounts of what people had seen and heard. Marie-Thérèse Kouao believed Victoria was possessed by demons. And that belief, shared and reinforced by parts of her religious community, had shaped everything that happened.

Victoria Adjo Climbié was born on 2nd November 1991 in Abobo, a shanty suburb of Abidjan, the Ivory Coast. She was the fifth of seven children born to Francis Climbié and his wife Berthe Amoissi. The family was poor, living in conditions where opportunity was scarce and the future uncertain. When Marie-Thérèse Kouao, Francis's aunt, visited in November 1998 and offered to take Victoria to Europe to give her an education and opportunities she'd never have in West Africa, the family saw it as a blessing.

Kouao was a French citizen, had three children of her own, and seemed established and capable. She'd been living in France, working at Charles de Gaulle airport, earning over £20,000 a year. The arrangement was straightforward: Victoria would live with her great-aunt, attend good schools, learn French and English, and build a better life. Her parents, struggling but hopeful, trusting a family member, agreed. Victoria left Abobo in November 1998, seven years old, "happy and excited" about her new life, according to relatives who saw her off.

They had no way of knowing what would happen once Victoria was in Kouao's care, isolated from anyone who might have protected her.

The reality was darker than the Climbié family could have imagined. Kouao had been living off state benefits and child support since her 1995 widowing. She'd been pursued by French authorities for benefit fraud. The job at Charles de Gaulle was gone or had never been as lucrative as she claimed. She'd used a false French passport to bring Victoria to Paris, listing the child as "Anna Kouao," her own daughter. Victoria became, in the prosecution's later words, part of "Operation Scrounge", a scheme to obtain benefits using children who weren't Kouao's own.

French authorities began investigating after Victoria's absences from school became concerning. By December 1998, social services were involved. Kouao fled to London in April 1999, Victoria in tow, running from French benefit fraud charges totalling £2,000. They arrived in England with forged documents, Kouao still claiming Victoria was her daughter Anna, and immediately applied for housing and benefits. Ealing Council gave them accommodation. The state provided £2,000 in support. Kouao got a job as a cleaner at Northwick Park Hospital in Harrow.

And the abuse began.

It's not known exactly when Kouao started hurting Victoria, though it likely escalated when they met Carl Manning. On 10th June 1999, Kouao was riding the Number 18 bus through North London when she struck up a conversation with the driver. Carl John Manning, twenty-eight years old, British-born of St Lucian descent, single, living alone in a tiny studio flat in Somerset Gardens, Tottenham. Within days, Kouao and Victoria had moved into Manning's one-bedroom flat. Within weeks, Victoria was being beaten.

The possession narrative emerged early. Kouao told people Victoria was wicked. Evil. Possessed by demons that made her misbehave. When Victoria wet herself, which she started doing constantly because she was terrified and traumatised, Kouao said it was the demons. When Victoria flinched away from her, when she wouldn't make eye contact, when she stood to attention whenever Kouao entered a room, when Kouao's very presence caused the child to urinate in fear, Kouao interpreted it as evidence of possession.

Carl Manning adopted the same interpretation, or at least the same language. In his diary, he referred to Victoria as "Satan." Whether he truly believed she was possessed or whether it was simply a convenient justification for the sadistic pleasure he clearly took in hurting her, the possession narrative shaped how they treated her. She wasn't a child who needed care and protection. She was a vessel for evil that needed punishment, isolation, and exorcism.

The abuse was systematic and escalating. They beat her with belts, wooden spoons, coat hangers, hammers, and bicycle chains. Manning later told police, his voice matter-of-fact: "You could beat her, and she would not cry at all. She could take the beatings and pain like anything." They scalded her with boiling water. Burned her with cigarettes, 128 injuries, many of them cigarette burns, Dr Carey would later document. They fed her like a dog, cold leftovers scattered on the floor, her hands bound with masking tape so she had to eat without using them.

At night, they tied her up and left her in the bathroom. First, they bound her in the bath itself, hands and feet secured so she couldn't move. When that caused skin breakdown, they put her in black bin liners instead, wrapping her like a package, leaving her there in the unheated bathroom through the night. Every night. In her own urine and faeces because she couldn't get out to use the toilet. In the cold because the flat had no heating in that room. Alone because neither

Kouao nor Manning wanted to hear, see or think about what they were doing to her.

By July 1999, Victoria's condition had visibly deteriorated. Her childminder, Avril Cameron, became alarmed. The little girl had cuts all over her body, weeping, infected wounds on her fingers, marks that looked suspiciously like they'd been deliberately inflicted. On 14th July 1999, Cameron took Victoria to Central Middlesex Hospital. The medical staff examined her, documented the injuries, and made a child protection referral.

Dr Ruby Schwartz, consultant paediatrician and child protection specialist, saw Victoria on 15th July. The child was cut and bruised. But Kouao had a story ready. Victoria had scabies, she explained. The child scratched constantly, couldn't help herself, and had inflicted these wounds by scratching too vigorously at the itchy sores. Dr Schwartz, incredibly, accepted this explanation. Diagnosed with scabies. Prescribed treatment. Released Victoria back into Kouao's care.

The child protection referral went to Haringey Council. Social worker Lisa Arthurworrey and PC Karen Jones were assigned to the case. They scheduled a home visit for 4th August. Then they heard about the scabies diagnosis and cancelled. Didn't want to risk catching scabies themselves, apparently. Decided the case could wait.

It couldn't. Ten days later, on 24th July 1999, Victoria was taken to North Middlesex Hospital's casualty department with scalding to her head and face. The injuries were so severe that doctors immediately suspected deliberate infliction. This time, the referral to child protection was more urgent. Lisa Arthurworrey and PC Jones became involved again.

Kouao had another story. Victoria had been scratching her scalp due to scabies. It was bleeding and wouldn't heal. So Kouao had poured hot water over the child's head to stop the scratching. To help her. The explanation was bizarre enough to have raised immediate red flags. But when Arthurworrey and Jones interviewed Kouao, she had something else to add.

Victoria was possessed by demons. The child hurt herself during demonic episodes. The scratching, the injuries, the strange behaviour, all evidence of possession. Kouao was trying to get the demons out. She needed help, spiritual help, not interference from authorities who didn't understand the situation.

And somehow that explanation muddied the waters enough that the investigation stalled.

This is where the possession narrative became actively dangerous rather than just tragically mistaken. Because everything about Victoria's behaviour was textbook evidence of severe abuse and trauma. Urinary incontinence is a classic response to chronic fear and stress in children. The withdrawal, the inability to make eye contact, the cowering when adults approached, the standing to attention in Kouao's presence, all were completely predictable responses to being beaten and scalded and starved. That she sometimes seemed distant or unresponsive was dissociation, her mind escaping a situation her body couldn't.

Any professional with basic training in child development or trauma recognition should have seen what was happening. But when you're looking through a lens where demons are real, and possession explains behaviour, those signs get reinterpreted. The child isn't traumatised; she's possessed. She doesn't need protection; she needs deliverance. And every failed intervention, every time the "demons" didn't leave, proved they were powerful, and more drastic measures were required.

Victoria was discharged from North Middlesex Hospital on 6th August 1999, collected by Kouao after her explanation for the injuries was accepted by child protection authorities. Arthurworrey made a home visit to the Somerset Gardens flat on 16th August. She later testified that Victoria seemed happy, that she saw no cause for alarm. How she missed the signs of severe abuse in a child who was being tortured daily remains one of the inquiry's most damning questions.

Between August 1999 and February 2000, Arthurworrey made several more attempts to visit. She received no answer when she knocked. She speculated to her supervisor, Carole Baptiste, that Kouao and Victoria had perhaps returned to France. Despite lacking evidence, Baptiste wrote in Victoria's file that they had left the area. On 18th February 2000, Haringey Council wrote to Kouao saying that if they didn't receive contact, they would close the case.

They closed it on 25th February 2000. The same day, Victoria died.

During those months between August 1999 and February 2000, Victoria endured intensifying torture. They smashed her toes with hammers. They beat her so badly that blood spattered the walls of Manning's flat. They starved her systematically by the time she died; she weighed just 52 pounds, her body skeletal. And they continued framing it as spiritual warfare.

Kouao took Victoria to churches. These weren't fringe groups or obscure cults. They were established churches in London's African Christian community, congregations of hundreds, pastors with theological training, ordinary people trying to live out their faith in a new country.

Pastor Pascal Orome of the Mission Ensemble Pour Christ church in Southeast London performed an exorcism on Victoria. The details of what exactly happened aren't fully documented in public records, but we know Orome prayed over the child, commanded demons to leave her, and pronounced her "delivered from witchcraft or wicked spirits." He saw angry wounds on Victoria's head. He saw that her hands were covered with scars. He did not believe the injuries were due to abuse. He prayed for Victoria in good faith, he said later, truly believed he was helping, and had no way of knowing what Kouao was doing to the child at home.

But he saw an eight-year-old child with visible injuries and treated her as possessed rather than abused. And nobody in that church community, apparently, thought to contact child protection services.

In February 2000, as Victoria's condition deteriorated to critical levels, Kouao took her to another church. The Universal Church of the Kingdom of God in North London. She brought Victoria on 24th February, the child barely conscious, hypothermic, suffering from multiple organ failure. Pastor Alvaro Lima was horrified by what he saw. He insisted Victoria should be taken to the hospital immediately. Not for exorcism. For medical care.

Kouao and Manning finally called for an ambulance. But even then, they tried to subvert help. Manning gave the driver directions to Seven Sisters Road, away from the nearest hospital. The taxi driver ignored him, suspicious of what he was seeing, and drove directly to an ambulance station instead. Victoria was rushed to North Middlesex Hospital, then transferred to St Mary's intensive care unit.

She was unconscious when she arrived. Body temperature 27 degrees Celsius, hypothermia so severe that doctors couldn't understand how she was still alive. She had burns covering much of her body. Second and third-degree burns from scalding. Cigarette burns. Wounds from beatings. Pressure sores from being tied up. Malnutrition was so extreme that her organs were shutting down. The ambulance crew who brought her in noted something strange about Kouao's behaviour. She kept saying "my baby, my baby," but her concern seemed "not quite enough." Manning seemed "almost as if he was not there."

Victoria died the next day at 3:15 pm. Her body had simply endured too much.

The trial of Marie-Thérèse Kouao and Carl Manning opened in November 2000. The prosecution made it clear that blame lay not only with the defendants in the dock but with child protection authorities who had been "blindingly incompetent." Manning denied murder but pleaded guilty to child cruelty and manslaughter. Kouao denied all charges.

During police interviews, both claimed Victoria had been possessed. Kouao was particularly insistent, maintaining that she was innocent, that she'd been trying to help the child, that she was the victim of a conspiracy. At the inquiry that followed her conviction, she ranted about her innocence whilst also criticising Victoria's devastated parents, suggesting they bore responsibility for what had happened.

Manning was more subdued. In video-recorded evidence played at the inquiry, he apologised for his part in Victoria's suffering. He also said, remarkably, that child protection agencies could not be blamed for what happened. This is from the man who'd beaten an eight-year-old child with a bicycle chain and referred to her as Satan in his diary.

The jury found both guilty of murder. The sentence of life imprisonment was mandatory. But the legal proceedings, whilst delivering justice in the narrow sense, didn't answer the deeper questions. How had this been allowed to happen? How had so many professionals seen Victoria and failed to save her? And what role had the possession narrative played in those failures?

The Laming Inquiry, which opened in May 2001, called over 230 witnesses. Social workers, police officers, doctors, nurses, housing officials, Kouao and Manning themselves. It heard about systemic failures, underfunded departments, poor communication between agencies, inadequate training, and racial tensions that made professionals hesitant to challenge Kouao. It heard about cultural sensitivity concerns, the fear of seeming racist or dismissive of African Christian beliefs that had made some workers uncertain how to respond when Kouao explained Victoria's behaviour through possession.

Was this a genuine religious belief they should respect? Was it a red flag they should have investigated? The uncertainty led to inaction. And Victoria died.

Lord Laming's report noted that some of the people who saw Victoria and didn't act decisively were themselves from African Christian backgrounds, where spiritual warfare and deliverance were familiar concepts. When Kouao said the child was possessed, it wasn't incomprehensible. It made sense within their worldview. That doesn't excuse the failures to protect Victoria, but it helps explain how multiple people could encounter a clearly abused child and not respond with the urgency the situation demanded.

There's a particularly painful detail in the case records. A church member, someone who'd seen Victoria at services, noticed the child looked unwell and frightened. This person approached Kouao and gently suggested that Victoria might need to see a doctor, that the child's behaviour might not be spiritual but medical in nature. Kouao became angry. Said the person didn't understand spiritual matters.

Accused them of interfering. The church member backed off. Didn't push harder. Didn't contact authorities.

That moment haunted them afterwards, according to testimony at the inquiry. They'd known something was wrong. They'd tried to help in a way that seemed appropriate to them. When Kouao rejected the suggestion and framed it as spiritual ignorance, they deferred to her interpretation. Maybe she did know better. Maybe it was spiritual. Maybe interfering would do more harm than good.

And Victoria died.

This is how religious lenses can enable abuse even when the people involved aren't abusers themselves. They're ordinary people, trying to be respectful of others' beliefs, not wanting to impose their own interpretations, trusting that carers know what's best for children in their care. But when the carer's interpretation is that the child is possessed and needs harsh treatment to drive out demons, that deference becomes deadly.

The psychological mechanisms at work in Kouao herself are harder to access. She's never been forthcoming about her inner state, her genuine beliefs, her motivations. Was she psychotic, experiencing delusions that Victoria was possessed? Was she using the possession narrative cynically to justify abuse she wanted to commit anyway? Was it some combination, where she half-believed the demons were real and half-knew she was using that belief to excuse her cruelty?

We know she had a history of erratic behaviour before Victoria came to live with her. She'd made odd claims, struggled with employment and housing, and manipulated benefit systems across two countries. Some people who knew her thought she was mentally ill. Others thought she was simply difficult and manipulative. She'd been married twice, divorced in 1978, and widowed in 1995. She'd had three children of her own, though their whereabouts and well-being were unclear. She was described in court as "a cunning, manipulative liar."

The possession narrative she constructed around Victoria could have been a genuine delusion, her troubled mind creating a reality where the child was evil and needed punishment. Or it could have been deliberate performance, a way to frame child abuse as spiritual warfare and garner support from religious communities whilst deflecting scrutiny from authorities.

Carl Manning's role is clearer, or at least more straightforward. He participated eagerly in the abuse. The diary entries, the bloodstains on his boots, the matter-of-fact way he described beating Victoria until she couldn't cry anymore all suggest someone who enjoyed the cruelty. The possession narrative gave him permission and justification, but the sadism appears to have been his own. Whether he genuinely believed Victoria was possessed is almost irrelevant. His behaviour suggests he would have found some reason to hurt her regardless.

What we can say with certainty is that the possession belief system made the abuse possible in ways that straightforward child abuse might not have been. If Kouao and Manning had simply been beating Victoria for no stated reason, people would have intervened more quickly. The claims of possession, the exorcisms, the religious language around it, created just enough ambiguity, just enough deference to spiritual matters, that people hesitated.

And children don't survive on hesitation.

The African Christian churches in London that had contact with Victoria and Kouao came under intense scrutiny after her death. Some defended their practices, argued that deliverance ministry was biblical and appropriate, and maintained that the problem was Kouao's abuse, not the church's theology. Others engaged in painful self-examination, asked hard questions about how their beliefs and practices might have contributed to a child's death, and implemented safeguarding measures.

Pastor Orome faced no criminal charges. Conducting an exorcism isn't illegal in the UK, even on a child, provided it doesn't involve assault or abuse. There wasn't any evidence that Orome himself had physically harmed Victoria during the prayer session. But the moral and ethical questions remain unanswered. What responsibility does he bear for treating an abused child as possessed rather than recognising the abuse and reporting it?

The broader African Christian community wrestled with Victoria's case in ways that were often divisive. Some churches became more cautious about deliverance ministry, especially involving children. Others doubled down, arguing that demons are real and children can be possessed like adults. The theological debates continue. But Victoria Climbié remains a reference point, a name invoked when discussing the potential harms of possession beliefs applied to vulnerable people.

What makes Victoria's case particularly significant is that it's not historical. This happened in London in 1999-2000, in a major Western city with robust child protection systems, in churches that weren't fringe cults but established congregations. The possession belief wasn't an ancient superstition. It was living theology, actively practised, capable of overriding obvious evidence that a child was being tortured.

And it's not an isolated case. Since Victoria's death, there have been others in the UK involving children abused or killed by carers who believed them possessed. Kristy Bamu, fifteen years old, was tortured and drowned by his sister and her partner in London on Christmas Day 2010 because they believed he was possessed by kindoki, witchcraft. Child B, whose identity remains protected, was subjected to exorcism rituals by her parents and was rescued by authorities before she could be seriously harmed. These are the cases that came to public attention. How many others exist where the abuse is ongoing or where children died without proper investigation?

The psychological question running through all these cases is how ordinary people convince themselves that torturing a child is not only acceptable but necessary and righteous. Because Marie-Thérèse Kouao, whatever else she was, wasn't unique in human psychology. She was capable of convincing herself that horrific abuse was spiritual warfare. She maintained that narrative not just to others but apparently to herself. And enough people around her found that narrative plausible that she continued having access to Victoria for months despite multiple red flags.

Belief is powerful. It shapes perception. When you're convinced demons are real, and a child is possessed, their fear looks like demonic resistance. Their withdrawal looks like evil taking hold. Their trauma responses look like confirmation that an exorcism is needed. The same behaviours that would immediately signal abuse to someone not looking through that lens get completely reinterpreted. And the reinterpretation is self-reinforcing: every failed exorcism, every time the "demons" don't leave, proves they're powerful, and more intervention is required.

This is where possession beliefs become particularly dangerous for children. Adults can sometimes escape situations where they're subjected to harmful exorcisms. They can leave, call for help, or resist. Children can't. They're dependent on the adults around them for survival. When those adults believe the child is possessed, the child has no recourse. They can't argue themselves out of being seen as demonically influenced. They can't escape the belief system that's been imposed on them.

Victoria Climbié couldn't tell anyone she wasn't possessed. She was eight years old, isolated from anyone who might have helped her, trapped with people who saw demons when they looked at her instead of a frightened child who needed protection. She couldn't make them see reality because they were looking through a lens that distorted everything. And that distortion, that ability of belief to override observable fact, killed her as surely as the scalding water and the beatings and the starvation.

The tragedy is that everything about Victoria's behaviour made sense if you understood trauma. She was displaying textbook responses to chronic abuse. Any professional with proper training should have recognised what they were seeing. But the possession narrative was powerful enough to create doubt, to make people hesitate, to prevent the decisive intervention that might have saved her.

Victoria Climbié died with 128 injuries on her body and a core temperature too low to measure. She was eight years old. She died not because demons were powerful but because every adult around her chose the wrong explanation when the right one was obvious. An abused child. Full stop.

The possession belief didn't cause the abuse in some simple, direct way. Marie-Thérèse Kouao's cruelty, Carl Manning's sadism, those came from somewhere deeper and darker than theology. But the possession framework made the abuse possible, which explained it to others, creating just enough confusion and deference that people didn't intervene as quickly or decisively as they should have.

That's how faith becomes fatal. Not because believing in demons automatically makes you abuse children, but because possession frameworks can enable abuse by reinterpreting its signs as spiritual warfare, by making witnesses hesitate to challenge religious explanations, by creating narratives where cruelty becomes righteous action.

Victoria Climbié died because people believed in demons more than they believed their own eyes when they saw an injured, frightened child. And unless religious communities grapple honestly with how their beliefs about possession can be weaponised, how their theological systems can enable harm, how their desire to respect spiritual experiences can prevent them from recognising abuse, she won't be the last.

Victoria deserved that honesty when she was alive. Nobody gave it to her.

CHAPTER XI

The Weight Of Faith

MILWAUKEE, WISCONSIN. SUMMER 2003.

Terrance Cottrell Jr. was eight years old when the people at Faith Temple Church of the Apostolic Faith held him face down on the floor and pressed on his chest until he stopped breathing. It was the ninth prayer service his mother had brought him to in over three weeks. Nine times she'd taken her son to this small storefront church in a Milwaukee strip mall, seeking help for behaviours she didn't understand. Nine times, Pastor Ray Hemphill and his congregation had prayed over Terrance, commanding the demons they believed caused his autism to leave his body.

The ninth time killed him.

Patricia Cooper had been told her son was possessed by evil spirits. The way he didn't speak much, mostly single words like "water" or "bathroom", wasn't typical of autism. That the way he moved his hands in repetitive patterns, the way he sometimes melted down when things got overwhelming, the way he occasionally played roughly with other kids, these weren't symptoms of a neurodevelopmental condition. This was a spiritual attack. And Faith Temple knew how to deal with spiritual attack.

That Friday night, Terrance was wrapped in sheets. His arms and legs were held down. Pastor Ray Hemphill, five feet seven inches tall, 150 to 170 pounds depending on which witness account you believe, lay across the boy's chest. Terrance weighed perhaps 70 pounds. Hemphill pressed his knee into the child's chest and held his hand across Terrance's forehead. Then he began to pray, calling on the power of Jesus Christ to cast out the evil spirits of autism.

Terrance struggled. Naturally, he struggled. He was eight years old, being held down by multiple adults, including his own mother, who gripped his feet, unable to breathe properly through the sheets and the weight on his body, terrified and confused about what was happening to him. But his struggles were interpreted as demons fighting back. His attempts to get free were seen as evil, resisting the power of God. So they held him tighter, prayed louder, kept the pressure on his small body.

The ritual lasted two hours. Somewhere during those two hours, Terrance Cottrell Jr. stopped breathing. When they finally released him, when one of the parishioners noticed the boy wasn't moving, it was too late. He was unresponsive. They called 911. Paramedics arrived and attempted resuscitation. Terrance was rushed to the hospital. He was pronounced dead shortly after arrival.

The medical examiner, Jeanne Wiedmeyer, ruled it a homicide by mechanical asphyxia due to external chest compression. The eight-year-old boy had suffocated under the weight of adults who were trying to drive demons out of him.

Patricia Cooper had to live with what happened. She'd brought her son to that church. She'd held his feet whilst others pressed on his chest. She'd believed what they told her about demons and possession. She'd trusted Pastor Hemphill and the congregation to help her child. And instead, they'd killed him. The guilt must be unbearable. The knowledge that your child died because you believed people who told you his autism was demonic possession, that devastation doesn't have words adequate to describe it.

Pastor Ray Hemphill, 47, a former maintenance worker with no formal religious education, ordained as a pastor by his brother, Bishop David Hemphill, who'd founded Faith Temple in 1977, was arrested and charged. Not with murder, though the medical examiner called it homicide. Prosecutors chose not to file murder charges because it would be difficult to prove Hemphill intended to kill Terrance. Instead, child abuse recklessly causes great bodily harm. The distinction mattered for the trial, for the potential sentence, for how the legal system processed what had happened.

Hemphill's defence was straightforward. He hadn't meant to harm the child. He'd been performing a religious ritual, trying to help, acting on sincerely held beliefs about demons and spiritual warfare. The fact that Terrance died was tragic, yes, but it wasn't criminal because there was no intent to kill. It was an accident during a religious practice, protected by the First Amendment, his lawyers argued. Freedom of religion meant he had the right to perform exorcisms, and the unfortunate outcome didn't change the fact that his actions were religiously motivated.

The prosecution's case was equally straightforward. Hemphill and the others had held an eight-year-old child face down with sheets wrapped around him, applied sustained pressure to his body for two hours, and ignored his struggling. Any reasonable person should have known this was dangerous. Children die from restraint asphyxiation. It's not mysterious or unforeseeable. When you compress a child's chest and restrict their breathing, death is a known risk. Religious motivation didn't excuse the recklessness.

The case highlighted painful questions about where religious freedom ends and child protection begins. If Hemphill had hit Terrance with a stick during the exorcism and the boy had died from head trauma, would that be a protected religious practice? If he'd withheld food and water for days as part of spiritual cleansing and the child had died of dehydration, would that be acceptable? At what point does religious ritual become criminal conduct, and who gets to decide where that line is?

In July 2004, the jury convicted Hemphill of child abuse, recklessly causing great bodily harm. On 17th August 2004, nearly one year to the day after Terrance's death, Milwaukee County Circuit Judge Jean DiMotto sentenced him. Two and a half years in prison. Seven and a half years under state supervision after release. Restitution of $1,224.75 to the family. And a curious provision: Hemphill was ordered to refrain from performing exorcisms until he received "extensive training" in them.

Two and a half years. That's what Ray Hemphill served for Terrance Cottrell Jr.'s death. The maximum possible sentence was ten years in prison and a $25,000 fine. Some people thought the sentence was too lenient. Others thought any prison time was persecution of religious practice. The legal outcome satisfied nobody, as is often the case. The law isn't particularly well-equipped to handle situations in which sincere religious belief leads to terrible outcomes.

Whilst not admitting guilt, Hemphill told the court at sentencing: "Your honour, I'm truly sorry for what happened to Terrance Cottrell

Jr. That is what I would like to say. Thanks." Assistant District Attorney Mark Williams noted that Hemphill and his brother still insisted Terrance had been possessed by demons. "There seems to be little or no remorse," the prosecutor said.

No charges were filed against any of the women who participated in holding Terrance down, including Patricia Cooper. All cited their Fifth Amendment right to refuse to testify to avoid incriminating themselves during Hemphill's trial.

But the legal case is almost the least interesting part of what happened to Terrance Cottrell. The question that haunts this case, the thing that makes it more than another tragic death, is how his autism got misinterpreted as demonic possession in the first place. And once that interpretation took hold, it made killing him seem not just acceptable but necessary and righteous to the adults who loved him and wanted to help him.

Terrance had been diagnosed with autism at age two. That wasn't a secret or controversial diagnosis. He'd been evaluated by medical professionals. He was receiving special education services in public school. His medical treatment was paid for by Social Security, and it included prescription psychiatric drugs. People knew. But in the community Patricia Cooper was part of, in the theological system Faith Temple Church operated within, autism wasn't understood primarily as a neurological condition. It was a spiritual problem.

The behaviours associated with autism, the stimming, the communication difficulties, the meltdowns, the way autistic children sometimes seem to exist in their own world, all of that looked like demonic influence if you were looking through a lens where demons were real and active.

This is particularly common in some African American Pentecostal and charismatic Christian communities, though it's not unique to them. There's a theological tradition that emphasises spiritual warfare, that sees demons as constantly active and looking for ways to attack believers, that interprets unusual behaviour or medical conditions through a supernatural lens. In that belief system, a child who doesn't behave typically, who has developmental differences, who struggles with things other children don't, isn't just neurodivergent. They're under spiritual attack or possessed by evil forces.

The interpretation isn't malicious. It comes from genuine belief. Bishop David Hemphill, Pastor Ray's brother and the church's founder, explained it to reporters after Terrance's death: "We were asking God to take this spirit that was tormenting this little boy to death. We were praying that hard, but not to kill." He cited Matthew 12:43, which states: "When an evil spirit comes out of a man, it goes through arid places seeking rest and does not find it."

Assistant Pastor Pamela Hemphill told investigators the idea to lie across Terrance came from the Revised Standard Version of the Bible, First Kings 17:21. The passage describes a prophet who lay across a child and cried out, "Let this child's soul come into him again."

If you think the spiritual realm is as real as the physical one, if you believe demons exist and can influence or possess people, if your theology teaches that deliverance is possible and necessary, then seeing autism as possession makes a certain kind of sense. The child is suffering. Something is causing that suffering. Medicine hasn't fixed it. Maybe the problem isn't medical; maybe it's spiritual. And if it's spiritual, then spiritual solutions are what's needed.

But autism isn't caused by demons. It's a neurological difference present from birth or early development, involving how the brain processes information and experiences the world. It's not curable through exorcism because there's nothing to cure in that sense. Autistic people aren't broken or possessed. They're people whose brains work differently from neurotypical brains, and whilst that creates challenges, particularly in a world designed for neurotypical people, it's not evil or demonic.

The behaviours Patricia Cooper and the people at Faith Temple interpreted as demonic were completely typical for an autistic eight-year-old. The stimming of those repetitive hand movements is a form of self-regulation. It's how many autistic people manage sensory input and emotional states. It's not demons moving through the body. It's neurology working differently.

The communication difficulties, the fact that Terrance mostly spoke in single words, that's how autism often manifests. Terrance's cousin, Luwanda Ward, twenty-four, explained it to reporters: "Instead of saying, 'I want soda,' he'd say, 'Soda.' Or for water, he'd say, 'Water.'" Language development and social communication work differently in autistic brains. It's not spirits preventing speech. It's a neurodevelopmental difference.

But at least once during the prayer sessions, Terrance had cried out, "Shoot me." This shook the congregation. Assistant Pastor Pamela Hemphill later asked reporters: "If you have an eight-year-old boy who can't say anything but 'water' and 'bathroom,' tell me why this boy would look at someone and say 'shoot me,' if it wasn't a demon? Demons are real."

The explanation is heartbreaking but straightforward. A child being held down by multiple adults, unable to breathe properly, experiencing overwhelming sensory input and terror, might cry out for death to stop the torture. Or he might have picked up the phrase from television, from conversations he'd overheard, repeating it the way autistic children sometimes do with scripted language. Either way, it wasn't demons. It was an eight-year-old in distress.

The meltdowns, which probably happened fairly often when Terrance was in environments that weren't accommodating to his needs, aren't demonic tantrums. Their nervous system is overwhelmed. When autistic people experience too much sensory input, too much unpredictability, too much demand on their processing capacity, their nervous systems can't handle it, and they melt down. It looks like a loss of control because, in a sense, it is, but it's neurological, not spiritual.

Everything about Terrance that his mother and the church interpreted as possession had straightforward neurological explanations. But if you don't know that, if your lens for understanding unusual behaviour is primarily spiritual, if the authorities you trust tell you demons are real, and your child is showing signs of possession, you believe them. Especially if you're scared and desperate and want help for your child who's struggling in ways you don't understand.

Patricia Cooper wasn't a bad mother. She wasn't neglectful or cruel. Denise Allison, twenty-five, a friend and neighbour, told reporters that Patricia had described to her how church leaders would restrain her son at services, Patricia called "like an exorcism." Patricia said, "They were trying to cast the demons out of him." But she kept bringing him back. For three weeks, she took him to Faith Temple three times a week for these "special prayer services."

Assistant Pastor Pamela Hemphill described Cooper as desperate. She'd often voiced concern that Terrance would be institutionalised. According to Dr Bennett Leventhal, chief of child and adolescent psychiatry at the University of Chicago, autism "impairs the ability to comprehend such social cues as a parent's command of 'no,' head shaking, or a family member's embrace. Those are the very tools you use to raise a child. It's a very difficult disorder for parents to manage. You need a lot of help and a lot of resources."

Family members said Cooper had little of either. She was a single mother living in the impoverished northwest side of Milwaukee. Terrance's father, Terrance Cottrell Sr., told the Milwaukee Journal Sentinel he hadn't seen his son for about two months and didn't see the boy often because he didn't get along with Patricia. She was navigating this alone, with limited resources, in a community where institutional support was scarce and cultural frameworks made demonic possession seem more plausible than what mainstream medicine offered.

Faith Temple Church of the Apostolic Faith wasn't a cult. It was an informal grouping of six families with two self-ordained ministers at the helm. A small storefront church that served a community. Pastor Ray Hemphill, a janitor by trade with no theological training, genuinely believed in demons and deliverance. The church members who participated in the exorcism weren't sadists. They thought they were helping. They were praying. Calling on God. Trying to save a child's soul from evil. And their sincere belief, their absolute conviction that they were doing the right thing, made them hold an eight-year-old down for two hours until he suffocated.

This is where the psychological mechanisms of belief become crucial for understanding what happened. When you're certain you're right, when your worldview doesn't have room for the possibility that you might be wrong, when the authority figures you trust confirm your interpretation, you can commit terrible acts whilst genuinely thinking you're doing good.

The adults holding Terrance down that night weren't experiencing cognitive dissonance about what they were doing. They weren't thinking "this seems wrong, but we'll do it anyway." They thought they were engaged in spiritual warfare. The child struggling beneath them wasn't an eight-year-old boy terrified and unable to breathe. He was a battlefield where God and demons were fighting, and their job was to help God win.

Confirmation bias played a massive role. Every behaviour Terrance displayed was interpreted through the lens of possession. When he struggled, that was demons resisting. When he made sounds, that was demons speaking. When he cried out, "Shoot me," that was the demons trying to manipulate them into stopping. The framework explained everything in ways that reinforced the belief they were doing the right thing.

Group dynamics made it worse. When multiple people share a belief, when everyone in the room agrees that this is demonic possession and exorcism is necessary, dissent becomes almost impossible. Even if someone had a flicker of doubt, even if someone thought, "this doesn't seem right," and spoke up against the group consensus, especially when the group is led by religious authority, it takes courage that most people don't have in the moment.

The religious authority structure mattered enormously. Pastor Ray Hemphill led this ritual. Bishop David Hemphill, who'd founded the church, supported it. When they said Terrance was possessed, when they decided exorcism was needed, and when they directed how it should be done, people deferred to them. Not because they were mindless followers but because, in their beliefs, pastors have discernment and spiritual authority that laypeople don't.

The length of time is significant. This wasn't a brief prayer over Terrance. It was two hours of sustained physical restraint. At some point during those two hours, someone should have thought, "This isn't working. We should stop." But stopping would have meant admitting the exorcism wasn't successful, that the demons were too powerful, that maybe they'd been wrong. So they continued. Made it more intense. Prayed harder. Pressed harder. Because giving up felt like letting evil win.

There's a terrible irony in the fact that the behaviours they were trying to stop, Terrance's autistic behaviours, were probably intensifying under the stress of the exorcism. Being restrained, unable to breathe properly, surrounded by loud voices and intense emotion, would make any autistic child's nervous system escalate. The stimming would increase. The distress would be obvious. He might have made sounds, tried to communicate his fear in whatever ways he could. And all of that would have been interpreted as demons fighting back, as proof that the exorcism was necessary and they needed to continue.

The sheets wrapped around Terrance added another layer of danger. Restraint asphyxiation happens when pressure on the chest prevents the lungs from expanding properly. Add sheets restricting airflow, add the 150-to-170-pound weight of an adult man lying across a 70-pound child's chest for two hours, add the panic that comes with not being able to breathe, and death becomes highly likely.

This isn't specialised medical knowledge. It's a basic understanding of how breathing works. But in the moment, focused on demons and spiritual warfare, apparently nobody thought about the physical reality of what they were doing to a child's body.

When Terrance stopped moving, when he went limp, they might have thought they'd succeeded. The demons had left. The child was delivered. Maybe there was even a moment of relief before they realised something was wrong. That transition from "we did it" to "something's wrong" to "he's not breathing" to "call 911" must have happened fast, confusion turning to horror as they realised the still child wasn't peaceful or delivered but dying.

The church released a statement expressing sorrow while downplaying its role. "Terrance's death is a great tragedy," Bishop David Hemphill said. "However, it was not a malicious act on the part of the church."

He told the Milwaukee Journal Sentinel: "We didn't do anything wrong. We did what the book of Matthew said in chapter 12. All we did was ask God to deliver him."

The paramedics arrived to find a dead eight-year-old boy and a church full of people who'd just realised they'd killed him. The statements given to the police in the aftermath are heartbreaking. People trying to explain what happened, what they'd been trying to do, why it had seemed right at the time. Patricia Cooper's grief, her confusion, her slow realisation that the people she'd trusted had killed her son whilst she held his feet.

The autopsy was unambiguous. Terrance died from mechanical asphyxia due to external chest compression. The medical examiner noted evidence consistent with sustained pressure on a small body, a clear indication this wasn't a natural death or an accident in any meaningful sense. Someone had decided to hold this child down. Multiple people had maintained that decision for two hours. And that decision had killed him.

The trial forced uncomfortable questions about religious freedom and harm. Hemphill's lawyers argued this was a protected religious practice. The prosecution countered that freedom of religion doesn't include the right to kill children. The jury had to decide whether sincere religious belief mitigated the crime of causing a child's death through dangerous restraint. They decided it didn't excuse the reck-lessness, but apparently, it mitigated enough that the sentence was rel-atively light.

After his release, Hemphill apparently continued ministry work. Faith Temple Church itself seems to have dissolved or changed. Some people in the community saw Hemphill as a victim of persecution, a man punished for his faith. Others saw him as someone who'd killed a child and gotten away with it because religion protected him from the consequences his actions deserved.

Neither narrative captures the complexity. Hemphill almost cer-tainly believed he was helping. His religious convictions were genuine. He didn't set out to kill a child. But his belief, his certainty, his belief system that interpreted autism as demonic possession, made him do something that any reasonable person should have known was danger-ous. An eight-year-old boy died because belief overrode basic common sense about how fragile children's bodies are and how easily restraint can kill.

Patricia Cooper had to bury her son. Had to live with the knowl-edge that she'd taken him to that church, that she'd believed them when they said he was possessed, that she'd held his feet whilst they pressed on his chest, that she'd trusted them to help him, and instead they'd killed him. The guilt, the grief, the second-guessing of every de-cision that led to that moment, that's a burden that doesn't end.

Terrance's father, Terrance Cottrell Sr., told reporters he wanted everyone involved in his son's death held responsible. But the legal sys-tem, unwilling or unable to charge multiple participants, focused on the pastor who'd led the ritual.

The African American autistic community responded to Ter-rance's death with grief and fury. Here was yet another case of a Black autistic child being seen as possessed rather than disabled, subjected to violence under the guise of help, dying because the adults around him couldn't or wouldn't recognise autism when they saw it. The intersecting vulnerabilities being Black, being autistic, and being in a religious community that interpreted neurodivergence as demonic made Terrance particularly at risk. And nobody had protected him.

Advocacy groups pushed for better awareness about autism in religious communities, for training that would help pastors and church leaders recognise neurodevelopmental conditions and respond appropriately. Some churches engaged with this, developed policies on when to call medical professionals rather than attempt spiritual intervention, and formed partnerships with disability organisations. Others resisted, saw it as a secular intrusion into religious matters, and maintained that demons are real and sometimes children need deliverance regardless of what medical diagnoses they might have.

William Stillman, a Pennsylvania author with Asperger's syndrome who'd written eight books on autism, including two dealing with spirituality, told reporters after Terrance's death: "Isn't a place of worship supposed to be a sanctuary for all who wish to practise their religious beliefs? One of the things I've been seeing become more common is parents being led to believe by members of their religious denomination that they need to consider an exorcism or a deliverance ceremony to rid their child of autism."

The case contributed to growing concerns about restraint-related deaths of autistic children. Terrance wasn't the first and wouldn't be the last autistic child killed by adults using restraint, whether during an exorcism or in schools or psychiatric facilities. The common thread is that when autistic children's behaviour escalates, often because their needs aren't being met or because they're in distress, adults respond with force meant to control them. And sometimes that force kills them.

There's a direct line between seeing autism as demonic and seeing autism as something that needs to be forcibly suppressed or controlled. Both frameworks treat autistic behaviour as wrong, as something to eliminate rather than understand and accommodate. Both put the burden on the autistic child to change rather than on adults to create environments where autistic children can exist safely. And both can lead to violence against vulnerable children who can't defend themselves or escape.

In 2006, filmmaker John Haderlein created a thirty-minute documentary about Terrance's life and death, titled "Junior: The Terrance Cottrell Story," using the nickname those who loved him called him by. The film took an uncompromising look at the bleak plight of autistic children, specifically Black autistic children in impoverished communities where resources are scarce and cultural frameworks make tragic outcomes more likely. The documentary was shown at conferences and advocacy events, but never received wide distribution. Most people have never heard of Terrance Cottrell Jr.

Terrance was eight years old and autistic. He couldn't explain to the adults holding him down why what they were doing was wrong. He couldn't make them see him. He died without anyone in that room understanding what they were looking at — not demons, not spiritual resistance, just a child who needed air.

The theological questions raised by his death are uncomfortable for religious communities that practise deliverance ministry. If Terrance wasn't possessed, if his autism was just autism, then the exorcism was based on misdiagnosis. But how do you know? What's the test for distinguishing between psychiatric or neurological conditions and genuine possession? If you get it wrong, if you perform an exorcism on someone who needs medical care, you've done tremendous harm. But if demons are real and you don't perform an exorcism on someone who genuinely needs it, haven't you also failed them?

The answer some churches arrived at is that medical and spiritual approaches shouldn't be either-or. You can pray for someone whilst also ensuring they get appropriate medical care. You can believe in demons whilst also recognising that most unusual behaviour has natural explanations. You can practise your faith whilst deferring to medical expertise about diagnoses and treatment. But that requires humility about spiritual discernment, a willingness to admit you might be wrong, prioritising the person's wellbeing over theological certainty.

Other churches rejected that compromise. Saw it as capitulation to secular thinking, as denying the reality of the spiritual realm, as a lack of faith. In their view, if you truly believe demons exist, if you truly trust God's power to deliver people, then medical interventions are at best supplementary and at worst evidence of insufficient faith. That certainty, that unwillingness to consider they might be wrong about spiritual interpretation, is what makes deliverance ministry so dangerous.

Terrance's case should have been a turning point. It should have made every church practising deliverance ministry pause and ask hard questions about their protocols, how they determine who needs exorcism, the physical safety measures they have in place, and when they involve medical professionals. Some churches did that. Many didn't. And children remain at risk because the theological belief system that killed Terrance Cottrell Jr. is still active in churches across America and around the world.

The weight of faith, when it's placed on a child's chest and maintained for two hours until he can't breathe anymore, is fatal. Not metaphorically. Literally. Faith killed Terrance. Not God, not demons, but human beings who believed so completely in their spiritual interpretation that they ignored physical reality until an eight-year-old boy was dead.

That's the tragedy underneath this case. The people who killed Terrance loved him. Patricia Cooper loved her son. The congregation thought they were helping. Pastor Hemphill genuinely believed he was saving the child's soul. Their intentions, from their perspective, were pure. And that made no difference to the outcome at all. Good intentions combined with dangerous practices and religious certainty killed him as thoroughly as malice would have. Maybe more thoroughly, because malice might have stopped when the child's distress became obvious. Faith kept going, certain that the suffering was necessary, that this was spiritual warfare, that God would protect the child if they were truly doing His work.

He didn't. God didn't protect Terrance Cottrell Jr. from the people who were praying whilst they compressed his chest for two hours. Eight years old, autistic, vulnerable, killed by faith that couldn't see past demons to recognise the frightened child suffocating beneath their hands.

CHAPTER XII

The Deliverance That Killed

LONDON, ENGLAND. WINTER 2010.

Kristy Bamu was fifteen years old when his sister and her boyfriend drowned him in a bathtub filled with freezing water, convinced he was possessed by Kindoki witchcraft and needed deliverance. He'd been in their flat in Newham, East London, for nine days. Nine days that had started as a Christmas holiday visit and ended with Kristy begging his older sister Magalie to kill him, to make the pain stop, whilst she stood by and watched her boyfriend Eric Bikubi torture him with hammers, metal bars, pliers, and knives.

By the time Kristy slipped beneath the water that Christmas evening, he'd suffered 130 separate injuries. His teeth had been knocked out. His skull was fractured. His ears had been twisted with pliers until they bled. Ceramic floor tiles had been smashed over his head. He'd been beaten with metal bars until bones broke, stabbed with knives, denied food and water and sleep for days. And through it all, Magalie and Eric had been performing what they believed was an exorcism, a "deliverance ceremony" to drive the evil spirits out of him.

When paramedics arrived at the eighth-floor flat on Manor Road, they found Kristy's body still in the bath. Eric Bikubi had attempted resuscitation after realising the boy wasn't moving, but it was far too late. Kristy had been dead for some time, drowned and beaten, a fifteen-year-old child who'd travelled from Paris expecting to celebrate Christmas with family and instead died because the people he loved and trusted believed he was a witch.

The medical examiner's report documented what had been done to him. Over 130 injuries. Blunt force trauma to the head. Multiple fractures. Lacerations. Burns. Evidence of sustained, systematic torture over multiple days. The cause of death: drowning, but only after the prolonged abuse had left him too weak to resist, too broken to fight back, begging for death as a mercy.

Magalie Bamu, 29, Kristy's eldest sister, was arrested immediately. So was Eric Bikubi, twenty-eight, a football coach originally from the Democratic Republic of Congo. Both were charged with murder. The investigation that followed would reveal not just what happened to Kristy, but how belief in witchcraft, Kindoki in the Lingala language of the DRC, had turned a family Christmas into a four-day ordeal of torture culminating in a child's death.

And Kristy wasn't the only victim. His siblings had been there too, forced to watch, forced to participate, terrorised into believing they were also possessed and needed violent cleansing to survive.

Kristy Bamu was born in the Democratic Republic of Congo, but his family had moved to Paris when he was young. By December 2010, he was living there with his parents, Pierre and Jacqueline Bamu, and his siblings: Kelly (twenty years old), Yves, and two younger children whose names were protected during legal proceedings. The family was working-class, struggling financially but close-knit. Pierre and Jacqueline worked hard to provide for their children, and the siblings looked out for each other.

Magalie was the oldest. She'd moved to London years earlier with her boyfriend, Eric Bikubi. The couple lived in a flat in a tower block in Newham, East London, that housed dozens of families. Eric worked as a football coach. He was known in the community and seemed ordinary enough on the surface. But Eric Bikubi had what would later be described in court as an obsession with Kindoki, witchcraft and possession.

This wasn't his first accusation. In 2008, two years before Kristy's murder, a young woman named Naomi Ilonga had stayed with Eric and Magalie for three months. Naomi was nineteen years old. During her stay, Eric became convinced she was possessed by Kindoki. His evidence? She bit her nails.

For three days at the end of her visit, Eric deprived Naomi of food and sleep, forced her to sit and pray with Magalie for hours, and accused her of bringing evil into his home. He told her the nail-biting was a sign that demons were making her do it, that she needed deliverance. Naomi, terrified, managed to call her mother, who came and rescued her. She escaped. Kristy Bamu would not be so lucky.

In December 2010, Kristy and four of his siblings decided to visit Magalie and Eric for Christmas. Pierre and Jacqueline couldn't get time off work immediately, so they planned to join the children a few days after Christmas. The siblings travelled from Paris to London on 16th December 2010. Kelly was twenty, responsible and protective of her younger siblings. Yves was in his teens. The two youngest children were eleven and younger. And Kristy, fifteen years old, quiet, possibly on the autism spectrum though never formally diagnosed, excited about seeing his oldest sister.

The first few days were lovely, according to Kelly's later testimony. Normal family time. Chatting, catching up, preparing for Christmas. Magalie seemed pleased to see them. Eric was welcoming. There was no indication of what was coming.

Then, a few days after they arrived, something shifted. Eric started watching the children closely. Started making comments about their behaviour. Started using the word Kindoki. Kelly, who'd been raised partly in the DRC before the family moved to France, understood what that meant. The younger children, raised entirely in Paris, didn't. But they all sensed the change in atmosphere, the way Eric's gaze had become suspicious, the way Magalie deferred to him completely.

Eric Bikubi's accusations started small. The children were behaving oddly, he said. They were bringing negative energy into the flat. They needed to pray. So, they prayed. Hours of prayer, Eric leading them, demanding confessions of wrongdoing, insisting they ask God to cleanse them of evil. Still relatively benign, if increasingly unsettling.

Then Kristy wet himself. He'd been under enormous stress, frightened, and sleep-deprived from the constant praying. Bedwetting is a common response to anxiety and trauma, especially in young people. But Eric interpreted it as confirmation of possession. A child wetting himself could only mean one thing: demons were inside him, making him lose control, marking him as possessed.

From that point, Eric's focus narrowed to Kristy. The boy became the primary target, the one Eric believed was most deeply infected with Kindoki, the source of the evil threatening his home. And over the next four days, 21st to 25th December 2010, Eric Bikubi subjected

Kristy to what the trial prosecutor would later describe as "a prolonged attack of unspeakable savagery and brutality."

The "deliverance ceremony" began with prayer. Forced, relentless prayer. Eric made Kristy and his siblings pray for hours, denying them food, water, and sleep. If they tried to rest, he woke them violently. If they said they were hungry, he told them demons didn't deserve food. If they cried, he said that was the demons crying, resisting God's power.

Then the beatings started. Eric used whatever was to hand. Sticks. Metal bars, the kind used for weightlifting. A hammer. A chisel. Ceramic floor tiles that he smashed over Kristy's head. Bottles. Knives. He forced Kristy's siblings to participate, to hit their brother, telling them it was necessary, that they had to help drive the demons out, or the whole family would be infected.

Kelly, 20, tried to protect Kristy. But Eric was a grown man, physically powerful, completely convinced of his righteous purpose. And Magalie, Kristy's own sister, wasn't intervening. Wasn't stopping Eric. Was, in fact, participating. She beat Kristy herself. Used pliers to twist his ear until it tore. Encouraged Eric when he seemed to be wavering. "He deserves it," she told Kelly when Kelly begged her to make it stop. "We are witches. We deserve this."

At one point, Eric tried to force Kristy, Kelly, and their eleven-year-old sister to jump out of the window to prove they could fly. If they were really witches, he reasoned, they should be able to fly. When they refused, terrified, he beat them harder for their "disobedience."

The flat was in chaos. Blood on the walls, on the floors. Kristy's younger siblings were forced to clean it up whilst Eric played loud music to drown out the screaming. A neighbour complained about the noise on Christmas Eve, but didn't follow through or investigate further. Just another noise complaint in a busy tower block.

Kelly and the eleven-year-old sister eventually "confessed" to being witches, hoping it would end the torture. It worked for them. Eric eased off, satisfied they'd repented. But Kristy refused to confess. Maybe he didn't understand what was being asked of him. Maybe he couldn't bring himself to admit to something that wasn't true. Maybe he was too traumatised to respond coherently. Whatever the reason, his refusal to confess convinced Eric that the demons in him were particularly strong, particularly resistant to deliverance. The torture intensified.

By Christmas Eve, Kristy was broken. Physically destroyed from the days of beating. Emotionally shattered from the betrayal of his sister, from the realisation nobody was coming to save him. He was begging to die. "Please kill me," he told Magalie. "Please make it stop." His sister did nothing.

That evening, Eric called Pierre and Jacqueline in Paris. Magalie spoke first, telling her father that he needed to come collect the children immediately because they were witches. Then Eric got on the phone. His message was clear and chilling: "If you don't come get him, I'm going to kill him."

Kristy also spoke to his father. His final words: "Eric will kill me."

Pierre Bamu, six hours away in Paris, panicked. He'd trusted Eric, thought of him as a son, believed his daughter was in good hands. But now Eric was threatening to murder his child, and Kristy was warning him that he was going to die. Pierre and Jacqueline frantically searched for a last-minute hire car to drive to London immediately. It was Christmas Eve. Everything was booked. They couldn't find transport.

They decided they'd have to wait and arrive as planned two days later, on the 27th.

They didn't know they'd already run out of time.

Christmas Day 2010. The flat on Manor Road was a scene of carnage. Kristy could barely stand. His face was destroyed, teeth knocked out, skull fractured. His body was covered in cuts, bruises, and broken bones. He'd had no food or water for days. He was, in the words the court would later hear, "begging to die" from the pain.

Eric decided the final deliverance would be ritual cleansing in water. He forced Kristy into the bathtub. Turned on the cold water freezing, because the hot water wasn't working or because Eric believed cold water was part of the ritual. Forced Kristy's siblings into the bath as well, making them watch and participate.

As the water level rose, Kristy, too weak to hold himself up, slipped beneath the surface. Kelly noticed he wasn't breathing. Screamed for Eric to do something. Eric finally realised something was wrong, that the boy wasn't fighting anymore, wasn't moving, that the "deliverance" had gone further than intended.

He pulled Kristy from the bath and attempted CPR. But Kristy Bamu was dead. Drowned, beaten to death, tortured by his sister and her boyfriend, who believed they were saving his soul whilst destroying his body.

Magalie called 999. Paramedics arrived rapidly. Tried to resuscitate Kristy. But he'd been dead too long. Brain death from drowning, compounded by the trauma his body had endured over four days. There was nothing they could do.

At 8 pm on Christmas Day, Kelly Bamu called her parents in Paris. Told them Kristy was dead. Pierre and Jacqueline, who'd been preparing to drive to London the next morning, fell apart. Their son was gone. Killed by their eldest daughter and the man they'd trusted as family.

Police arrested Eric Bikubi and Magalie Bamu immediately. The flat was secured as a crime scene. The evidence was overwhelming. Blood everywhere. The weapons used in the beating. Kristy's body bore the marks of sustained torture. The surviving siblings, as witnesses, were traumatised but able to describe what had happened.

The case went to trial at the Old Bailey in early 2012. The prosecution was led by Brian Altman QC. The charges: murder for both defendants, plus two counts of actual bodily harm for the abuse of Kelly and the eleven-year-old sister.

Eric Bikubi didn't deny killing Kristy. His defence instead argued diminished responsibility due to mental illness. Brain scans showed lesions that his lawyers claimed "probably contributed to an abnormal mental state." He genuinely believed Kristy was possessed by Kindoki, they argued. He was trying to help, trying to save the child from demonic influence. The killing was tragic but not criminal in intent.

Magalie Bamu's defence was that she'd acted under duress, that Eric had terrorised her into participating, that she was as much a victim as perpetrator. She claimed she didn't believe in witchcraft, that Eric had forced her to go along with his delusions through the threat of violence.

The prosecution dismantled both defences. Kelly's testimony was devastating. Her older sister, she said, had actively participated in the torture. Had beaten Kristy herself. Had encouraged Eric when he seemed uncertain. Had shown no pity, no mercy, no recognition that what they were doing was wrong.

"It was as if they were obsessed by witchcraft," Kelly told the court, frequently breaking down. "They decided we had come there to kill them. Kristy asked for forgiveness. He asked again and again. Magalie did absolutely nothing. She didn't give a damn. She said we deserved it."

Kelly called her sister "an idiot," said she was certain Magalie still believed, even now, that they were witches. "I have no pity for her," Kelly said. "She had no pity for us."

The prosecution presented medical evidence of Kristy's injuries. Over 130 separate wounds. The systematic nature of the torture. The weapons used. The duration of four days of sustained abuse. Expert witnesses testified about Kindoki beliefs, about possession belief systems in Congolese communities, and about how those beliefs could lead to violence when combined with mental illness, paranoia, and unchecked authority.

They also presented evidence of Eric's previous accusations against Naomi Ilonga in 2008, establishing a pattern of behaviour, proving this wasn't an isolated psychotic break but a sustained belief system that had led to abuse before.

The trial lasted eight weeks. The jury heard evidence so disturbing that Judge David Paget, who was presiding over his final trial before retirement, told them it was so "harrowing" he was exempting them all from jury service for the rest of their lives. "It is a case we will all remember," he said. "Court staff will speak to you and offer help to you."

On 1st March 2012, the jury returned guilty verdicts for both defendants. Eric Bikubi: guilty of murder. Magalie Bamu: guilty of murder by a 10-2 majority verdict. Both were also found guilty of actual bodily harm against Kelly and the younger sister.

Sentencing took place on 5th March 2012. Judge Paget addressed the court, describing the murder as having "a sadistic element," calling it "prolonged torture involving mental and physical suffering being inflicted before death." He said the ordeal the children were subjected to "almost passes belief."

He accepted Eric's defence that he had brain damage and genuinely believed Kristy was a witch. But, the judge emphasised, "The belief in witchcraft, however genuine, cannot excuse an assault on another person, let alone the killing of another human being."

To Magalie, the judge said she'd shown no remorse at any point during the trial, had never apologised, and her claim that Eric forced her to participate was not credible. Kelly's testimony proved Magalie had acted of her own accord, had encouraged and participated in the violence willingly.

Eric Bikubi was sentenced to life imprisonment with a minimum term of 30 years. Magalie Bamu was sentenced to life imprisonment with a minimum term of 25 years. Both were remanded in custody immediately.

Pierre Bamu's statement, read aloud in court, left jury members in tears. "I feel betrayed," he wrote. "To know that Kristy's own sister, Magalie, did nothing to save him makes the pain that much worse. We were always fond of Eric and regarded him as a son. Kristy died in unimaginable circumstances at the hands of people who he loved and trusted. People whom we all loved and trusted."

But then, in a gesture of extraordinary grace, the family added: "We will never forget, but to put our lives back into sync, we must forgive. We take no comfort in the verdicts; we have been robbed of a beloved son, a daughter, a son-in-law. Christmas, a festival of joy and Jacqueline's birthday, will always be scarred by these terrible events."

The case sparked a national conversation about child abuse linked to witchcraft and possession beliefs in the UK. Scotland Yard revealed they'd carried out 83 investigations into faith-based child abuse over the previous ten years. Kristy's case was the most extreme, but it wasn't isolated.

Detective Superintendent Terry Sharpe of the Metropolitan Police said: "Child abuse in any form, including that based on a belief in witchcraft or spirit possession, is a horrific crime which is condemned by people of all cultures, communities and faith, and is never acceptable in any circumstances."

In August 2012, the UK government launched an action plan to tackle child abuse linked to witchcraft or possession. The plan aimed to raise awareness, provide training for frontline workers, reach out to faith organisations, and set out practical steps to identify and protect children at risk.

But critics argued the action plan didn't go far enough because it failed to address the root cause: the branding of vulnerable children as witches or possessed. In African contexts where these beliefs are prevalent, witch-branding is tantamount to violence. Once a child is labelled as possessed, the actions that follow neglect, physical abuse, emotional abuse, sexual abuse, denial of medical care, and withdrawal from school become justified in the minds of the abusers as necessary deliverance.

Kristy's case highlighted how these beliefs could transplant to Western countries through migration, carrying the same deadly potential when combined with isolation, a lack of oversight, and authority figures who believe their spiritual interpretation overrides physical reality.

Understanding what happened to Kristy requires understanding Kindoki. In the Democratic Republic of Congo and surrounding regions, Kindoki means witchcraft or sorcery. It's believed that certain people, often children, can be possessed by evil spirits that give them supernatural powers to harm others. The belief is deeply embedded in cultural and spiritual frameworks, where the supernatural and physical worlds are understood as interconnected.

Kindoki isn't specifically part of Islam (like djinn) or Christianity (like Western demon possession), though it exists alongside both religions in the DRC. It's an indigenous African belief system that predates colonial religions and has persisted through them, sometimes blending with Christian or Islamic frameworks.

Children accused of Kindoki face terrible consequences. They're seen as dangerous, as vessels for evil that must be cleansed through violent exorcism rituals. The symptoms that "prove" possession are often just normal childhood behaviours reinterpreted through a supernatural lens: bedwetting, nightmares, illness, behavioural difficulties, even just being different or difficult.

Eric Bikubi's belief in Kindoki was genuine, according to all evidence. The brain lesions documented in his scans suggested organic pathology, structural damage that can disrupt normal cognitive processing, impair reality testing, and generate paranoid ideation. In psychiatric terms, Eric likely suffered from a delusional disorder with persecutory features, his conviction that others were using witchcraft against him meeting the clinical criteria for a fixed, false belief resistant to contrary evidence.

The lesions may have contributed to what psychiatrists call "impaired theory of mind", difficulty understanding that other people have internal states different from one's own. When Eric looked at Kristy, he couldn't see a frightened fifteen-year-old; he saw only the threat his damaged brain insisted was there. The paranoid psychosis made him certain, absolutely convinced, that demons were present and violence was a necessary defence.

This type of delusional disorder often features hypervigilance, the constant scanning for threats, and the reinterpretation of innocent behaviours as evidence of malevolence. Kristy's every action got filtered through Eric's paranoid lens. A quiet child became suspiciously withdrawn. Normal teenage awkwardness became evidence of demonic influence. Bedwetting from stress became proof of possession. Eric's damaged brain couldn't distinguish between his fears and reality, couldn't recognise that the threat he perceived wasn't there.

But genuine belief doesn't excuse violence. Doesn't make the torture less real or the child less dead. Kristy Bamu suffered because Eric believed he was possessed, yes, but he died because Eric acted on that belief with systematic brutality for four days, and because Magalie, Kristy's own sister, believed it too or at least believed Eric enough to participate in killing her brother.

Magalie's role reveals something more disturbing than psychosis: folie à deux, shared psychotic disorder, where a delusional belief system transfers from one person to another through close association. In psychiatric literature, this typically occurs when a dominant partner (the "inducer") imposes their delusions on a more passive, suggestible partner (the "acceptor") who's psychologically or emotionally dependent on them.

Eric was the inducer. His paranoid conviction about Kindoki, backed by his authority as an older man and Magalie's partner, created a worldview she adopted. But folie à deux requires more than just proximity to delusion. It requires isolation from reality checks, dependence on the delusional person, and often an underlying vulnerability in the acceptor, low self-esteem, limited social connections outside the relationship, and a need to maintain the bond at any cost.

Magalie ticked every box. She'd moved to London, away from her family support system. Eric was her primary relationship, her household, her life. When he started seeing demons, when he interpreted her siblings' visit through his paranoid lens, she faced a choice: believe Eric and maintain the relationship or challenge him and risk everything. She chose belief. Or more precisely, she chose Eric, and belief came with him.

This is trauma bonding in action. Trauma bonds form when intermittent reinforcement, kindness mixed with cruelty, affection alternating with threat, creates a powerful psychological attachment. Abusers don't abuse constantly; they cycle between harm and care, keeping their victims hooked through unpredictability. Magalie had likely experienced this pattern with Eric for years. He could be loving, then paranoid. Gentle, then violent. And her survival strategy became compliance, agreement, and participation in whatever he believed to keep herself safe.

But trauma bonding doesn't fully explain Magalie beating her own brother with pliers, watching him beg for death and doing nothing. That requires something darker: identification with the aggressor, a defence mechanism where the victim internalises the abuser's perspective to reduce anxiety. If Magalie couldn't stop Eric, couldn't protect Kristy without endangering herself, then perhaps the way to survive psychologically was to believe Eric was right. That Kristy really was possessed. That the torture was necessary. That she was helping, not harming.

This is how ordinary people participate in atrocities. Not through malice, not through inherent evil, but through psychological mechanisms that allow them to live with themselves whilst committing terrible acts. Magalie remade reality to match Eric's delusions because that was less painful than acknowledging she was helping torture her brother to death, whilst doing nothing to save him.

The prosecution argued Magalie acted independently, encouraged Eric, and showed no coercion. Kelly's testimony confirmed this. But that doesn't mean Magalie wasn't psychologically trapped. Abused partners who become abusers themselves exist in a grey area where victimhood and perpetration blur. She was both a victim of Eric's psychological control and perpetrator of Kristy's torture. The judge rejected her duress defence because her actions went beyond mere compliance; she initiated violence, showed enthusiasm, and displayed none of the reluctance that genuine duress produces. She'd internalised Eric's worldview so completely that it became her own.

This makes her, in some ways, more culpable than Eric. He had brain damage, structural pathology impairing his judgment. She had psychological dependence, trauma bonding, shared delusion, all real, all documented, all insufficient to excuse watching your brother beg for death and feeling no pity. The jury recognised this in their verdict. Magalie chose Eric over Kristy, chose maintaining her relationship over protecting a child, chose belief in demons over the evidence of her brother's agony. Those were choices, however constrained by psychology, and she made them repeatedly for four days.

And then there's Kristy himself. The quiet fifteen-year-old was possibly occupied somewhere on the autism spectrum, though never formally diagnosed. His family noticed he was different, quieter than his siblings, sometimes seeming to exist in his own world, processing social interactions in ways that didn't quite match neurotypical expectations. In another context, with proper assessment and support, he might have thrived. In Eric Bikubi's paranoid framework, those differences became evidence of possession.

Autistic people are particularly vulnerable to possession accusations because their neurodivergent behaviours can seem inexplicable to those who don't understand autism. The stimming repetitive movements that help regulate sensory input look like involuntary actions caused by external forces. The communication differences look like something blocking normal speech. The sensory sensitivities that cause meltdowns look like rage or distress from demonic influence. The tendency to retreat into special interests or internal worlds seems to be controlled by something else.

Kristy's possible autism made him a perfect target for Eric's delusions. His quietness became suspicious withdrawal. His difficulty with social reciprocity became a demonic interference with normal human connection. His fear responses to bedwetting and his inability to explain himself in ways Eric expected became proof of possession. Every neurological difference was reframed as a spiritual affliction.

And autistic people often can't advocate for themselves effectively in these situations. They might struggle to articulate what they're experiencing, to explain that their behaviours are neurological rather than spiritual, to make people understand that what looks like "demons" is a brain that works differently. Kristy tried to defend himself, "I'm not a witch," he told Eric repeatedly. But he couldn't make Eric understand, couldn't find the words or the framework to explain his neurodivergence in ways Eric's paranoid psychosis would accept. His difference became his death sentence.

The psychological mechanisms at work here mirror those in other possession-based killings. Confirmation bias turned Kristy's every behaviour into evidence of demons. When he wet himself: possession. When he seemed withdrawn: demons taking hold. When he cried, demons resisted. When he begged for mercy, the demons tried to manipulate them into stopping the deliverance. The framework explained everything in ways that made continued torture seem necessary.

Group dynamics intensified the violence. Eric and Magalie reinforced each other's beliefs in a closed loop where doubt became impossible. The younger children were forced to participate, creating a group consensus that this was right and necessary, that resistance to the "deliverance" would mark them as possessed, too. When everyone in the room agrees that an exorcism is happening, that demons are being fought, dissent becomes impossible.

The flat's isolation meant there were no witnesses who might have challenged their interpretation. No outside perspectives to say, "this is a child being tortured, not a demon being exorcised." The children had nowhere to go, no way to call for help without Eric or Magalie knowing. They were trapped in a closed system where Eric's authority and Magalie's complicity created a reality where torture was deliverance.

The forced participation traumatised Kristy's siblings in ways they'll carry forever. Being made to hit your brother whilst he begs for mercy creates psychological damage that persists decades later. Kelly, who tried to protect Kristy, lives with survivor's guilt, the knowledge that she couldn't save him, that she was forced to hurt him, that she confessed to witchcraft to make her torture stop, whilst Kristy refused and died for it. The younger siblings watched their brother being murdered, participated under threat, and will spend their lives processing that trauma.

This is intergenerational harm. Eric's psychosis and Magalie's complicity didn't just kill Kristy; they damaged every child in that flat, destroyed Pierre and Jacqueline's family, left Kelly and her siblings with PTSD, attachment disorders, and profound mistrust of authority figures who claim to be helping. The psychological aftermath of possession-based abuse extends far beyond the person who dies.

Kristy came to London to spend Christmas with family. He died in a bathtub on Christmas Day, fifteen years old, because the people who should have loved him decided to destroy him instead.

The theological and psychological questions his death raises are uncomfortable. If Eric genuinely believed Kristy was possessed, if his brain lesions impaired his ability to recognise reality, is he responsible? The court said yes. Belief doesn't excuse violence. Mental illness doesn't erase culpability when you torture someone for four days. Even if demons were real, even if Kristy had been possessed, the "deliverance" Eric performed was just torture dressed up in religious language.

And Magalie had no such excuse. No brain damage. No documented mental illness beyond the shared psychosis she'd adopted from Eric. Just a woman who believed her boyfriend's accusations more than her brother's screams, who beat her sibling because someone told her he was possessed, who stood by whilst a child begged to die and did nothing to save him. Trauma bonding explains her psychological state, but doesn't excuse her actions. Understanding how she became capable of such cruelty doesn't make the cruelty less real, doesn't make Kristy less dead.

Child protection failed Kristy. The neighbour who complained about noise but didn't investigate. The systems in place to identify at-risk children somehow missed five kids being tortured in a London flat for four days. The cultural competency gaps meant social services and police didn't always recognise when "deliverance ceremonies" were child abuse.

After Kristy's death, there were calls for better training, better awareness, and better intervention. Some churches engaged with this, created safeguarding policies, and partnered with child protection agencies. Others resisted, saw it as interference in religious matters, and maintained that spiritual beliefs couldn't be questioned by secular authorities.

But Kindoki killed Kristy. Not metaphorically. Not indirectly. The belief system, combined with Eric's paranoid psychosis, Magalie's trauma-bonded compliance, and Kristy's neurodivergent vulnerability, created conditions where a fifteen-year-old boy was tortured to death whilst his siblings watched, whilst his parents were six hours away in Paris desperately trying to find transport to save him, whilst Christmas Day 2010 became the day a family was destroyed because possession seemed more plausible than recognising a child in need of protection.

The weight of belief, when placed on a child's body in the form of hammers and pliers and metal bars, kills. When belief drives you to hold a fifteen-year-old underwater until he drowns, it's not faith. It's violence. And no amount of genuine conviction about demons makes the violence righteous, makes the dead child less dead, makes the torture less real.

Kristy Bamu died because people believed in Kindoki more than they believed their own eyes, their own hearts, their basic human obligation not to torture children. Fifteen years old. Visiting family for Christmas. He died in a bathtub because his sister and her boyfriend saw demons instead of seeing him.

CHAPTER XIII

The Cross She Couldn't Escape

Tanacu, Romania, Spring 2005

Maricica Irina Cornici, twenty-three years old, died chained to a wooden cross in the basement of the Holy Trinity Monastery. No food for three days. No water. A towel was stuffed in her mouth to stop her cursing. Her wrists and ankles were raw from restraints. When the nuns finally called an ambulance, she was already dead, killed during an exorcism meant to save her soul.

Father Daniel Petru Corogeanu, the twenty-nine-year-old priest who led the ritual, initially believed he'd succeeded. "She was cured," he told police. The devils had left her body. She'd simply fainted from exhaustion. Except Irina never woke up. When doctors examined her corpse at the hospital, they found ligature marks on her wrists, ankles and stomach. The autopsy concluded she'd died from dehydration, exhaustion and lack of oxygen. The police investigation that followed would expose how a young woman with schizophrenia became trapped in a medieval nightmare, sacrificed to a belief system that saw demons where psychiatry saw illness.

Irina's life had been precarious from the start. Born into a broken family in rural Romania, she lost her father to suicide while still a child. She and her brother Vasile grew up in an orphanage, one of thousands of Romanian children abandoned to the state during Nicolae Ceaușescu's brutal communist regime. The orphanages were grim, overcrowded, understaffed, offering little beyond basic survival. Irina emerged from that system damaged but determined. At nineteen, she found work as a nanny in Germany, then later in Banat, a region in western Romania. She sent money home. She tried building a life.

In January 2005, Irina visited a friend who'd become a nun at the Holy Trinity Monastery in Tanacu, a tiny village of about a thousand people in Vaslui County, north-eastern Romania. The monastery sat on a hilltop overlooking rolling vineyards and cornfields, isolated, austere, recently built by a private donor. Irina's friend encouraged her to stay, to join the order. Perhaps Irina saw an escape from her difficult past, a community to belong to, stability she'd never known. Perhaps she simply had nowhere else to go. She moved into the convent and began training as a nun.

Within weeks, something went wrong. Irina started giggling inappropriately during Mass. Then the giggling became disturbing behaviour, talking to herself, claiming she heard voices, acting in ways that frightened the other nuns. By April 2005, her mental state had deteriorated enough that she was admitted to the psychiatric unit in Vaslui, the nearest city.

Dr Gheorghe Silvestrovici, the psychiatrist who treated her, later told journalists what he'd observed. "She thought the devil was talking to her and told her that she was a sinful person. It's a symptom of schizophrenia, and she was probably having her first episode." The diagnosis was clear. Irina was experiencing psychosis auditory hallucinations, paranoid delusions, the classic presentation of schizophrenia in a young adult. The doctors prescribed antipsychotic medication and kept her in the hospital for two weeks. When they released her on 20th April, they gave her explicit instructions: continue taking the medication, return for follow-up appointments in ten days. They remitted her to the care of the monastery, assuming the nuns would ensure she attended her appointments and took her pills.

She never returned to the hospital. Back at the monastery, Father Corogeanu reached a different conclusion about what was wrong with Irina. The voices she heard weren't symptoms of mental illness. They were demons. Satan himself had taken possession of her body and was tormenting her soul. The inappropriate giggling, the disturbing statements, and the refusal to drink holy water are all evidence of demonic influence. Medical treatment was irrelevant. "You can't take the Devil out of people with pills," Corogeanu would later tell the court. What Irina needed wasn't psychiatry. She needed an exorcism.

Corogeanu's background should have raised concerns long before Irina arrived. He'd been ordained as a priest without finishing his theological studies, a shortcut facilitated by the post-communist religious revival that saw hundreds of new monasteries and churches erected across Romania in the 1990s and early 2000s. Under Ceaușescu, Orthodox Christianity had been suppressed, churches closed, and priests persecuted. When the regime fell in 1989, there was an explosion of religious fervour and a desperate shortage of clergy. Men like Corogeanu, minimally trained but enthusiastic, filled the gap. The Romanian Orthodox Church, scrambling to meet demand, overlooked gaps in education and orthodoxy. Corogeanu reportedly performed exorcisms in ways not approved by Church authorities and even accused his own bishop of promoting Freemasonry, a sign of his conspiratorial thinking and willingness to operate outside official channels.

But in Tanacu, isolated from oversight, Corogeanu had authority. He was the priest. His word was spiritual law. And when he decided Irina was possessed, the four nuns assisting him, Nicoleta Arcalianu, Adina Cepraga, Elena Otel and Simona Bardanas accepted his diagnosis without question. The medication was stopped. The follow-up appointments were ignored. Irina's psychosis, untreated, intensified.

Even Irina's brother Vasile, who visited her at the monastery, became convinced she was possessed. He later testified in court that he'd been with her when he saw Satan "go into her." The entity taunted her, he claimed, calling her "girl" and "girly" during her first communion. This testimony reveals how possession narratives shape perception. Vasile interpreted his sister's psychotic symptoms through a supernatural lens because that was the framework everyone around him used. If the priest said Satan was present, if the nuns agreed, if Irina herself was describing the devil speaking to her, then possession became the shared reality. The psychiatric diagnosis, delivered by trained doctors in a hospital, carried no weight against the collective belief of the religious community.

The exorcism itself was brutal and prolonged. Initially, the nuns simply bound Irina's hands and feet and locked her in her room whilst they celebrated the Ascension of Jesus. When that didn't "cure" her, Corogeanu escalated. He had the nuns construct a makeshift wooden cross board nailed together to form a cruciform structure. They chained Irina to it, her arms stretched out, her body exposed. They carried her into the church for the ritual.

For three days, Irina remained bound to that cross. Her wrists and forehead were anointed with holy oil. A towel was stuffed into her mouth to stop her from cursing because the curses, in Corogeanu's theology, came from demons speaking through her. The nuns and priest prayed over her continuously, sprinkling her lips with holy water, conducting prayers to cast out the Devil. No food. No water beyond the symbolic droplets on her lips. No medical attention. Just prayers and chains and the certainty that they were saving her eternal soul.

Sister Nicoleta Arcalianu, who received the longest sentence among the nuns, later defended their actions in court. "Irina was very aggressive and violent, and we did not know what to do with her. I spoke with Father Corogeanu, and we decided to isolate her. She could have either killed herself or killed someone else had we not done that. I have seen the same kind of ritual in other monasteries, and the possessed were tied up and treated in the same way as we did with Irina. Irina knew that she was possessed by evil spirits because she was begging us to tie her up and help her."

That last claim that Irina begged to be restrained deserves scrutiny. People experiencing psychosis sometimes do ask for help controlling their behaviour, especially if they're terrified by their own symptoms. If Irina believed demons were tormenting her, if she was hearing voices commanding her to do things, she might have asked the nuns to physically prevent her from acting on those commands. But that plea for help, if it happened, was a request for treatment, not authorisation for torture. Begging someone to help you stop the voices doesn't mean you consent to being chained to a cross without food or water until you die.

The defence that they'd "seen the same ritual in other monasteries" is equally revealing. Arcalianu wasn't describing a standardised Orthodox exorcism approved by Church authorities. She was describing informal, violent practices that had spread through rural Romanian monasteries in the chaotic post-communist years. Corogeanu and others like him were making up their procedures, drawing on medieval folklore and fragments of liturgy, creating rituals that the official Church would later condemn as "abominable" and "illegal." But in isolated communities like Tanacu, these improvised exorcisms became normalised. If other monasteries were tying people to crosses, if other priests were using physical force to expel demons, then it seemed legitimate. Tradition, even recent and invented tradition, carries powerful authority.

After three days, Irina went limp. Corogeanu removed the chains and declared her cured. The demons had been expelled. She'd fainted from exhaustion but would recover. They gave her bread and tea. She didn't wake up. Her pulse grew weak. Finally, the nuns panicked and called an ambulance.

What happened next remains disputed. The paramedics found Irina unconscious, dehydrated, barely alive. In the ambulance, they administered adrenaline six times, according to some accounts, trying to revive her. She died en route to the hospital. Years later, the coroner who performed the exhumation, Dr Dan Gheorghiu, would claim that Irina died from an adrenaline overdose administered by the paramedics, not from the exorcism itself. "The woman died of an overdose of adrenaline," he insisted in 2014. "Don't ask me, I don't know why the judges did not take that into account."

Corogeanu seized on this claim. "My biggest mistake was that I called the ambulance when I saw she was not moving. I think she died because the medics who came with the ambulance tried to resuscitate her by giving her too much adrenaline. Had I not called the ambulance, she would have been well now." This is blame-shifting of a particularly vicious kind, suggesting that the woman he'd tortured for three days would have survived if only he'd continued neglecting her medical needs rather than allowing professionals to intervene.

The 2005 autopsy, conducted immediately after death, concluded that Irina died from dehydration, exhaustion and lack of oxygen, direct consequences of being chained to a cross without food or water for seventy-two hours. The adrenaline administered in the ambulance was a desperate attempt to save a woman already dying from the exorcism. Whether the exact mechanism of death was the prolonged torture itself or complications from emergency treatment doesn't change the fundamental reality: Irina would have been fine if anyone had simply given her the medication prescribed by Dr Silvestrovici.

When doctors at the hospital noticed the ligature marks on Irina's body, they immediately contacted the police. Anisoara Antohi, Irina's aunt, saw the corpse before burial. "She was disfigured, she had marks on her hands, her ankles and her stomach," she told reporters. Gheorghe Antohi, Irina's great-uncle, wept at her grave. "She was a good girl. It was too cruel, God, much too cruel. Those who killed her should all be crucified like her."

The family initially tried to bury Irina quietly, perhaps hoping to avoid scandal. But some reports say "a source" contacted police before the burial could proceed. When officers arrived at the cemetery, relatives resisted their attempts to take the body for post-mortem examination. Police eventually forced the issue, removing Irina's corpse for proper investigation. That resistance points to the complicated loyalties within the community; even family members who grieved Irina's death weren't certain the monastery had done anything wrong. Possession beliefs ran deep.

Corogeanu and the four nuns were arrested and charged with aggravated murder and depriving a person of liberty. The initial charges carried potential life sentences. Prosecutors argued the case showed intentional sadism that the defendants had deliberately caused Irina's death through prolonged torture. The defence countered that aggravated murder implied intent and malice, neither of which was present. "They believed they were helping the woman, that they were curing her from her pains," argued Aurelian Pavelescu, a lawyer and member of parliament. "They should face manslaughter charges, not murder. They didn't intend to kill anyone."

The trial became a national scandal. Romanian media ran headlines like "Romania in the Middle Ages," treating the case as an embarrassing throwback to a superstitious past that the modern nation was supposed to have left behind. The Romanian Orthodox Church moved swiftly to distance itself from the tragedy. On 7th July 2005, the Holy Synod issued a statement expressing "profound shock, dismay, and sorrow" over Irina's death, attributing it to "severe physical mistreatment by monk Daniel Corogeanu and four nuns under the pretext of expelling demons."

The Church's statement carefully acknowledged that it accepted demonic possession as real and exorcism as a valid sacramental practice, but strictly limited to prescribed liturgical elements. Proper Orthodox exorcism involved reciting prayers composed by early Church Fathers, sprinkling holy water, and anointing with sanctified oil. Any deviation, binding someone to a cross, gagging them, or prolonged isolation without food or water was categorically forbidden.

The Church defrocked Corogeanu and excommunicated the four nuns. The monastery at Tanacu was closed, its gates chained shut.

The trial, held in Vaslui, stretched over months. Corogeanu and the nuns pleaded not guilty. They maintained they'd acted properly, following procedures they'd seen in other monasteries, trying to help a woman they believed was genuinely possessed. Maria Ilisei, their defence lawyer, argued: "They do not have to pay criminally for what they did. A civil suit is a different story. But not all tragic events are criminal, and I aim to absolve them of criminal guilt."

The prosecution presented medical evidence: Irina's schizophrenia diagnosis, the prescribed treatment she never received, and the autopsy findings showing death from dehydration and lack of oxygen. They presented testimony from Dr Silvestrovici about Irina's psychiatric symptoms and his clear instructions for follow-up care. They documented the physical evidence: the chains, the wooden cross, the ligature marks on Irina's body. And they emphasised that even if the defendants sincerely believed in demonic possession, "belief in possession, however genuine, cannot excuse assault to another person, let alone killing of another human being."

In February 2007, the court delivered its verdict. All five defendants were found guilty. Corogeanu was sentenced to fourteen years in prison. Sister Nicoleta Arcalianu received eight years. Sisters Adina Cepraga, Simona Bardanas and Elena Otel were each sentenced to five years. They were also ordered to pay €1,700 compensation to Irina's parents, a sum that felt grimly inadequate for the loss of their daughter.

Dozens of Corogeanu's supporters packed the courtroom. When the verdict was announced, several burst into tears. They prayed for the priest, maintained his innocence, and insisted Irina had truly been possessed. The defendants' lawyers immediately filed appeals, arguing the sentences were too harsh. In the appeal, Corogeanu's sentence was reduced to seven years. He was released on parole in November 2011 after serving two-thirds of his sentence.

Upon release, Corogeanu initially announced plans to establish a new monastery dedicated to Irina's memory, a gesture that suggested he still didn't grasp what he'd done wrong. But when he attempted to return to Tanacu, angry villagers ran him out of town. He ended up living as a hermit in a wooden hut, isolated and essentially exiled. Even after serving his sentence, the public remained unwilling to forgive him. His transformation from a local folk hero, a priest who took demonic possession seriously in a region hungry for spiritual leadership, to a national folk devil was complete.

The case prompted the Romanian Orthodox Church to implement stricter rules for entering monasteries, including mandatory psychological testing for candidates. The reforms came too late for Irina but might prevent future tragedies. In 2012, Romanian director Cristian Mungiu adapted the case into the film "Beyond the Hills" (*După Dealuri*), which premiered at Cannes and won Best Screenplay and Best Actress awards. The film brought international attention to the case and sparked discussions about the dangers of fundamentalist religious practices in isolated communities.

Yet in Tanacu itself, many residents continue to believe Irina was genuinely possessed. They insist Corogeanu did his best to help her, that the real tragedy was calling the ambulance and allowing secular authorities to interfere with spiritual matters. This persistent belief, even after the trial and convictions, demonstrates how deeply embedded possession belief systems can be. Once a community accepts that demons are real and exorcism is necessary, evidence of harm doesn't disprove the framework; it shows that the exorcism wasn't done correctly, or that the demons were particularly powerful, or that outside interference ruined what would have been a successful spiritual intervention.

From a psychiatric perspective, Irina's case is tragically straightforward. She was experiencing her first psychotic episode, almost certainly schizophrenia based on her age, symptoms and the type of hallucinations described. Hearing voices that comment negatively on your behaviour, "you're a sinful person", is a classic auditory hallucination pattern. The religious content of her delusions reflected her environment; someone experiencing psychosis typically incorporates themes from their immediate cultural context into their delusional system. In a monastery, that means demons, sin, and divine punishment.

First-episode psychosis typically emerges in early adulthood, precisely Irina's age range. The prodromal phase, the early warning signs before a full psychotic break, might have included social withdrawal, increasing isolation, and the subtle changes in thinking that friends and family notice but can't quite name. Then comes the acute phase: hallucinations, delusions, disorganised thinking, frightening breaks from shared reality. This is what Dr Silvestrovici witnessed in April 2005: a young woman in the throes of her first major psychotic episode, terrified by voices she couldn't control, trying to make sense of experiences that felt overwhelmingly real.

The content of psychotic symptoms is culturally determined. Someone raised in a secular urban environment might hear voices from aliens or government agents. Someone embedded in a religious community hears demons and divine voices. The neurological process is identical, with disrupted dopamine pathways, misfiring neurons, and the brain generating percepts without external stimuli. But the narrative overlay, the story the person tells themselves about what's happening, comes from their cultural vocabulary. Irina grew up in an Orthodox Christian household, entered a monastery, and was immersed in liturgy and theology. When her brain started misfiring, the voices naturally spoke in theological language. They told her she was sinful, that the devil was present, that she needed spiritual cleansing. This made her symptoms seem like possession to everyone around her because the symptoms themselves were described in possession language.

The tragic irony is that schizophrenia is eminently treatable, especially in first episodes. Antipsychotic medications, typically drugs like risperidone, olanzapine, or quetiapine, work by modulating dopamine receptors in the brain. They don't cure schizophrenia, but they can dramatically reduce or eliminate positive symptoms like hallucinations and delusions within weeks. The earlier treatment begins, the better the long-term outcome. People who receive prompt, appropriate treatment for first-episode psychosis have significantly better prognoses than those whose treatment is delayed or denied.

With proper medication management, therapy, and support, many people with schizophrenia go on to live productive, fulfilling lives. They manage their symptoms the way someone with diabetes manages blood sugar through consistent treatment, monitoring, and lifestyle adjustments. Some experience only one or two psychotic episodes in their lifetime if medication is maintained. Others have more chronic courses but achieve stability with proper care. The key is early intervention and consistent treatment.

Irina's prognosis, had she stayed on her medication and attended follow-up appointments, would likely have been good. She was young, physically healthy despite her difficult childhood. She had some social support from the monastery community and her brother. The doctors had diagnosed her quickly and prescribed appropriate medication. She had everything she needed to recover, except for one thing she couldn't control: the beliefs of the people around her.

Instead, she died because the people around her rejected psychiatric explanations in favour of supernatural ones. And that rejection wasn't random or irrational within their worldview; it was the logical conclusion of a religious lens that takes demonic possession seriously. If demons are real, if they can inhabit human bodies and cause disturbing behaviour, then symptoms that look exactly like demonic possession are probably exactly that. Corogeanu and the nuns weren't ignorant of medicine. They knew doctors existed, knew about hospitals, and knew Irina had been diagnosed with something. They rejected that diagnosis because their theological commitments required them to. Accepting that Irina had schizophrenia would mean accepting that demons aren't real, that exorcism doesn't work, that their entire spiritual framework is mistaken. That's psychologically untenable for true believers.

This is why psychiatric education alone won't solve the problem. You can teach communities about mental illness, explain neurotransmitters and brain chemistry, and demonstrate that medication works. But if people's deepest commitments involve supernatural causation, if their identity and community are built around beliefs in spiritual warfare, they'll find ways to preserve those beliefs. They might acknowledge that some conditions are medical, whilst maintaining that others are demonic. They might accept that medication helps, but credit prayer said alongside the pills. They might create elaborate theories about how demons exploit medical vulnerabilities or how mental illness makes people susceptible to possession. The framework adapts to accommodate contradictory evidence rather than being abandoned.

The isolation Irina experienced once identified as possessed made everything worse. Physical isolation, locked in rooms, and chained to crosses prevented her from accessing alternative perspectives or help. Social isolation meant the only people interpreting her behaviour were those already committed to the possession diagnosis. Psychological isolation meant her own attempts to explain her experience were dismissed or reinterpreted through the possession lens. When she said the devil was talking to her, a straightforward description of auditory hallucinations, they heard confirmation of demonic presence rather than a symptom requiring treatment.

This isolation also deprived her of the most basic human comforts during a terrifying experience. Psychosis is frightening. You're hearing voices others can't hear, experiencing things that feel real but that everyone insists aren't happening, losing your grip on shared reality. Most people having their first psychotic episode are terrified, confused, desperate for help, and trying to make sense of what's happening to them. They need reassurance, support, and gentle guidance back toward stability. Instead, Irina got chains and accusations that demons were inside her, which could only have intensified her terror and confusion. Every attempt to cry out, to explain her fear, to beg for help was interpreted as demons speaking. Her suffering became evidence against her rather than a call for compassion.

The mechanism by which possession beliefs killed Irina reveals a pattern seen across cases worldwide. First, symptoms are reinterpreted as spiritual problems. Second, medical treatment is discontinued or never initiated because it's deemed irrelevant to the "real" problem. Third, spiritual treatments are applied treatments that, however well-intentioned, often involve harmful practices like restraint, isolation, food deprivation or physical violence. Fourth, when the victim's condition worsens (as untreated psychosis inevitably will), this is taken as evidence that the spiritual affliction is powerful and requires more aggressive intervention. Fifth, the victim dies from the accumulated physical and psychological trauma or from complications of their untreated mental illness.

At each step, the possession framework makes harming the victim seem not just acceptable but necessary. Chaining someone to a cross sounds barbaric in psychiatric terms, but makes perfect sense in exorcism logic. You're not restraining a person; you're preventing a demon from using that person's body to cause harm. Withholding food and water sounds like torture, but if you believe the demon draws strength from physical sustenance, starving the body seems like tactical spiritual warfare. The worse the victim suffers, the more it confirms the demon's power, justifying further escalation.

Corogeanu's statement that "you can't take the Devil out of people with pills" encapsulates the fundamental incompatibility between possession belief and medical treatment. If you're certain someone is possessed, then medication isn't just useless, it's a category error, like trying to fix a spiritual problem with physical tools. This conviction makes possession believers resistant to evidence that medical treatment works. When antipsychotics eliminate hallucinations, they might credit prayer said alongside the medication, or suggest the demons were only temporarily suppressed and will return. The framework is self-sealing.

The testimony from Irina's brother, Vasile, that he witnessed Satan entering her, illustrates how possession beliefs spread within families and communities. Vasile loved his sister. He wanted her well.

When she started exhibiting disturbing symptoms, he sought explanations. The medical explanation that her brain chemistry was disrupted, that she had a treatable medical condition, might have felt insufficient or frightening. The possession explanation offered clarity, cosmic meaning, and a clear course of action: exorcism. It also connected him to a community of believers who validated his interpretation and offered support through shared ritual.

Once Vasile accepted the possession framework, every subsequent observation confirmed it. Irina's frightened behaviour looked like demonic torment rather than psychotic terror. Her verbal expressions looked like demons speaking through her rather than delusional content. Her deterioration under the stress of restraint and isolation looked like the demons fighting back rather than her mental state worsening due to trauma and lack of treatment. Confirmation bias, operating within a shared belief system, made alternative explanations psychologically unavailable.

Sister Nicoleta Arcalianu's claims that she'd "seen the same kind of ritual in other monasteries" points to a disturbing reality: Irina wasn't the only person subjected to such treatment. During the post-communist religious revival, informal exorcism practices proliferated across rural Romania without oversight. How many others were restrained, starved, tortured in the name of casting out demons? How many survived? How many died? The Tanacu case only came to light because someone reported it to the police before Irina could be buried. How many similar deaths went unreported, accepted by families and communities as tragic outcomes of spiritual warfare rather than preventable results of medical neglect?

The defence lawyer's argument that "not all tragic events are criminal" raises important questions about culpability when sincere religious belief motivates harmful actions. Legally, the court concluded that a sincere belief doesn't excuse causing death through torture, even torture framed as a religious ritual. Morally and ethically, the case is more complicated. Corogeanu and the nuns weren't sadists enjoying Irina's suffering. They genuinely believed they were saving her soul from eternal damnation. Their intentions were good. Their theology was lethal.

This is the crux of why possession beliefs are so dangerous: they allow good people to commit atrocities whilst maintaining their self-image as helpers and saviours. The cognitive dissonance that normally prevents humans from torturing others is resolved by the possession framework. You're not hurting a person; you're fighting a demon. The victim's suffering isn't your fault; it's the demon's resistance. And if the victim dies, it's not murder, it's either spiritual triumph (the demons left, taking the person's life with them) or tragic proof that the demons were too powerful (but you tried your best).

Irina's case should have been a turning point for Romanian Orthodoxy and for global discussions about exorcism practices. The Church's reforms, such as psychological testing for monastics, stricter oversight of ritual practices, and condemnation of unauthorised exorcisms, were steps forward. But they don't address the fundamental problem: as long as possession is accepted as real, as long as exorcism is practised as valid spiritual medicine, vulnerable people with mental health conditions will be at risk.

The coroner's later claim that adrenaline killed Irina, not the exorcism, is a distraction from the central issue. Even if true, and the initial autopsy contradicted it, focusing on the exact medical mechanism of death obscures the bigger picture. Irina needed medical care. She received torture instead. That she might have technically died from a medication administered in a desperate attempt to save her doesn't absolve anyone of responsibility for putting her in that situation.

The film adaptation, "Beyond the Hills," brought Irina's story to international audiences and sparked important discussions. But in Romania itself, particularly in rural communities like Tanacu, the underlying beliefs haven't fundamentally changed. People still consult exorcists. Monasteries still perform rituals to cast out demons. The infrastructure for psychiatric care in rural areas remains inadequate. And when someone develops schizophrenia or another psychotic disorder, the pull toward supernatural explanations, especially in deeply religious communities, remains strong.

Irina Cornici should be alive. She should have been able to manage her schizophrenia with medication and support, to build a life beyond the trauma of her orphanage childhood, to find the belonging and purpose she sought when she joined the monastery. Instead, she died chained to a cross, her mouth stuffed with cloth to silence her cries, whilst people who claimed to love her tortured her in the name of salvation. And in Tanacu, where she's buried under a simple wooden cross marked "Sister Irina," many still believe the demons were real, and the exorcism was justified.

That's the horror central to possession beliefs when they collide with mental illness. The cruelty becomes righteousness. The torture becomes mercy. The victim becomes invisible behind the theological certainty that evil spirits must be cast out at any cost. And when the cost is a human life, when a young woman dies afraid and in pain because the people around her chose medieval superstition over modern medicine, those same people can convince themselves they did nothing wrong. They were fighting Satan. They were saving her soul. They called the ambulance when things went wrong, which proves they cared.

Irina deserved better. Every person with schizophrenia deserves better than to have their illness reinterpreted as demon possession. Every family facing a loved one's psychiatric crisis deserves access to proper care, not isolation with a priest who believes pills are useless against the Devil. And every religious community needs to reckon with the damage caused when faith overrides evidence, when spiritual certainty justifies physical harm, and when the most vulnerable among us die because ancient fears trump modern understanding.

Until possession beliefs are recognised as fundamentally incompatible with ethical treatment of mental illness, until exorcism as a response to symptoms is universally condemned rather than conditionally permitted, the tragedies will continue. Someone, somewhere, is experiencing their first psychotic episode. Someone around them is concluding they're possessed. And someone is preparing chains, constructing a cross, convinced that what comes next is necessary spiritual warfare rather than preventable harm. Irina's death should have made this impossible. Instead, it's another case study in how supernatural beliefs enable cruelty, another life lost to the conviction that demons are real and suffering is salvation.

CHAPTER XIV

When Mothers Hear Demons

C LEAR LAKE, TEXAS. SPRING 2001.

Andrea Yates, thirty-seven years old, drowned her five children in the bathtub of their suburban Houston home. Noah, aged seven. John, five. Paul, three. Luke, two. Mary is six months old. One by one, methodically, between 9:00 and 10:00 in the morning, whilst her husband was at work and before her mother-in-law arrived to help. She filled the tub, held each child under the water until they stopped struggling, then laid their bodies on the master bedroom bed. Noah, the eldest and strongest, fought hardest. He managed to get his head above water and said, "I'm sorry, Mommy," before she pushed him back down. When it was finished, she called 911. "I just killed my kids," she told the operator.

A police officer arrived within minutes. Andrea answered the door, breathing heavily, her hair and clothes soaked. "I killed my kids," she repeated. She led him to the bedroom, where four small bodies lay, Mary cradled in John's arm because he'd been a particularly good big brother and could protect her in the afterlife. Noah's body was still floating face down in the bathtub. The officer later testified that Andrea showed no emotion or distress. Just a flat, robotic calm that made the scene even more horrifying.

Andrea Yates wasn't a monster. She was a woman experiencing severe postpartum psychosis with religious delusions, untreated because her medication had been discontinued two weeks earlier. She believed Satan himself was literally inside her body. She believed her children were doomed to perish in the fires of hell because she was an inadequate mother who'd raised them in sin. She believed the only way to save their souls was to kill them during their "innocent years" before they reached the age of accountability, so God would take them to heaven. And she believed that after killing them, the state of Texas would execute her, eliminating Satan from the world. In her psychotic reasoning, murdering her children was the most loving act she could perform, sacrificing herself to eternal damnation so they could have eternal life.

This wasn't Andrea's first psychotic episode. Her mental illness had a well-documented history spanning years, marked by multiple psychiatric hospitalisations, two suicide attempts, and clear diagnoses from multiple psychiatrists. The tragedy is that everyone knew she was severely mentally ill. The doctors knew. Her husband knew. Her family knew. And yet on 20th June 2001, she was left alone with five children despite explicit medical instructions that she required constant supervision. In that gap of care, psychosis commanded, and obedience followed.

Andrea Pia Kennedy was born on 2nd July 1964 in Houston, the youngest of five children in a close-knit middle-class family. She grew up in a traditional Christian household, though not particularly fundamentalist. She was a bright student, captain of her high school swim team, and valedictorian of her class. She attended the University of Houston, earned a nursing degree, and worked in cancer wards at the University of Texas MD Anderson Cancer Centre. By all accounts, she was compassionate, dedicated, and quietly competent. She met Russell "Rusty" Yates in 1989 at their shared apartment complex. They married in 1993.

The Yateses' marriage was built on evangelical Christianity, but of an increasingly extreme variety. Before meeting Andrea, Rusty had encountered Michael Woroniecki, an itinerant preacher who operated with his family in a converted bus, travelling across America delivering apocalyptic messages about sin, damnation, and the corruption of modern Christianity. Woroniecki's theology was harsh and unforgiving. He taught that women derived from Eve's original sin and were inherently corrupt. He preached that children were better off dying before age twelve because afterwards they'd reached the age of accountability and could be condemned to hell for their sins. He insisted that modern churches were apostate, that true Christians must separate themselves from worldly influence, and that suffering and deprivation were marks of authentic faith.

Rusty became a follower, receiving Woroniecki's newsletter *The Perilous Times* and maintaining correspondence. After marriage, Andrea was drawn into this theological framework. She read Woroniecki's materials and absorbed his teachings on female sinfulness and the spiritual dangers facing children. Later, both Rusty and Woroniecki would deny that these teachings influenced Andrea's psychosis or the murders. But psychiatrists who evaluated her found that her delusions were saturated with Woroniecki's specific theological language and concerns, particularly the conviction that she was irredeemably sinful and that her inadequacy as a mother would condemn her children to hell.

Andrea wanted to be a good wife and mother. She embraced fundamentalist Christianity with characteristic intensity, reading Scripture obsessively, praying for hours, trying to embody perfect Christian motherhood. The Yateses decided to have as many children "as nature would allow," rejecting contraception. Noah was born in 1994. John in 1995. Paul in 1997. Luke in 1999. They lived in a bus for a time, inspired by Woroniecki's example, before moving into a small house and then a four-bedroom home in Clear Lake.

Home-schooling five children whilst living according to strict fundamentalist principles created immense pressure. Andrea was responsible for all childcare, all household management, and all education. Rusty worked long hours as a NASA computer engineer. Andrea had no breaks, no help beyond occasional assistance from her mother-in-law, no respite from the relentless demands of caring for very young children. And beneath the surface, her mental health was deteriorating.

After Luke's birth in February 1999, Andrea crashed. The postpartum period is biologically and psychologically vulnerable, with dramatic hormonal shifts, sleep deprivation, physical recovery from childbirth, and the stress of caring for a newborn. For women with underlying psychiatric vulnerability, it can trigger severe mental illness. Andrea developed what psychiatrists would later diagnose as postpartum depression with psychotic features, later refined to postpartum psychosis and schizophrenia.

In June 1999, Rusty found Andrea in the bathroom, holding a knife to her throat, begging to die. She'd already attempted suicide once by overdosing on Trazodone, an antidepressant, and had landed in a coma for ten days. This second attempt prompted mental health utilisation. Dr Eileen Starbranch, the psychiatrist who treated Andrea, later testified that Andrea was "among the five sickest patients" she'd ever encountered. She was diagnosed with postpartum psychosis and prescribed Haldol, an antipsychotic medication. The medication worked. Andrea's symptoms improved dramatically. She began functioning again, resumed exercise, and maintained a stable routine.

Dr Starbranch gave the Yateses explicit instructions: Andrea must continue taking Haldol indefinitely, and she must not have any more children. Another pregnancy would "guarantee future psychotic depression." The warning was clear, unambiguous, and medically sound. Postpartum psychosis has high recurrence rates. Women who've experienced one episode are at significant risk for another with subsequent pregnancies, especially if they discontinue medication.

The Yateses ignored this advice. Seven weeks after Andrea's hospital discharge, she became pregnant again. She stopped taking Haldol in March 2000, either because she was pregnant or planning a pregnancy. On 30th November 2000, she gave birth to Mary. For several months, she seemed stable. But after her father's death on 12th March 2001, everything unravelled.

Andrea stopped eating. She stopped feeding Mary. She began mutilating herself, clawing at her scalp until she had circular bald patches. She thought she saw the mark of the Beast, 666, on her head and wanted to shave her head to check. She read the Bible obsessively, searching for understanding of what was happening to her. She became catatonic, sitting motionless for hours, unresponsive, trapped inside her deteriorating mind. On 1st April 2001, she was admitted to Devereux Texas Treatment Network, a psychiatric facility.

Dr Mohammed Saeed became her treating psychiatrist. He prescribed a series of psychotropic medications, including restarting Haldol. Andrea improved enough to be discharged in May 2001, but Dr Saeed gave explicit instructions: she required twenty-four-hour supervision around her children. She was not stable enough to be left alone with them. Rusty arranged for his mother, Dora Yates, to assist during the day.

But then Dr Saeed decided that multiple experts would later question: he tapered Andrea off Haldol due to concerns about side effects. Haldol isn't a benign drug; it can cause significant adverse effects, including movement disorders. But it had been keeping Andrea's psychosis in check. Discontinuing it was medically defensible in theory but catastrophic in practice. Within two weeks of stopping Haldol, Andrea's psychosis returned with devastating force.

By early June 2001, Andrea's family noticed she was deteriorating again. She was withdrawn, robotic in her movements, barely responsive. On 3rd May, she'd filled the bathtub in the middle of the day. She later confessed to police that she'd planned to drown the children that day but changed her mind at the last moment. When Dr Saeed saw her on 4th May, he assumed the filled tub meant she was planning to drown herself, not her children. He didn't hospitalise her. On 18th June, two days before the murders, Dr Saeed examined Andrea again and documented seeing no evidence of psychosis. Either he missed the signs or Andrea had learned to hide them.

Meanwhile, Rusty had decided Andrea needed to become more independent. Despite Dr Saeed's explicit instructions for constant supervision, Rusty began leaving her alone with the children for short periods. He announced at a family gathering the weekend before the murders that he'd decided to leave Andrea alone for an hour each morning and evening to prevent her from becoming "totally dependent" on him and his mother. Andrea's own mother, present at that gathering, expressed shock that Andrea wasn't stable enough for this. Brian Kennedy, Andrea's brother, later claimed Rusty told him, whilst driving Andrea to a mental health facility, that depressed people just needed "a swift kick in the pants" to get motivated.

Whether Rusty genuinely believed Andrea was improving or simply couldn't face the reality of her illness remains unclear. What's certain is that on the morning of 20th June 2001, he left for work at 9:00, leaving Andrea alone with five children. Dora was scheduled to arrive at 10:00. In that hour of unsupervised time, Andrea drowned all five.

She started with Mary, the baby. Then Luke, Paul, and John. She laid each body on the bed after drowning them, arranging them carefully. Noah, the seven-year-old, was the hardest. He was bigger, stronger, and more aware of what was happening. He fought. He managed to surface and gasped, "I'm sorry, Mommy", perhaps thinking that if he apologised for whatever he'd done wrong, she'd stop. She pushed him back under and held him there until he drowned. His body was left floating face down in the tub.

At 9:34, Andrea called 911. "I need a police officer," she said calmly. When asked why, she replied, "I just killed my kids." The dispatcher thought she'd misheard. Andrea repeated it. A Houston police officer arrived four minutes later. Andrea, soaking wet, answered the door and led him to the carnage. She showed no emotion, no remorse, no distress. Just mechanical compliance.

At the Harris County Jail psychiatric unit, placed on suicide watch, Andrea began explaining her reasoning to doctors. "My children weren't righteous," she told the director of mental health services the day after her arrest. "They stumbled because I was evil. The way I was raising them, they could never be saved. They were doomed to perish in the fires of hell." She believed killing them whilst they were still in their "innocent years" allowed God to take them to heaven. She believed she would be executed by the state and that her execution would eliminate Satan, who she believed was literally inside her body, from the world. In her psychotic calculus, five dead children plus her own execution equalled universal salvation.

Andrea also revealed the extent of her delusions in the months before the murders. She'd believed television cameras were hidden throughout her house since 1999, monitoring her mothering. She thought her mother-in-law's glasses contained a camera. She believed television commercials were speaking directly to her, calling her a "fat pig" for giving her children too much candy. She saw personal messages from Satan in the films *Seven* and *O Brother, Where Art Thou?* innocent movies that anyone could watch, but Andrea believed they were Satan's specific torments directed at her. She "knew" that Noah would grow up to be a serial killer, that Paul would become a deaf, mute homosexual prostitute, specific delusional knowledge about her children's futures that proved they were damned.

Most chilling, she believed Satan could hear spoken words but couldn't read her mind. That's why she never told anyone about her plan to kill the children; speaking it aloud would alert Satan, who would stop her from saving her children's souls. The concealment that prosecutors would cite as proof of guilt was actually integral to her delusion.

Andrea's trial began in February 2002. The prosecution, led by Harris County District Attorney Chuck Rosenthal, sought the death penalty. Their theory: Andrea killed her children not because of psychosis but because she didn't want to care for them anymore. She was overwhelmed, exhausted, and resentful of the burden. The drownings were a selfish act of escape framed as mental illness after the fact. To prove this, they needed to demonstrate that Andrea knew her actions were wrong, that she understood drowning children was illegal and morally condemned.

Texas law uses a modified version of the M'Naghten Rules for determining insanity: a defendant is not guilty by reason of insanity if, at the time of the crime, they didn't know their conduct was wrong due to severe mental disease or defect. The legal question wasn't whether Andrea was mentally ill; she was. The question was whether her mental illness prevented her from knowing that killing children was wrong.

The prosecution emphasised Andrea's behaviour after the murders: she called 911, she waited for police, she didn't attempt to flee or destroy evidence. These actions, they argued, showed she understood she'd done something illegal and accepted consequences. During cross-examination of defence experts, prosecutors hammered on the point that Andrea concealed her plan from family and friends, which meant she knew society viewed killing children as wrong.

The defence, led by attorneys George Parnham and Wendell Odom, presented overwhelming psychiatric evidence. Dr Phillip Resnick, a leading forensic psychiatrist, testified as their expert witness. He'd conducted extensive interviews with Andrea and reviewed all medical and police records. His conclusion: Andrea suffered from severe postpartum psychosis with schizophrenia, manifesting in command hallucinations and religious delusions. She believed killing her children was right, not legally right, but morally and spiritually right in the delusional framework psychosis had created. She understood Texas law prohibited killing children. She knew society condemned it. But in her psychotic perception of reality, she had access to higher knowledge, spiritual truth that superseded earthly law. She was fighting Satan. She was saving her children's souls. She was obeying what she believed were divine imperatives.

Dr Resnick explained: "A person can do an illegal act, but still believe the act is right. She knew it was against the law, but she did what she thought was right in the world she perceived through her psychotic eyes at the time."

Dr Ellen Allbritton, who'd treated Andrea at Devereux, described her as "someone who had declined to the point of nonfunction, just there, a shell." Dr Starbranch testified about the 1999 psychotic episode and her explicit warnings about future pregnancies. The medical evidence was consistent and compelling: Andrea Yates was profoundly mentally ill and had been for years.

The prosecution countered with Dr Park Dietz, a forensic psychiatrist who examined Andrea in November 2001. Dietz testified that whilst Andrea suffered severe mental illness, she knew her actions were wrong. As evidence, he pointed to an episode of the television show *Law & Order* that had recently aired, in which a woman suffering from postpartum depression drowned her children and was found not guilty by reason of insanity. Dietz suggested Andrea might have gotten the idea from this episode and crafted her insanity defence accordingly.

There was one problem: the episode didn't exist. Dietz had confused a *Law & Order* episode he'd consulted on with something that never aired. His testimony was false. But the jury didn't know that in February 2002.

After thirteen hours of deliberation, the jury found Andrea Yates guilty of capital murder. They rejected the death penalty but sentenced her to life in prison with the possibility of parole after forty years. She was thirty-seven years old. She'd spend the rest of her life incarcerated for murders committed during psychotic delusions.

Rusty Yates, throughout the trial, insisted it was the illness that killed the children, not Andrea. He stood by his wife. But the conviction devastated him. By 2004, unable to sustain the marriage under the weight of grief and Andrea's imprisonment, Rusty divorced her. He remarried in 2006.

Andrea's appellate lawyers discovered Dr Dietz's false testimony and filed for appeal. On 6th January 2005, the Texas Court of Appeals overturned the conviction, ruling that Dietz's erroneous testimony about the non-existent *Law & Order* episode was prejudicial. The prosecution had used it to suggest Andrea fabricated her insanity defence, but it was based on a falsehood. Andrea was granted a new trial.

The retrial began in June 2006. This time, the focus was squarely on Andrea's mental state. Dr George Ringholz and other psychiatrists testified about her delusions of Satanic influence, her command hallucinations, and her psychotic belief system. The prosecution still argued she knew her actions were wrong, but without the false *Law & Order* testimony, their case was weaker.

On 26th July 2006, after 13 hours of deliberation, the jury returned a verdict of not guilty by reason of insanity. Andrea Yates had killed her five children, but she'd done so whilst so profoundly mentally ill that she couldn't distinguish right from wrong in the moral sense required by Texas law.

Andrea was committed to Kerrville State Hospital, a maximum-security psychiatric facility, for indefinite treatment. She remains there today, twenty-three years later. Annual reviews assess her mental state and danger to public safety. She has consistently declined release hearings. In interviews conducted years after the murders, Andrea has expressed understanding that what she did was terrible, but she remains somewhat detached from the full emotional reality, a common outcome in cases where someone commits horrific acts during psychosis and later regains some clarity but never fully integrates what happened.

The question haunting Andrea Yates' case is how preventable it was. At every stage, warning signs were visible and documented. In 1999, Dr Starbranch explicitly warned against future pregnancies. That warning was ignored. In early 2001, Dr Saeed ordered twenty-four-hour supervision. That order was violated. Two weeks before the murders, Haldol, the medication keeping Andrea's psychosis controlled, was discontinued. On 20th June, Andrea was left alone with five children despite clear medical instructions against it.

Rusty Yates bears responsibility for his decisions, particularly the choice to leave Andrea unsupervised. But he was also operating within a religious lens that stigmatised mental illness and emphasised faith over treatment. The Woronieckis' influence, though denied by Rusty, clearly shaped the family's understanding of Andrea's symptoms. When she became withdrawn and strange, when she filled bathtubs and clawed at her scalp, these behaviours could be interpreted as a spiritual crisis rather than a medical emergency. Prayer and Bible reading seemed like appropriate responses within their theological framework, even as Andrea's psychosis deepened.

The case raises profound questions about postpartum mental illness, religious delusion, and systemic failures. Postpartum psychosis affects approximately one to two women per thousand births, rare but not vanishingly so. Symptoms typically appear within the first few weeks after delivery and can include hallucinations, delusions, severe mood swings, confusion, and, in the worst cases, thoughts of harming the baby or suicide. It's a medical emergency requiring immediate intervention, usually hospitalisation and antipsychotic medication. With proper treatment, most women recover completely.

The biological mechanism underlying postpartum psychosis involves dramatic hormonal shifts following childbirth. During pregnancy, levels of oestrogen and progesterone increase significantly. After delivery, these hormones plummet precipitously within forty-eight hours, a neurochemical shock that can trigger mental illness symptoms in vulnerable women. Sleep deprivation, common in the postpartum period, further destabilises brain function. The stress of caring for a newborn, particularly for women with perfectionist tendencies or limited support, adds psychological pressure. In Andrea's case, all these factors converged: hormonal chaos, severe sleep deprivation from caring for multiple young children, the psychological burden of fundamentalist expectations about motherhood, and underlying genetic vulnerability to psychosis.

Research suggests women with a personal or family history of bipolar disorder or schizophrenia face an elevated risk for postpartum psychosis. Andrea's family history included mental illness, though details weren't extensively documented during her trials. Her adolescent struggles with bulimia and suicidal ideation suggested underlying psychiatric vulnerability that predated motherhood. When the biological stress of repeated pregnancies activated that vulnerability, the results were catastrophic.

Understanding postpartum psychosis requires distinguishing it from the more common postpartum depression. Postpartum depression affects ten to fifteen percent of new mothers, significantly more common than psychosis. Symptoms include persistent sadness, anxiety, difficulty bonding with the baby, changes in appetite and sleep beyond what's normal postpartum, feelings of worthlessness or guilt. It's serious and debilitating, but doesn't typically involve the hallucinations, delusions, or complete breaks from reality that characterise psychosis. Women with postpartum depression know their thoughts are their own, even if those thoughts are distressing. Women with postpartum psychosis lose the insight that they can't distinguish psychotic symptoms from reality.

Andrea's 1999 episode clearly met criteria for postpartum psychosis, not just depression. She heard voices. She believed cameras were monitoring her. She attempted suicide not once but twice because she genuinely believed she was so fundamentally evil that her children would be better off without her. These aren't depressive symptoms; they're psychotic symptoms with depressive content. The diagnosis of schizophrenia that later emerged suggests her psychosis wasn't just postpartum triggered but represented an ongoing psychotic disorder that pregnancy and childbirth activated or exacerbated.

Schizophrenia typically emerges in late adolescence or early adulthood, though women often develop symptoms later than men. Andrea was twenty-six when she married, thirty-five when her first clear psychotic episode occurred. This timing is consistent with late-onset schizophrenia in women, where hormonal factors may delay symptom emergence until a biological stressor, such as pregnancy, childbirth, or menopause, triggers the illness. Her specific symptom pattern, paranoid delusions, auditory hallucinations, religious preoccupation, and disorganised behaviour fit the paranoid subtype of schizophrenia, the most common presentation.

The religious content of her delusions wasn't unusual. Studies consistently show that twenty-five to forty percent of people with schizophrenia experience religious delusions or hallucinations. The specific theological themes vary by culture and personal background. In predominantly Christian societies, patients commonly believe they're Jesus, the Antichrist, being tested by God, or receiving divine commands. The brain experiencing psychosis doesn't create new conceptual frameworks; it draws on existing beliefs and distorts them. Andrea's immersion in fundamentalist Christianity meant her psychosis manifested through theological language. Had she been raised Buddhist, Hindu, or secular, the delusions would have taken different forms whilst the underlying psychotic process remained identical.

But postpartum psychosis is frequently misunderstood, even by medical professionals. New mothers experiencing bizarre thoughts or hallucinations may not report them because they fear being seen as bad mothers or having their children removed. Family members may dismiss symptoms as normal postpartum adjustment or sleep deprivation. Religious communities may interpret symptoms as a spiritual attack rather than illness. And even when the condition is recognised and treated, as Andrea's was in 1999, ongoing vigilance is required because the risk of recurrence is high.

The recurrence risk is what makes Dr Starbranch's warning so critical. Women who've experienced one episode of postpartum psychosis face approximately a twenty-five to fifty percent chance of recurrence with subsequent pregnancies. That's why psychiatrists typically advise against future pregnancies unless the woman maintains consistent medical treatment, has strong family support, and accepts significant medical monitoring throughout pregnancy and postpartum. Andrea had none of these protective factors in 2000 when she became pregnant with Mary. She'd discontinued Haldol. She had minimal psychiatric follow-up. Her husband's decision to have more children despite medical advice represented either a profound misunderstanding of the risks or a religious conviction that God would protect them regardless of psychiatric warnings.

The question of medication management during pregnancy is genuinely complex. Most psychiatric medications carry some fetal risk, though those risks are often lower than the risks of untreated maternal mental illness. Women face impossible choices: take medication that might harm the developing baby, or risk psychotic relapse that could result in suicide or infanticide. Andrea's doctors in 1999 recommended continuing medication and avoiding future pregnancy. She became pregnant anyway and stopped medication. That decision, whether made by Andrea, Rusty, or both together, set the stage for the 2001 tragedy.

The religious content of Andrea's delusions made them particularly difficult to address. She believed Satan was real, that hell was real, that her children's souls were in mortal danger. For someone raised in evangelical Christianity, these aren't obviously delusional concepts; they're doctrinal truths. The line between intense religious conviction and psychotic delusion is context-dependent. When Andrea said Satan was inside her, how should family and friends have distinguished between metaphorical spiritual struggle and literal delusional belief in demonic possession?

Dr Resnick, in his testimony, noted that Andrea's specific delusions, particularly her detailed "knowledge" about her children's damned futures and her belief that Satan could hear spoken words but not read thoughts, went beyond ordinary religious belief into clear psychotic territory. But those discernments require psychiatric expertise. For family members embedded in fundamentalist religious communities where Satan is understood as a real, active presence in the world, Andrea's claims might have seemed extreme but not obviously impossible.

Michael Woroniecki's theology created a framework wherein Andrea's psychotic delusions could flourish. His teachings emphasised female sinfulness, the spiritual dangers facing children, and the inadequacy of human mothering to ensure salvation. These themes directly echo Andrea's delusional beliefs about being an evil mother who'd doomed her children to hell. Woroniecki's insistence that children were better off dying before age twelve provided the exact theological justification Andrea used for killing her children while they were still in their "innocent years."

Both Woroniecki and Rusty have denied any causal connection, insisting Andrea's psychosis came from biology, not theology. And they're partially right, Andrea's illness was biological, rooted in postpartum hormonal chaos and underlying psychiatric vulnerability. But delusions don't emerge in a vacuum. The brain experiencing psychosis draws on the individual's existing knowledge, beliefs, and cultural framework to construct its delusional narratives. Andrea's delusions were saturated with Woroniecki's specific theological language because that was the religious vocabulary she'd been immersed in for years. Someone from a different religious background might have developed entirely different delusions, perhaps messages from ancestors, or persecution by government agencies, or alien abduction. The psychotic process is similar; the content varies.

The tragedy is compounded by what Andrea's case revealed about systemic failures in mental health care and family support. She was seeing psychiatrists. She was receiving treatment. She had a documented history of severe postpartum psychosis. Yet she was still left alone with five children two weeks after discontinuing the antipsychotic medication that kept her stable. That gap between knowing someone is severely mentally ill and ensuring adequate safety measures speaks to broader problems: inadequate psychiatric follow-up, insufficient support for families managing severe mental illness at home, societal and religious stigma that prevents people from accepting the seriousness of psychiatric conditions, and medical decisions like discontinuing Haldol that prioritise managing side effects over preventing psychotic relapse.

Andrea Yates's five children, Noah, John, Paul, Luke, and Mary, would now be adults had they lived. Noah would be thirty, John twenty-eight, Paul twenty-six, Luke twenty-three, and Mary twenty-three. They might have had families of their own. Instead, they drowned in a bathtub because their mother's brain, devastated by postpartum psychosis and untreated schizophrenia, constructed a delusional reality in which killing them was an act of salvation.

The case's legacy includes the Andrea Yates Law, passed by the Texas Legislature in 2003, requiring hospitals and medical professionals to inform patients about postpartum mental illness. The Yates Children Memorial Fund, established by Andrea's defence attorney George Parnham and his wife Mary, has trained more than 2,500 medical professionals and distributed over 575,000 brochures about postpartum depression and psychosis. These efforts aim to prevent future tragedies by improving early detection and treatment.

But awareness campaigns, whilst valuable, don't address the deeper theological and structural problems Andrea's case exposed. Religious communities that emphasise spiritual warfare, demonic influence, and the sinfulness of human nature create environments where psychotic delusions can seem like spiritual reality. Medical systems that allow severely mentally ill women to be discharged with inadequate follow-up put families at risk. Cultural expectations that mothers should naturally cope with childcare demands regardless of mental state prevent women from seeking help.

Andrea Yates didn't choose to be psychotic. She didn't choose to believe Satan was inside her or that her children were damned. Those beliefs were symptoms of severe mental illness, no more voluntary than hallucinations in schizophrenia or mania in bipolar disorder. What she needed was consistent medical treatment, proper medication management, and family support that prioritised medical reality over religious interpretation. What she got instead was discontinued medication, unsupervised time with her children, and immersion in a theological belief system that made her psychotic delusions seem plausible.

She sits in Kerrville State Hospital, medicated now, stable. Living with the knowledge that, whilst psychotic, she methodically drowned five children. Her mind no longer constructs delusional realities about Satan and salvation. Intellectually, she understands that what she did was wrong. But the emotional and moral reckoning is complicated by the gap between the person she is now, treated, rational, no longer psychotic and the person she was then, lost in delusions, unable to distinguish her brain's psychotic narratives from reality.

The lesson from Andrea Yates' case, if there is one, is that postpartum psychosis is a medical emergency requiring aggressive intervention, that religious frameworks emphasising demons and damnation can make psychotic delusions worse, and that leaving severely mentally ill people in charge of vulnerable dependents without adequate supervision is catastrophically dangerous. Five children died because those lessons hadn't been learned in 2001. The question is whether they've been learned now, or whether somewhere today a woman experiencing postpartum psychosis is being told to pray harder whilst her medication is discontinued, her warning signs are dismissed as spiritual struggle, and her children remain in her care despite the catastrophic risk her untreated illness poses to everyone around her.

Andrea Yates' children deserved better. Andrea Yates deserved better, consistent treatment, proper medication, and recognition that discontinuing Haldol whilst caring for five young children was inviting disaster. The psychiatric profession, the religious community, and the family system all failed catastrophically. And five children drowned whilst their mother heard Satan commanding their salvation through death

CHAPTER XV

When The State Believed

Gary, Indiana, 2011–2012

The boy walked backwards up a wall.

That is the sentence that put the Latoya Ammons case in the public eye. Not the flies in the dead of winter. Not the footsteps on the basement stairs. Not the shadowy figure Rosa Campbell watched pace the living room at midnight, disappearing when she switched on the lights. All of that had been building for months inside a rented house on Carolina Street in Gary, Indiana, accumulating, as these things do, one strange event on top of another, each explicable on its own, the weight of them together becoming harder to dismiss. But a nine-year-old boy walking backwards up a wall in a hospital examination room, witnessed by a DCS case manager and a registered nurse, was filed in official documents signed by state employees, which is what made this different.

Every other case in this book involves the state arriving too late. Police were called after a death. Courts convening after a crime. Doctors are finding injuries that should have been prevented. The apparatus of secular authority, looking at what belief had already done and trying to construct accountability from the wreckage. The Ammons case is the one in which the apparatus appeared while it was happening, was carefully examined with trained eyes, and, in several documented instances, came away uncertain about what it had seen.

Not everyone. Not all of them. The clinical psychologists who assessed the children were clear. The sceptical voices in the file were firm. But a DCS family case manager put in writing that a child had walked backwards up a wall, a behaviour she could not explain. A 36-year veteran of the police force told the Indianapolis Star, "I am a believer." A Catholic bishop, for the first time in his 21 years in the Diocese of Gary, authorised an exorcism. These are not credulous people operating outside institutional frameworks. These are people inside the system, filing reports, following procedures, and describing something they could not account for through ordinary means.

That is what makes this case worth its own chapter. Not because the demons were real. They weren't. But because the question of why professional, trained, sceptical-by-default individuals ended up reporting events in the language of possession tells us something important about how that framework spreads not only through communities of belief, but through anyone who spends enough time in a room where the framework is already operating and the alternative explanations feel insufficient.

Latoya Ammons moved into the house on Carolina Street in November 2011. She was an Indianapolis resident in her thirties, a mother of three children: a 12-year-old daughter, a 9-year-old son, and a 7-year-old son. Her mother, Rosa Campbell, moved in with her. The house was a modest one-storey rental in Gary, Indiana, a city that had been in slow economic decline for decades, its steel industry long gone, its population shrunk to a fraction of its mid-century peak. Carolina Street was quiet. The house had three bedrooms, one bathroom, a concrete basement, and a screened-in porch. It was the kind of place you took because you could afford it, not because it was where you'd have chosen to be.

The first strange event was the flies. December, in Indiana, means frozen ground and bitter cold, not conditions in which large black flies appear on a screened porch and resist all attempts to kill them. Rosa Campbell remembers it clearly. "We killed them and killed them and killed them, but they kept coming back." This is not, in itself, evidence of anything supernatural. Flies can overwinter in wall cavities, emerge when the heating warms the interior, and return in volume if the source isn't found. But it unsettled the family, particularly given the timing and the season, and unsettlement, once it begins, tends to find more to feed on.

Then came the footsteps. After midnight, the family heard steady sounds ascending the basement stairs, the measured tread of someone coming up, followed by the creak of the door opening into the kitchen. Nobody was there when they checked. Rosa also reported waking in the night to find a large set of wet boot prints crossing the living room floor, with no explanation for how they had appeared. The family's sleep grew fractured. The house, which had seemed ordinary enough in daylight, began to feel different after dark.

These are the conditions under which belief becomes scaffolding. When you cannot sleep reliably, when every night brings sounds and sights that ordinary explanation doesn't account for, when the adults in the household are frightened, and the children can see that the adults are frightened, the framework that makes sense of what is happening becomes very important. For the Ammons family, that framework was religious. Latoya and Rosa were churchgoing women. They prayed. They read scripture. They understood the world in terms that included the real existence of spiritual forces, benevolent and malevolent. When strange things happen within that framework, the vocabulary used to explain them is not psychiatric or neurological. It is theological.

By early spring 2012, the family was describing a situation that had escalated considerably. The children, according to later DCS records, began exhibiting behaviour that alarmed the adults: speaking in low, altered voices, going into what the family described as trances, and making statements they would not remember afterwards. The 12-year-old daughter said she twice went into unconscious states. She reported seeing shadowy figures in the house. She said she felt at times as though invisible hands were choking her and holding her down, and that a voice had told her she had twenty minutes to live and would never see her family again. The seven-year-old sat in a closet speaking to someone no one else could see, describing what it was like to be murdered.

Read those accounts in isolation, and they describe a family in serious psychological distress, possibly a child in crisis, possibly multiple children who had been living with frightened adults in an atmosphere saturated with fear for long enough that their own perceptions had been shaped by it. Read them through the framework the family was using, and they described children under demonic attack.

On 19th April 2012, Latoya Ammons took her children to see their family physician, Dr Geoffrey Onyeukwu, at his practice in the Gary area. She wanted him to examine them. What happened in that office produced the first wave of witness accounts that would make the case nationally significant.

According to the DCS report, while the children were in Dr Onyeuk-wu's office, the youngest boy began cursing in what witnesses described as a demonic voice. Medical staff reported that he was then lifted and thrown into the wall by an unseen force, striking it hard enough to knock him unconscious. When he regained consciousness, it took five grown adults to restrain him. Dr Onyeukwu, who had been a physician for twenty years, later told the Indianapolis Star: "I was scared myself when I walked into the room." He described the children's behaviour as unlike anything he had encountered in two decades of practice.

The accuracy of exactly who witnessed what matters here, and it is worth being precise about it. The throwing of the child against the wall is documented in the DCS intake report. Whether Dr Onyeukwu himself personally witnessed the child being thrown, or whether he was describing what medical staff told him had occurred, is not entirely clear from the available accounts. The doctor's own statement focuses on the children's demonic voices and altered behaviour. What is clear is that the intake documentation created that day described events that were immediately interpreted through a possession framework, and that this interpretation was not challenged by the medical staff at the scene.

DCS was contacted. The case was assigned to family case manager Valerie Washington. She came to the hospital to interview the family and assess the children. In the examination room, while speaking to the seven-year-old boy, Washington noticed him growl and gnash his teeth. His eyes rolled back in his head. He grabbed his older brother's throat with both hands and squeezed. Staff had to intervene physically. Washington remained with the family. Later that same day, she and registered nurse Willie Lee Walker brought the boys into a small room for a further interview with a psychologist.

What happened next is what the case is remembered for.

According to Washington's signed DCS report, the seven-year-old, the younger of the two boys, got a strange grin on his face. He began to walk backwards. He walked up the wall. He flipped over his grandmother's head and landed on his feet. Washington and nurse Walker, according to the documentation, were so frightened that they ran out of the room.

That report is in the official DCS case file. Valerie Washington's name is on it. It is not a rumour or a tabloid claim. It is a signed document prepared by a state employee that describes events she said she witnessed in a medical setting on a specific date.

It is also worth examining very carefully what that document actually contains, and what it doesn't.

The most widely repeated version of this event, the version that circulated in media reports, which made Captain Austin a self-described believer, that prompted the bishop to authorise an exorcism, describes a child walking backwards up a wall entirely unaided. What Washington's actual report describes, upon close examination, is somewhat different. A journalist's investigation of the case later established that, at the moment the boy climbed up the wall, his grandmother, Rosa Campbell, was in the room and holding his hand. A child holding an adult's hand, bracing against a wall with his feet and walking himself upward while the adult's grip provides counterbalance, can absolutely walk up a wall and flip over. It is something children do. It is physically explicable. It does not require supernatural agency.

Washington apparently did not mention the grandmother's role in her initial report. Joe Nickell, a senior research fellow at the Centre for

Inquiry who investigated the case in depth, interviewed witnesses and concluded that the supposed supernatural events were either misreported, embellished, or had straightforward natural explanations. The levitation of the 12-year-old daughter, another widely cited incident, was described by the family as something that "raised her up off the bed," which Nickell observed was consistent with the girl simply throwing herself upward, rather than any external force acting on her. The child who had been "thrown against the wall" at the doctor's office: no account places Dr Onyeukwu as a direct witness to the act of throwing, only to the aftermath.

None of this makes Washington a liar. The more interesting question is how a trained DCS case manager came to produce a report describing a child walking backwards up a wall, omitting the grandmother's presence and describing the event in language that strongly implied something inexplicable had occurred.

The answer is probably not dishonesty. The answer is probably the atmosphere.

By the time Washington arrived at the hospital to interview the Ammons family on 19th April 2012, she was walking into a situation in which everyone present had already been discussing possession for months. Latoya and Rosa had been living inside the framework of demonic attack since December. The family doctor had just described being frightened by what he'd seen in his examination room. The children had been exhibiting distressing behaviour that the adults around them were interpreting through a specific lens. Washington stepped into that room carrying all the ordinary human susceptibility to context and expectation that any person carries. When the seven-year-old did something unusual with the wall, something that had a physical explanation, she saw it through the only framework that had been presented to her that day.

This is not frailty or stupidity. This is how human perception works. We interpret what we see through the context we bring to it. When that context has been saturated in one particular framework, our interpretation follows. Psychologists call it priming. You can prime people to see faces in ambiguous images, or meaningful patterns in random noise, or supernatural events in unusual but explicable behaviour. Washington had been thoroughly primed. So had the nurse. So, in the weeks that followed, several police officers and a bishop were involved. The case was passed to DCS supervisor Samantha Ilic, who took over coordinating the investigation. DCS removed the three children from Latoya's custody in May 2012, citing concerns about the children's welfare and the need to assess the household. Latoya, separated from her children, moved temporarily to Indianapolis. Ilic and other DCS staff conducted multiple visits to the Carolina Street house. On 10th May 2012, a group including Captain Austin, Rosa Campbell, Latoya, Father Michael Maginot, Samantha Ilic, and two Lake County officers visited the property together. Austin had initially approached the case as a likely fraud, a family manufacturing supernatural claims to generate sympathy or money. Multiple visits to the house had changed his view. He told the Indianapolis Star simply: "I am a believer." He also told them that after nightfall, he would not stay in the house. "I have been shot at. I have investigated homicides, rapes, and robberies," he said. "This is different."

During the May visit, police observed what they described as an oil-like substance dripping from the venetian blinds in a bedroom. The room was sealed for 25 minutes after two officers cleaned the substance off and stood nearby to ensure no one entered. When they re-opened the room, the substance had returned. Austin's own records note radio malfunctions, a photo that appeared to show a shadowy figure taken when nobody was in the house, and his car seat moving independently after he left. Whether any of these events were genuinely inexplicable or had prosaic explanations, old house, settling structures, photographic artefacts, and mechanical faults, is another question the file does not answer.

Father Michael Maginot, a Catholic priest from the neighbouring city of Merrillville, had been brought in at the family's request. He spent four hours in the house interviewing Latoya and Rosa and described coming away convinced the family was being "tormented by demons." He requested permission from Bishop Dale Melczek of the Diocese of Gary to perform an exorcism on Latoya. Bishop Melczek granted the request for the first time in his 21 years as bishop. Maginot performed three exorcisms in total: two in English and one in Latin, conducted at his church in Merrillville in June 2012. Police officers were present at the exorcisms.

The clinical psychologists who examined the children had a different view of the situation.

Stacy Wright, who assessed the youngest boy, noted in her report that his behaviour, the demonic voices, the threats, and the apparent episodes of altered consciousness appeared to be performative. He "tends to act possessed upon being challenged or asked questions he doesn't want to answer," Wright wrote. Her conclusion was blunt: this appeared to be "an unfortunate and sad case of a child who has been induced into a delusional system perpetuated by his mother and potentially reinforced" by other adults in the household.

Joel Schwartz, who evaluated the older two children, reached similar conclusions. He noted the need to assess the extent to which the 12-year-old daughter had been "unduly influenced by her mother's concerns that the family was exposed to paranormal activity." The DCS psychological evaluations consistently described not possession but a family system in which adults had been terrified, children had absorbed that terror and learned to perform within its expectations, and the result was behaviour that looked alarming out of context and was deeply concerning in terms of child welfare.

The landlord, Charles Reed, who had owned the property for 33 years, stated unambiguously that he had never experienced any paranormal events in the house and that the tenants before the Ammons family had reported nothing unusual. The tenant who moved in after Ammons left also reported no disturbances.

By November 2012, Latoya had met the DCS requirements for reunification: she had found a new home and secured employment. The children were returned to her custody. DCS continued monitoring visits through early 2013. The case manager who conducted the follow-up visits in January 2013, Christina Olejnik, noted in her records: "No demonic presences or spirits in the home. The family is no longer fixated on religion to explain or cope with the children's behaviour issues." That sentence, buried in a bureaucratic follow-up report, may be the most important line in the entire 800-page file. The demonic framework had been the primary lens through which the family understood and explained the children's distress. Once the family moved out of that house, once the DCS involvement shifted the context away from possession and toward welfare assessment, the framework apparently lost its grip. The children's distress, in whatever form it took, resolved.

In 2014, the case attracted renewed national attention when the Indianapolis Star published its investigation, drawing on the nearly 800 pages of official documentation. Paranormal TV presenter Zak Bagans purchased the Carolina Street house for $35,000 and began filming a documentary he called Demon House. He later described the experience as deeply disturbing and said it had affected him personally in ways he had not anticipated. In 2016, he had the house demolished. He told reporters: "Something was inside that house that had the ability to do things that I have never seen before, things that others carrying the highest forms of credibility couldn't explain either." He moved the basement staircase to his Haunted Museum in Las Vegas, where it remains on display.

Nobody was ever charged with any crime. No child died. No crime was committed. This is the Ammons case's most significant structural difference from every other case in this book: nothing criminal happened. Three children were temporarily removed from their mother's care, assessed as exhibiting trauma responses consistent with being raised in an atmosphere of fear, and returned once the atmosphere changed. Their mother believed her family had been under demonic attack. The state investigated and produced 800 pages of documentation. Some of those pages describe events that remain genuinely puzzling when read uncritically. Others, when examined with care, reveal how those events were shaped and interpreted in ways that made them appear more inexplicable than they were.

The psychology of what happened on Carolina Street is, in many ways, more interesting than any supernatural explanation could be.

Consider the sequence. A family moves into a house in November. By December, they are reporting strange events. By spring, the events have intensified dramatically. The children are exhibiting disturbing behaviour. State professionals arrive and find the situation alarming enough to remove the children. Some of those professionals report witnessing things they cannot explain. A bishop authorises an exorcism. A senior police officer publicly declares himself a believer. And then, within months of the family leaving the house and the DCS focus shifting to welfare rather than possession, everything stops.

That sequence maps almost perfectly onto what psychologists call folie à famille, shared psychotic belief within a family unit. It is not that the family members were individually delusional in a clinical sense. It is that they had been living together, in a context of fear, sleep deprivation, and genuine distress, interpreting events through a framework that every adult in the household endorsed, for long enough that the framework had become the only available way to make sense of experience. When something strange happened, a fly, a creak, a child's nightmare, a boy's aggressive episode at the doctor's office, the framework explained it instantly and completely. That completeness is both the framework's greatest strength and its greatest danger. An explanation that accounts for everything perfectly, that converts every piece of new evidence into confirmation of itself, is not a theory that can be disproved. It is a closed system. And closed systems, once established in a frightened household, are very difficult to escape from the inside.

The children had been inside that system for months. Wright and Schwartz, the clinical psychologists, described children who had learned to perform within it. The youngest boy who growled and threatened his brother and tried to strangle him in front of Valerie Washington, that child had spent months in a household where demonic behaviour was the dominant explanatory category for distress. Children are extraordinarily good at learning which behaviours attract adult attention and concern, and at reproducing those behaviours when they are stressed, frightened, or want something to stop. He was seven years old. He was terrified. The adults around him had been modelling a specific script for months. He learned it.

That is not cynicism about the child. It is an acknowledgement of how much children absorb from the adults around them, and how powerfully an environment of fear can shape behaviour in ways that then appear to confirm the fear.

The professionals who found themselves uncertain, Washington, Austin, and Dr Onyeukwu are equally worth understanding rather than dismissing. All three arrived in situations that were already saturated with the possession framework. Washington was interviewing a family whose doctor had just used language of supernatural fear. Austin was investigating a household where every resident was in genuine distress, and where every physical anomaly had been interpreted and narrated through a coherent, emotionally compelling story. Dr Onyeukwu described his own fear, not just the children's behaviour, which tells you something about the atmosphere created in that examination room before he even walked in. The psychological research on suggestion and expectation is extensive: context shapes perception in ways that are not conscious and not easily corrected. These were not people who chose to believe. They were people whose perceptual systems were working exactly as designed, finding patterns, being influenced by context, and interpreting ambiguous events through the most available explanatory framework.

What the Ammons case actually demonstrates is not the reality of demonic possession. It demonstrates how thoroughly that framework can colonise the perceptions of people who enter its gravitational field without their own clear alternative framework in place. The DCS system failed to provide that alternative quickly enough. The initial responders, the doctor, the nurse, and the first case manager arrived without adequate protocols for distinguishing between a family in psychological crisis, a family constructing a supernatural narrative for other reasons, and a situation requiring immediate psychiatric intervention. They were assessing child welfare in circumstances where the relevant expertise was psychiatry, and the psychiatric assessment did not happen until after the possession framework had already infected several official reports.

The lesson the Ammons case offers to the book's larger argument is precise and uncomfortable: the possession framework is not limited to communities of religious belief. Given the right conditions, sustained fear, sleep disruption, a coherent explanatory narrative applied consistently over time, and an absence of competing frameworks with institutional authority, it can reach into the secular apparatus designed to prevent exactly this kind of harm and temporarily reorganise how that apparatus sees.

Captain Austin is a good man who spent 36 years investigating crimes. He walked into a situation that had been carefully, if unconsciously, prepared to make even a sceptic uncertain. He left believing.

The follow-up DCS report from January 2013 closes the file on Carolina Street: no demonic presences, family no longer fixated on religion to explain the children's behaviour. Nine words that contain the entire story. The children needed help. They got it, eventually, imperfectly, after a great deal of institutional confusion. They are presumably adults now, living ordinary lives somewhere in Indiana.

The house is gone. Zak Bagans had it demolished in 2016. The lot on Carolina Street is empty. The staircase from the basement, "the staircase to hell," as it was called in media coverage, is now in a museum in Las Vegas, where people pay to stand near it.

Something was wrong in that house. Not demons. But something a family in serious distress, children exhibiting trauma responses, adults paralysed by fear and reinforcing each other's terror over months, a context so thoroughly saturated in one explanatory framework that professionals arriving to assess it got temporarily lost inside it. That is real. That happened. The records are there.

Whether that counts as haunted is a question each reader will answer for themselves. The more important question, the one this book keeps returning to, is this: when the secular institutions designed to protect vulnerable people encounter the possession framework in operation, what happens to those institutions? The Ammons case suggests the answer is more troubling than anyone would like to admit.

They don't always stay outside it.

There is one further dimension to the Ammons case that the official documentation captures only partially, and it matters.

The 800-page file primarily documents what the state apparatus observed and concluded. It is less good at capturing what it felt like to be Latoya Ammons. A woman who had moved her family into a house she could afford, who had spent months in a state of genuine terror, who had watched her children exhibit behaviour she could not explain through any framework available to her, who had then watched state officials remove those children from her custody while simultaneously conducting exorcisms with her Catholic priest. The institutional response to the Ammons case was fragmented and self-contradictory in ways that must have been bewildering to experience. DCS was investigating potential child neglect at the same moment that a bishop was authorising an exorcism at the request of another state official. The clinical psychologists were concluding that the children had been induced into a delusional system by their mother at the same time that a police captain was publicly declaring himself a believer in the demonic.

Latoya Ammons was not charged with anything. She was not found to have abused or neglected her children. She met all the DCS requirements for reunification and had her children returned to her. She told the Indianapolis Star, after the case went public, that she had never expected the attention it received. "I figured that we would get some type of uproar from my hometown, but I never imagined that it would go viral." She now lives in Indianapolis. She has declined most media requests.

What she believed happened to her family, and what actually happened, are questions the official record does not fully separate. The official record says the children showed trauma responses consistent with being raised in an atmosphere of fear. It does not say that Latoya Ammons deliberately created that atmosphere. It does not say she was lying. It does not even say she was wrong; it says the clinical framework did not support the possession interpretation, and that once the family left the house and the focus shifted, the behaviour resolved.

A family was frightened. A community of professionals was temporarily lost inside the same framework that had frightened the family. And the most powerful institutional response turned out to be, in the end, the most boring one: get the family out of that house, get the children into welfare assessment, stop talking about demons and start talking about behaviour and support. The follow-up worker who wrote "no demonic presences or spirits" in January 2013 probably thought she was closing a bureaucratic file. She was also, without quite knowing it, describing how the possession framework loses its grip when the conditions that sustained it change.

That is the Ammons case's final lesson. Possession belief is not robust to ordinary life. It thrives in conditions of isolation, fear, sleep deprivation, and the absence of competing explanatory frameworks. Change the conditions, and it fades. The house on Carolina Street produced nearly 800 pages of official documentation about demons. The follow-up welfare visits produced a single line: the family is no longer fixated on religion to explain the children's behaviour issues.

Nine words. The exorcism is over.

The children who lived through those months on Carolina Street are carrying something. Children who grow up inside a sustained atmosphere of supernatural terror who are told, repeatedly, by the adults they love and trust, that demonic forces are attacking their family, that the house they sleep in is under siege, that their own behaviour is evidence of spiritual attack those children carry that framework into adulthood in ways that may not be visible in a welfare follow-up report. The trauma of the experience is real regardless of what caused it. The fear was real. The nights of disrupted sleep were real. The months of watching their mother and grandmother interpret ordinary events as evidence of evil were real. Whatever the DCS case manager meant when she wrote that the family was no longer fixated on religion to explain the children's behaviour, and it was the right observation, it does not mean the fixation left no trace.

And the lot on Carolina Street remains empty. No plaque. No monument. The staircase lives in Las Vegas under theatrical lighting, and tourists pay to photograph themselves beside it, and the story gets told and retold as evidence of supernatural forces that a family in a Gary rental house encountered in the winter of 2011. Most tellings do not mention Stacy Wright's clinical assessment, or Joel Schwartz's report, or Christina Olejnik's follow-up notes. They mention Captain Austin saying he is a believer. They mention the boy walking up the wall. They leave out the grandmother's hand.

The grandmother's hand is the whole story.

CHAPTER XVI

The Girl Nobody Recorded

Natal, South Africa, 1906

The year 1906 is the year Natal burned.

The Bambatha Rebellion erupted that spring, a Zulu uprising against British colonial taxation, land seizure, and the accumulated brutality of a system designed to reduce an entire people to administered labour. The British response was swift and catastrophic. Thousands of Zulu men were killed. Thousands more were imprisoned. The Chiefs were stripped of authority. The colony of Natal, already a structure built on conquest and dispossession, tightened its grip on everything within it.

At St. Michael's Mission in Umzinto, a Catholic compound on the rolling green hills of the Natal interior, a sixteen-year-old orphan named Clara Germana Cele watched all of this from behind convent walls. She had lived inside those walls since the age of four. The world beyond them, the burning kraals, the reprisals, the quiet erasure of the culture she had been born into, reached her as rumour, as smoke on the horizon, as the lowered voices of the nuns. The mission was her entire world. The Church was everything she had.

And then, in the summer of 1906, something cracked inside her.

Clara was Zulu by birth and Catholic by circumstance, orphaned as an infant and placed at the Mariannhill mission, one of a network of Trappist stations established across Natal to educate, convert, and in the language of the day, civilise, the region's indigenous people. She had been baptised, catechised, trained in choir singing and domestic labour, immersed from earliest childhood in a theology of sin, contrition, and the ever-present struggle between God and the devil. She knew no other framework. She had no other language for inner experience. She had never, as far as anyone recorded, travelled beyond the mission's grounds.

This is the context that every account of the Clara Germana Cele case overlooks, and it is the one that matters most. A Zulu girl, orphaned and institutionalised, raised entirely within a colonial Catholic structure, in the year that structure's parent empire was using artillery against her people. Her possession, when it came, was Catholic in its imagery, its vocabulary, its named adversaries. There is a reason for that. It is the only spiritual language she has been given.

What we know of Clara's life before the summer of 1906 fits on a single page, and most of it comes from mission records written by European priests and nuns. She was known as devout, kind, and unremarkable. She sang in the choir. She attended confession. She received Holy Communion. She gave no cause for concern. This is the portrait that institutional memory preserves: a good girl, obedient, quietly faithful, the successful product of the mission's educational programme. Whether that portrait is accurate, or whether it is simply the portrait a Catholic mission in colonial Natal would have been likely to compose of a girl whose inner life it had no means or interest in examining carefully, is a question the sources cannot answer.

What the sources do tell us is that sometime in mid-1906, Clara approached her confessor, Father Erasmus Hörner, and told him she had made a pact with Satan. One account of the case, drawing on research into the mission's history, records that the confession followed what Clara described as a traumatic encounter in which a local sangoma, a Zulu traditional healer, had violated her. The specific nature of that violation is not recorded in the official Catholic documentation. The pact with Satan, however, is. The mission, in the way that institutions do, recorded the theological fact and left the human one to silence.

Father Hörner was a German-born Trappist who had arrived at Mariannhill in the 1890s, part of the wave of European missionaries who came to Natal with faith, discipline, and a profound conviction that the spiritual world was as real as the physical one. He heard Clara's confession and initially did not act on it further. Confessions were confidential. He absolved her. He sent her back to the dormitory. The ordinary business of a Catholic mission in colonial Africa continued.

Then, on 20th August 1906, the ordinary stopped.

The nuns heard it first. A sound from Clara's direction that one attending sister later described in words that still arrest the reader: "No animal had ever made such sounds. Neither the lions of East Africa nor the angry bulls. At times, it sounded like a veritable herd of wild beasts orchestrated by Satan had formed a hellish choir." Clara was ripping at her clothes. She was growling. She was speaking to entities that nobody else could see, holding what appeared to be extended conversations with invisible presences. At one point, she turned to the nearest sister and said, in a voice that did not sound like hers: "Sister, please call Father Erasmus. I must confess and tell everything. But quick, quick, or Satan will kill me. He has me in his power. Nothing blessed is with me. I have thrown away all the medals you gave me."

Father Hörner was summoned. What he found in that room was not the girl he had known.

Clara had always been, by the mission's account, gentle and controllable. Now she was not. She possessed what witnesses described as strength far beyond what her slight frame should have been able to produce, overpowering nuns who tried to hold her, throwing them aside. She could not approach sacred objects without convulsing. Holy water on her skin produced what the witnesses called burning, though no physical mark was visible. She refused all blessed food, saying she could detect the blessing. She began to levitate.

That is the claim that draws the most attention and the most scepticism, and it requires careful handling. Father Hörner himself later wrote: "Germana often floated three, four, and up to five feet in the air, sometimes vertically and at other times horizontally." The eyewitness reports are consistent across multiple witnesses. But "consistent" and "accurate" are different things, and the condition under which those witnesses were observing extreme emotional distress, intense religious expectation, a mission culture saturated in the reality of supernatural forces produced exactly the kind of perceptual environment in which shared error is most likely to occur. A girl in a severe dissociative episode, thrashing violently against the nuns holding her, might rise from a bed. In the hands of people holding her arms and legs, with sufficient convulsive force, that rising might appear to be levitation. This does not make the witnesses liars. It makes them human.

What cannot be so easily explained are the languages.

Clara had spent her entire life within St. Michael's Mission. She spoke

Zulu and, after 12 years at the mission school, had limited English and Afrikaans, necessary for her education and daily life. She had never had contact, as far as anyone could establish, with native speakers of Polish, German, French, or Norwegian. Yet witnesses recorded that she spoke in all of these languages during her episodes, with fluency and what they described as native command. Other students and nuns who knew those languages confirmed what they were hearing. The phenomenon, known in theological literature as xenoglossia, speaking in languages not previously learned, is one of the criteria the Catholic Church considers in assessing claimed possession.

The secular explanations for xenoglossia are not wholly satisfying. Cryptomnesia, the emergence of forgotten memories, can produce the illusion of knowledge that the person believes they never acquired. It is possible that Clara, living in a mission staffed by European priests and nuns from multiple countries, had absorbed more language than anyone had tracked. The mission was linguistically diverse, with German Trappists, Italian priests, and sisters from across Europe, all conducting their work and private conversations within earshot of the students. A girl with a facility for language and a lifetime of immersed exposure might produce approximations that sounded more fluent than they were. The reports of her languages come from the same witnesses who reported the levitation: believers already primed to interpret what they saw.

That said, the phenomenon at St. Michael's was witnessed and confirmed by people who themselves spoke those languages. This is not equivalent to an accurate account of levitation. It is harder to explain away.

The mission community had no psychiatric framework. In 1906, Natal had no accessible mental health services for indigenous people.

The concept of dissociative identity disorder was not yet formalised. Conversion disorder, the production of neurological symptoms without neurological cause, driven by psychological distress, was barely understood even in European medical circles, and its understanding certainly had not reached a mission compound in the Natal hills. What the priests and nuns had was the Rituale Romanum, centuries of Catholic teaching about demonic possession, and a girl whose behaviour matched the theological criteria precisely.

Father Hörner and the mission director, Father Martinus Mansueti, compiled their observations and sent them up the ecclesiastical chain of command. The Vicar General reviewed the case and authorised it. Two priests were appointed to perform the major exorcism rite. Both fasted in preparation, eating only bread and water for days. They gathered crucifixes, containers of holy water, consecrated oil, and the Rituale Romanum itself. The chapel at St. Michael's Mission was selected as the location: consecrated ground, the house of God, the place where the demon's power would be weakest and the priests' strongest. On 11th September 1906, the exorcism began at dawn.

It continued until midday. Then it resumed at three in the afternoon and continued into the night. What happened inside that chapel over those hours was recorded by the attending nuns in terms that have not diminished in their strangeness across more than a century. Clara tried to strangle Father Mansueti with his own stole, wrapping the liturgical garment around his throat with both hands while he recited the Latin prayers. She knocked a Bible from Father Hörner's hands with a force that witnesses said looked impossible. Her body, during the worst of her episodes, contorted in ways the nuns described as serpentine, as though her spine had lost its structure, as though she were moving like a snake rather than a human being. One witness reported that she appeared to physically transform during these moments, though the accounts are not specific about what the transformation looked like.

The exorcism continued through the second morning. And then, before approximately 170 people who had gathered in and around the chapel, students, nuns, priests, and local community members, Clara levitated one final time. The priests administered the rite. The presence that the witnesses described as inhabiting her announced that it was leaving. Clara came down from wherever she had been. She opened her eyes. She asked for water. The exorcism was declared complete.

The 170 witnesses are important. This is not an intimate gathering of committed believers behind closed doors. This is a public event. A mission chapel packed with people, including students who had no reason to lie about what they saw, who were themselves as frightened as anyone else. If the levitation at the conclusion of the exorcism was a fabrication, it was a fabrication maintained consistently by a large number of independent observers across decades. Whether or not that constitutes evidence of anything supernatural is a question each reader must resolve for themselves. There is, at a minimum, evidence that something occurred that those 170 people found remarkable enough to talk about for the rest of their lives.

Clara came back to herself. She was intensely embarrassed and wanted no one to speak of what had happened. She returned to her place in the mission's life: the choir, the dormitory, the schoolroom, the regulated rhythms of a Catholic institution in colonial Natal. For a time, it seemed finished.

Then, in January 1907, she confessed again. Another pact with Satan. Another descent into the states the nuns had hoped never to witness again.

The second exorcism followed. This time it lasted ten days. The Vicar Apostolic, Henri Delalle, presided over a more senior figure than had been present the first time, and one who, sources note, had been initially sceptical of the whole affair. His involvement suggests that the Church did not simply rubber-stamp the first proceedings and move on. There was official scrutiny. There was institutional caution. Delalle came, observed, concluded that what he was witnessing fell within the Church's categories of genuine possession, and completed the rite.

This time, when the presence departed, witnesses reported an overwhelming smell. Not the smell of something sacred, but of something rotting, an odour of putrescence that filled the chapel and took time to clear. This sensory detail, appearing in multiple independent accounts, is one of the case's most unusual features. Putrid smells accompanying the departure of possessing entities have been documented in other cases. Their explanation, whether psychosomatic, atmospheric, or something else entirely, remains genuinely puzzling even to those who approach the case without any theological commitment.

After the second exorcism, the disturbances stopped. Clara Germana Cele returned to her life at St. Michael's Mission and was not reported to exhibit any further episodes. She died in 1912, at approximately twenty-two years old, of heart failure. The mission held a quiet funeral. The record of her death is as sparse as the record of her life.

She deserves more than that sparseness. Not because she was possessed by a demon. But because she was a human being whose inner crisis, whatever it was, was experienced in the most isolated and powerless circumstances imaginable, and who has since been used, again and again, as a piece of evidence in someone else's argument about the supernatural, while the actual texture of her life goes unexamined.

Consider what Clara's psychology might have actually looked like through a clinical lens that Natal simply did not possess in 1906.

She was an orphan. She had been institutionalised since infancy. She had no family, no personal history outside the mission, no experience of a world beyond its walls. She was sixteen years old in 1906, an age at which the pressures of developing identity are intense even in support-ive, stable environments and Clara's environment, while providing material care, was neither culturally continuous with her identity nor psychologically equipped to support the kind of self-construction that adolescence demands. She was Zulu in a mission run entirely by European priests and nuns, in a colony that had just spent the year suppressing a Zulu uprising with extreme violence. She had no elders, no community of origin, no ancestral framework to draw on. She had the Church.

The Church had given her a model of the world in which evil was real, embodied, and active. It had given her the concepts of Satan, of pacts, of demonic possession, of exorcism and deliverance. These were not abstract theological categories for someone who had lived inside Catholic doctrine since the age of four. They were the architecture of reality. When something unbearable happened to Clara, and the ac-count that places sexual violence at the origin of her crisis is consistent with what typically precipitates severe dissociative episodes in young women, she had exactly one framework available to explain it. That framework told her she had been touched by evil, that evil could in-habit a body, that the inhabiting evil could be named, confronted, and cast out.

She named it. She confronted it. She asked for the ritual that could cast it out.

This is not manipulation. This is a young woman doing exactly what her entire upbringing had prepared her to do with unbearable experience: placing it within a system of meaning that made it, if not comprehensible, then at least addressable. The exorcism gave her a means of action. The prayers gave the priests and nuns a sense of purpose. The collective ritual gave the mission community a way to participate in her crisis rather than stand helplessly outside it. And after two days, Clara said the thing was gone, and the community believed her, and for months it stayed gone.

Until it wasn't.

The second pact, the second possession, the second exorcism, these repeat the pattern in ways that should give any thoughtful reader pause. A one-time crisis resolved by ritual and returning after several months is consistent with a dissociative episode that was not fully resolved by the initial intervention, or with a cycle of psychological distress that the ritual addressed only temporarily. It is also consistent with the theological interpretation: a young woman re-engaging with forces she had called once and found she could not fully expel. The documents do not permit certainty on this point. What they do reveal is that whatever Clara experienced, it was not a single contained event but a pattern, a repeating cycle of crisis, ritual, and imperfect resolution that only ended when her body gave out six years later.

The clinical vocabulary that would have helped Clara in 1906 did not exist in any form she could have accessed. Conversion disorder, in which psychological distress produces genuine physical and neurological symptoms, including loss of sensation, paralysis, involuntary movements, and altered states of consciousness, was described by Jean-Martin Charcot in France in the 1880s and was being studied by Freud and Breuer in the 1890s, but that knowledge had not crossed the distance between Vienna and Umzinto. What those studies have established is that conversion symptoms are real in the sense that the person experiencing them is not performing or faking; the brain is producing the symptoms through channels that bypass conscious control. The guttural voice is not put on. The convulsions are not theatrical. The altered state of consciousness in which a different voice speaks through the same person's throat is as genuine a neurological event as an epileptic seizure, even though it has no organic cause in the sense a neurologist would identify.

Clara Germana Cele was almost certainly experiencing conversion disorder layered on severe dissociative episodes, triggered by trauma in an environment that offered no psychological support and no framework for understanding what was happening except a theological one. The theological framework turned her crisis into a narrative of demonic possession, shaped her symptoms into the expected pattern of the possessed, the aversion to sacred objects, the speaking in tongues, the levitation, the demonic voice and then resolved it, at least temporarily, through the ritual of exorcism. The resolution was real, too. The relief she felt when she said the demon had gone was genuine. The brain, having been given a narrative framework that made the crisis survivable, could temporarily reorganise itself around that resolution.

The xenoglossia, the foreign languages, remains the element of the case that sits most uncomfortably with a straightforward conversion disorder reading. If the languages were real, if Clara were genuinely producing fluent Polish, French, German, and Norwegian in states she did not consciously control, then something was happening in that mission chapel in 1906 that our current neuroscience does not fully account for. Whether that something requires a supernatural explanation is a question that science cannot answer. What it does require is acknowledgement that the human brain's capacity to store and retrieve information through channels that bypass conscious awareness is not yet fully mapped. Cryptomnesia is real. Its outer limits are not yet known.

The case of Clara Germana Cele sits at a precise intersection of colonial history, trauma psychology, and religious faith, making simple conclusions impossible and demanding careful thought. She was a colonised orphan in a year of colonial violence, experiencing what was probably a trauma response in an institution whose only model for unusual mental states was theological. The priests who helped her were not cruel. Father Hörner, by all accounts, was a conscientious man who took her distress seriously and responded to it with the only tools he had. The ritual may genuinely have provided relief. It did not provide a cure. She died at twenty-two, of heart failure, in the only home she had ever known, having spent her final years in the quiet embarrassment she had asked for all along.

Nobody who lives in the West today and watches horror films that feature levitating girls in institutional settings thinks of Clara Germana Cele. They think of The Exorcist. They think of Emily Rose. They do not think of a sixteen-year-old Zulu orphan in a colonial mission compound in the same year as the Bambatha Rebellion, whose inner crisis was witnessed by 170 people and recorded in the documents of a European Church, and whose life and death are summarised in a Find a Grave entry and a few paragraphs on Wikipedia.

She was not a supernatural demonstration. She was not evidence for or against the existence of demons. She was a teenager with no resources, no support, no framework beyond what the mission had given her, managing something unbearable with the only tools available, in a world that had already taken everything else from her.

The strange choir of sounds that the nun recorded, no animal had ever made such sounds, was the voice of all of that. Of orphanhood, of colonial displacement, of violence that had no name and no healing available to it. Of a girl alone with something she could not bear, in a language she had been taught, crying out.

The priests answered her. In the language they had. In the only way they knew.

Whether that was enough is the question the case leaves open. Clinically, it was not. Humanly, it may have been the best that 1906 could do.

Clara Germana Cele died in 1912. She was twenty-two years old. She had asked, above all things, that people forget. The most accurate thing we can say about her, more than a century later, is that she deserved far more than the world she was given and that the story told about her, the story of the girl who levitated and spoke in tongues and was twice delivered from Satan, is so much larger and louder than the story of the girl herself that Clara Germana Cele has effectively vanished inside it.

Which, if you think about it, is its own kind of possession.

There is one further dimension to the Cele case that almost never receives the attention it merits, and it is the dimension that connects it most directly to the book's larger argument about what possession belief does to the people it touches.

Clara, unlike many of the subjects in these pages, survived. She was not killed by her exorcism. She was not harmed by the priests who administered it. Father Hörner and Father Mansueti were not Michael Taylor's Fellowship Group, were not the pastor who burned Vilma Trujillo García, were not the Bikubis. They fasted before the ritual. They obtained institutional authorisation. They performed the rite as the Church prescribed it, with the care, training, and doctrinal framework provided by the Rituale Romanum. And when it was over, Clara was returned to her life.

This is worth holding carefully, because the book has dwelt at length on cases where the possession framework killed. Clara's case is different. The framework gave her a name for the crisis, gave the community a means to respond to it, and ultimately gave her a resolution that was at least partially functional. For two days in September 1906 and for ten more days in April 1907, something was done about the unbearable thing inside her. Whether that something addressed the actual cause of the trauma, the institutional isolation, the colonial violence that had shaped every dimension of her existence, is another question. It did not. But it gave her a way of living with it that the available alternatives could not have provided.

This is the Lukins' argument, rendered in different conditions. George Lukins, the eighteenth-century Somerset tailor whose case appears earlier in this book, found in the possession framework a way of living with something that medicine had abandoned. Clara Germana Cele found in it a way of surviving something that no available institution had the tools to understand. The framework did not explain the underlying reality in either case. But it provided a structure, a community, a ritual of address that created enough of a resolution to allow ordinary life to resume.

The critical difference, and it is the difference this book has been built around, is that in Clara's case, the possession framework did not replace existing treatment. There was no existing treatment. There was no diagnostic vocabulary. There was no psychiatric service accessible to a Zulu orphan in colonial Natal in 1906. The framework filled a space that medicine had not yet occupied. It becomes deadly when it occupies the space medicine already occupies, displacing care that exists rather than substituting for care that doesn't. In 1906, Natal, for Clara Germana Cele, it was the latter.

That matters. It does not make the framework true. It does not mean the demon was real. It does not mean the Catholic exorcism rite is a clinically validated treatment for dissociative disorder. What it means is that the relationship between spiritual frameworks and human suffering is not always one of displacement and harm. Sometimes, in specific historical and cultural conditions, with specific individuals, within the constraints of what is actually available, it is all there is. And all there is can be enough to allow a person to go on.

Clara went on. For six more years, in the chapel and the choir and the dormitory and the schoolroom, she went on. She sang. She prayed. She grew, presumably, from sixteen toward twenty-two in the way that young women grow, in ways the mission's records did not bother to observe. And then she died, quietly, of heart failure, in Umzinto, in the only country she had ever lived in and the only home she had ever known.

Father Hörner outlived her. He continued his ministry at Mariannhill. He wrote his account of the possession and the exorcisms, and that account was eventually gathered and published, and the case passed into Catholic literature as one of the more thoroughly documented possession cases of the modern era. His name is on the record. Clara Germana Cele is on the record under a Catholic name given to her, not the Zulu name her parents gave her, which is not recorded anywhere by a Church that baptised infants into its own taxonomy. Even her name belongs to someone else's story.

In the end, what we have is this: a girl, a crisis, a ritual that helped partially and temporarily, and a death at twenty-two that ended whatever it was she had been carrying. The sounds that the nun described, the impossible choir of animal voices from one girl's throat, were quiet at last.

She asked people to forget. They didn't. But perhaps what they should have remembered, and didn't, was not the levitation or the languages or the exorcism. What they should have remembered was the girl herself, her name, her people, her particular aloneness in that place, in that year, in that world. The crisis was extraordinary. Life was ordinary. Both deserved to be kept.

The mission at Mariannhill continues to operate today, more than a century after Clara's crisis played out within its walls. It runs schools, a hospital, and a radio station. The chapel where 170 people witnessed what they described as a levitation has been rebuilt, reordered, and used for ordinary worship for 117 years. The dormitory where Clara tore her clothes, growled, and begged Father Erasmus is long gone. The hillside remains. The green interior of Natal remains. The descendants of the people who were there in 1906, who survived the Bambatha Rebellion and the decades of dispossession that followed, remain.

What makes the Cele case useful to this book is precisely that it sits at the boundary between harm and help, showing that the same framework that kills people in other chapters can, under specific conditions, serve as a genuine resource. Understanding when it does and when it doesn't is a theological question. It is a structural one. The variables are the availability of alternatives, the degree of institutional oversight, the training and restraint of the practitioners, the subject's consent, and the cultural context that makes one explanation or another feel adequate to the experience.

In 1906, Natal, at St. Michael's Mission, most of those variables aligned in ways that made the exorcism survivable and partially effective. The priests were trained, the ritual was authorised, the restraint used was physical rather than fatal, the subject was alive at the end and remained so for six years. This is a different outcome from Earling, Iowa, where the subject's symptoms returned within a year, and the triumph was fabricated in print. It is a vastly different outcome from Klingenberg, where Anneliese Michel starved to death. It is a different country from Gary, Indiana, where a DCS worker filed a report about a boy walking up a wall, and an entire institutional response was temporarily organised around the wrong explanation.

The Cele case does not redeem the possession framework. It contextualises it. Shows that the framework's relationship to harm is not inevitable but conditionally dependent on what else is available, who is doing the interpreting, and what happens after the ritual is over.

Clara Germana Cele lived. For six years she lived. The choir went on. The dormitory went on. The schoolroom went on. Umzinto went on, out there beyond the mission walls, in all its ordinary, complicated, colonial, living reality.

And then she died, at twenty-two. Heart failure.

The record ends there. It should not end so thin.

CHAPTER XVII

The Longest Exorcism

Q UEBEC, CANADA, 1940S–1960S

They called the era La Grande Noirceur. The Great Darkness.

It lasted for more than two decades, from the mid-1930s into the early 1960s, and it was not darkness in the poetic sense. It was deliberate. Administrative. Signed into law, countersigned by the Church, and managed by the Sisters of Providence, the Grey Nuns, the Brothers of Charity, and dozens of other religious orders whose charitable façades concealed institutions that operated, behind their locked wards and bolted doors, as something very close to human processing facilities.

At the centre of it was Maurice Duplessis, Premier of Quebec, childless bachelor, political autocrat, and devoted son of the Catholic Church. He ran the province the way a medieval lord ran his territory: through patronage, fear, and the alliance of temporal and spiritual power. The Church administered Quebec's schools, hospitals, and social services. Duplessis kept the arrangement intact and profitable.

What they built together, with the full participation of the province's medical establishment, was a machine for erasing children.

This is not the story of a single exorcism. It is the story of the longest one. Twenty years of children held inside asylums they didn't belong in, subjected to treatments that had no clinical justification, labelled with diagnoses that were fabricated for financial reasons, and left to carry what was done to them for the rest of their lives. No single moment of death. No dramatic collapse before an altar. Just the steady, bureaucratic destruction of thousands of ordinary children, conducted with the full authority of the state and the blessing of the Church, in the name of moral order and the saving of souls.

The mechanism was simple. In the late 1940s, the federal government introduced subsidy programmes for provincial health services. Quebec received $0.75 per day per child in an orphanage. A child classified as mentally deficient in a psychiatric hospital received $2.25 or more. The mathematics required no refinement. Within a short period, the province had many fewer orphans than before and dramatically more mental patients. Orphanages were redesignated as hospitals. Children sleeping in the same dormitory beds, eating the same food, attended by the same staff, were reclassified overnight as psychiatric cases. The reclassification required a physician's signature. The signatures were provided.

The 1962 Bédard Commission, convened after Duplessis's death in 1959 to investigate the province's psychiatric institutions, found that one-third of the 22,000 patients classified as mentally ill in Quebec's hospitals had been classified for financial reasons, not clinical ones. This was not an allegation. This was a commission finding, reported to the government. The commission carefully noted it, recommended reforms, and moved on. No criminal charges were laid. No religious order faced prosecution. The children, by then young adults, many of them institutionalised for more than a decade, were quietly released into communities they had never known, without education, without preparation, without any of the tools needed to function in a world they had been deliberately kept from.

Hervé Bertrand was sent to a Catholic orphanage as a young child, one of thousands whose mothers had been pressured into surrendering infants deemed illegitimate. He was among the luckier cases, routed to a reform school rather than a psychiatric ward, where he learned to read and write, and eventually became a plumber. When he emerged in the early 1960s, he at least had a trade. Most of his peers had nothing. They had spent their formative years scrubbing floors, painting walls, doing laundry, cooking not for themselves, but for the institutions that warehoused them. The nuns ate filet mignon, as several survivors reported, while the children ate noodles. The rest of the time was filled with prayers, punishments, and the particular terror of existing without any adult in the institution who had a meaningful interest in your survival.

The children who passed from orphanages into psychiatric wards entered a different world entirely. The wards at Saint-Jean-de-Dieu in Montreal, run by the Sisters of Providence, were not medical environments in any recognisable sense. They were containment facilities that had acquired the administrative classification of hospitals without acquiring much of the corresponding medical ethics. Electroshock therapy was administered routinely to children who had no psychotic illness, sometimes first thing in the morning, before staff moved on to other tasks. Denis Lazure, a physician who interned at the facility in the early 1950s and later became a government minister, described in his own memoirs pushing the button on the electrical box that sent currents through dozens of sedated patients before heading to the insulin coma rooms, where he would inject doses strong enough to induce unconsciousness. He described this without evident distress. It was simply the morning routine.

What was being treated? Nothing, in many cases. The children had been certified as mentally deficient to qualify their institutions for federal funding. Once inside the psychiatric ward, the diagnosis became their identity. Behaviours that were normal responses to institutional trauma, crying, anger, withdrawal, attempts to escape, were recorded as evidence of mental pathology and treated accordingly. The treatment itself induced further trauma. The further trauma produced further behaviours that were treated further. The cycle was self-reinforcing and had no natural stopping point. It stopped only when the institution decided to release a patient or when the patient died.

Some died. The question of how many is one that has never been formally answered, because the records were managed by the institutions themselves, the deaths were investigated by hospital police rather than external authorities, and in 1942, the Legislative Assembly of Quebec had passed a law permitting religious orders to sell the unclaimed bodies of orphans to medical schools for ten dollars. Survivors testified that they were assigned the job of transporting bodies to unmarked graves near the institutions. The site adjacent to Saint-Jean-de-Dieu became known colloquially as the pigsty cemetery, because it sat near a hog farm and had no headstones. Ground-penetrating radar surveys in recent years have identified anomalies consistent with human remains in quantities that match the scale described by survivors. The bodies have not been exhumed. The Church and the government have so far not permitted it.

Bruno Roy, a writer who had himself been institutionalised as a child, led the Duplessis Orphans' Committee when it was organised in the early 1990s. He was one of the very few survivors who had built a professional life from inside the catastrophe of his childhood. Most were doing less well. In the psychiatric study completed by one of the hospitals involved, middle-aged Duplessis Orphans reported more physical and mental impairments than matched control groups. Eighty percent reported suffering traumatic experiences between the ages of seven and eighteen. More than half reported physical, mental, or sexual abuse. Nearly four in five reported difficulty functioning socially or emotionally as adults. These figures describe a generation whose inner lives had been systematically dismantled, who had grown up without the foundational experiences of safety, continuity, love, and education that make adult functioning possible.

Rod Vienneau of Joliette, one of the more outspoken survivors, gave interviews and testimony for decades. He described the hospitals as places where children were selected for electroshock and experimental drug treatments based not on clinical criteria but on whether they had family members who might ask questions. Parentless children, children with no one to advocate for them, were chosen precisely because they were safe to harm. No one would come looking. No one had come looking before. A physician's report from 1967, recorded in court documents, describes examining a Duplessis Orphan as an outpatient at Saint-Jean-de-Dieu, by then renamed Louis-Hyppolite-Lafontaine Hospital and continuing to administer chlorpromazine years after the institutions had theoretically been reformed. The drug, a powerful antipsychotic that had been used experimentally on children since the mid-1940s, was effective at ensuring compliance. A compliant patient is an easy patient. A child on heavy antipsychotics does not fight, does not ask for its mother, and does not create administrative inconvenience.

The connection to this book's central subject requires careful articulation, because the Duplessis Orphans case does not fit neatly into the pattern of the earlier chapters. There was no single exorcism, no possessed woman chained to a cross, no priest reciting Latin over a convulsing child. The possession logic operated differently here. It was embedded in the institutional theology that ran Quebec's social services: the conviction that illegitimacy was sin, that the children of unwed mothers were morally compromised, that poverty itself was evidence of spiritual failure, that the suffering of the poor was not social injustice but divine correction. Children labelled as mentally deficient in these institutions were not simply being reclassified for subsidy purposes. They were also, within the theology of the nuns who ran the wards, being classified in a way that made the withdrawal of ordinary human consideration seem righteous.

This is possession logic without the dramatic ritual. The child is not inhabited by a demon in the theatrical sense. But the child is classified as other, as not-fully-human, as defective, as beyond the reach of ordinary compassion, and once that classification is in place, what can be done to the child becomes unthinkable by ordinary standards. The straitjacket, the ice bath, the electroshock, the hunger, the sexual abuse by staff: all of these require that the person doing them has already stopped seeing the child as simply a child. The psychiatric label provides exactly that permission. You are not hurting a person. You are treating a patient. The patient is incurable, is dangerous, and is better confined. The treatment, however it feels to the child, is necessary for the good of the institution, which is the good of the Church, which is the good of God.

This is the machinery underneath. The possession is not declared. It does not need to be. The children born in sin, classified as defective, warehoused in institutions, treated as experimental material they are possessed by their very existence within a theology that has no category for their innocence.

One survivor's account, published in a 1999 New York Times interview, describes being placed in a straitjacket and tied to a bed frame for weeks, surviving on food that was force-fed. The woman's abuser was a sister belonging to the Grey Nuns. When asked why she was being restrained, the sister's answer, as the survivor recalled it, was theological in its simplicity: for her own protection. This is the language of every exorcism in this book. The chains are protective. The torture is mercy. The victim is being saved from something worse than the suffering being inflicted.

What was being saved? In a psychiatric ward in mid-century Quebec, the answer would have involved a vocabulary of mental hygiene and institutional order. But underneath that modern administrative language was the older logic: the children were being disciplined because they were inherently disordered, because their very existence was a problem, because the Church's authority to impose order on chaos was not only a right but a duty. The nuns who administered ice baths and electroshock to children who had no pathology were not merely complying with a corrupt financial system. They were, within their own framework, performing an act of institutional exorcism: driving out the disorder, the deviance, the dangerous other-ness that they believed these children represented.

The complicity extended across three institutions. The Quebec government provided the financial incentive and signed the administrative orders. The Catholic Church provided the infrastructure, the staff, and the theological framework that made the treatment of children as less-than-human feel acceptable. The medical establishment provided the signatures, the diagnoses, the clinical language that dressed the whole enterprise in the respectability of science. None of these three could have accomplished what they accomplished alone. The power of the system lay precisely in the overlap, in the reinforcement of each pillar by the other two, in the way that state authority, ecclesiastical authority, and medical authority combined to make dissent not merely difficult but effectively invisible.

Several children wrote books in the early 1960s, after their release. The books attracted minimal attention. A 1962 commission found that sane children were kept in psychiatric institutions and made recommendations. The recommendations were quietly implemented, and the story was considered closed. It did not resurface publicly until 1989, when a Radio-Québec television programme invited survivors to speak on air. The accounts poured out the electroshock, the abuse, the bodies they had carried to unmarked graves, the years they had spent in wards that should not have held them. The following year, Pauline Gill published her exposé on one survivor's case. By 1991, the Duplessis Orphans' Committee had formed, and the legal campaign had begun.

The campaign encountered, at every turn, the institutional management of information that appears in different forms throughout this book. The hospital records had been lost or destroyed. The criminal charges the committee sought to bring against the nuns and monks responsible for specific abuses were rejected by the courts, largely because the evidence that might have supported them no longer existed in retrievable form. The Quebec Superior Court rejected a class action petition. The government offered $1,000 per surviving orphan, approximately the same amount that the bureaucrats processing the applications were paid per day. Premier Lucien Bouchard's 1999 apology was qualified, offered no individual compensation, and came with no offer of investigation. The Catholic Church, separately, created a fund but refused to acknowledge specific wrongdoing. Under subsequent premier Bernard Landry, a further programme provided compensation to some survivors, but required them to sign a waiver agreeing not to take legal action against the Church.

The waiver is the part that demands careful reading. Quebec's government would provide compensation to survivors but only if they agreed, in signing for that compensation, to surrender any legal claims against the religious institutions that had caused the harm. This is not reconciliation. This is the management of liability. The Church was not facing accountability. It was purchasing immunity, using public funds administered by a sympathetic government, from the people it had destroyed.

A 2018 class action brought by some survivors, seeking $875,000 each from eight religious communities, was rejected by the Superior Court of Quebec. The court's reasoning included the observation that too much time had passed. The harm, in other words, was real enough that the court did not dispute it. The harm was simply too old for the legal system's mechanisms to apply. The people who had designed the system, who had signed the administrative orders, who had pushed the button on the electroshock machines, who had sold children's bodies to medical schools they had largely died of natural causes, having faced no criminal proceedings, no professional sanctions, and in most cases no public naming of their actions.

Rod Vienneau continued giving interviews well into his later years. He called what had been done a crime against humanity. In 2010, the Duplessis Orphans brought their case before the United Nations Human

Rights Council. The Council heard them. Nothing enforceable followed.

What the psychiatric literature knows about the long-term effects of early institutional trauma does not require the Duplessis Orphans' specific history to be documented. The general pattern is well-established. Children who experience severe abuse and neglect in institutional settings before the age of five show measurable changes in brain architecture, including reduced volume in the prefrontal cortex and limbic structures associated with emotional regulation, stress response, and the capacity for attachment. The earlier the abuse begins, and the longer it persists, the more profound these neurological effects tend to be. Children who experienced neglect in institutionalised settings the kind of neglect that comes from wards where each nun was responsible for more than ten children under the age of two, where children could not speak properly until the age of four or six, where no individual adult had the time or the inclination to form a consistent bond show the neurological profile associated with severe attachment disruption.

Attachment disruption is not merely a psychological description. It describes how the developing brain wires itself. The infant brain, encountering a consistent caregiver who responds to its distress, learns that the world is predictable, that distress can be relieved, and that other people can be trusted to be there. This learning is encoded neurologically. When the consistent caregiver is absent when the child's cries are not answered, when the face that appears is hostile or indifferent, when distress is met not with comfort but with punishment or restraint the brain encodes a different map of the world: one where distress cannot be relieved, where other people are unpredictable or threatening, where the only reliable response to danger is to become invisible or to dissociate.

This is the psychological reality underneath the 78% of Duplessis Orphans who reported difficulty functioning socially or emotionally as adults. It is not a weakness. It is not a moral failure. It is the predictable neurological consequence of a developmental environment designed, whether deliberately or through indifference, to produce exactly this outcome. The same children who could not form attachments in infancy were later unable to sustain relationships as adults, were more likely to experience addiction and homelessness, and were more likely to encounter mental health difficulties that were, by grim irony, interpreted as confirmation of the original false diagnosis. Mentally deficient children, it turns out, become adults with mental health difficulties when you expose them to decades of trauma. The prophecy fulfils itself through the mechanism of the harm done in its name.

The bodies in the ground are the fact that the chapter returns to, because they are the fact that still waits for an accounting. Ground-penetrating radar surveys have identified potential burial sites adjacent to former psychiatric institutions. The Catholic Church and the Quebec government have not authorised systematic exhumation and identification. The surviving orphans in 2010, estimated at between three and four hundred, and declining every year, have asked, and continue to ask, that the dead be given their names back. That the graves be opened. That the records, such as they are, be examined. That someone, finally, counted the bodies.

Bruno Roy, who led the committee for years, died in 2012. He had written his own account of his institutionalisation, had used his relative success to advocate for those whose success had been less, and had watched the legal campaign produce inadequate settlements and no criminal accountability. He did not live to see the ground-penetrating radar surveys or the renewed calls for exhumation that followed the discovery of unmarked graves at residential schools across Canada in 2021. That discovery prompted fresh public attention to the Duplessis case, as advocates pointed out that the same logic that had operated in Catholic institutions, indigenous or marginalised children, and unmarked burials had operated in Quebec decades before anyone paid attention to residential schools. The parallel was exact. The institutional response, from both the Church and the province, was similarly characterised by acknowledgement of harm in the abstract and resistance to accountability in the specific.

The chapter is titled The Longest Exorcism. The title requires justification.

In every other case in this book, possession is declared. Someone, a priest, a pastor, a parent, an uncle, identifies a person as inhabited by something evil and proceeds to expel it. The harm is direct and concentrated. There is a ritual. There is a victim. There is a perpetrator. When the courts convict, they have a specific act to address.

The Duplessis Orphans case has no single ritual. What it has instead is a twenty-year deployment of the same underlying logic across tens of thousands of individual children: the identification of a population as morally compromised, the stripping of their ordinary human status, the application of harm in the name of institutional and theological order, and the insistence, maintained for decades after the fact, that what was done was done for their benefit. Father Corogeanu said the same thing about Irina Cornici. The nuns said the same thing about the children they chained to bed frames. The Church said the same thing about the children whose bodies they sold for ten dollars to medical school anatomy departments.

The mechanism is identical. The scale is different.

In Tanacu, one woman died over three days. In Quebec, thousands of children were processed through a system that destroyed their development, erased their identities, and left them unable to fully inhabit adulthood. Some died from the treatments. Some died in unmarked graves. Many survived in the way that people survive when survival is the only option available: damaged, under-resourced, carrying wounds that the world declined to name as wounds.

What Nestor, one of the surviving orphans who participated in the 2021 video conference with Irish Mother and Baby Home survivors, said into the microphone was this: "We did nothing wrong to God."

It is as exact a description of what was done to them as any legal document produces. The children had done nothing wrong. They were born to the wrong mothers, in the wrong province, at the wrong moment in the wrong political arrangement. They were labelled sinful and defective by a system that needed them to be sinful and defective in order to function financially. They were held inside institutions that treated the label as a clinical reality, and the clinical reality as justification for everything that followed. And when it was over, when the wards quietly emptied in the early 1960s and the children were discharged into a world they had been kept from, no one in authority said to them what Nestor understood to be true and needed someone else to confirm: that they had done nothing wrong.

The Church has not offered a formal apology. The College of Physicians sent a letter of regret in 2012. The Quebec government's apologies have been partial, procedural, and attached to compensation programmes that required survivors to surrender further legal claims as a condition of receiving them. The unmarked graves have not been opened. The records that were not destroyed remain largely inaccessible. The religious orders that ran the institutions continue to exist, in reduced but ongoing form, and have not faced criminal prosecution for what happened inside their walls.

The longest exorcism. It ran for two decades. Its subjects were children who had committed no transgression against God or man beyond the fact of existing. Its perpetrators were three intersecting institutions: government, the Church, and medicine, each providing cover for the other, each insisting that what was being done was necessary and good. Its victims carry the evidence in their bodies, their brain chemistry, their inability to form relationships, their difficulty trusting institutions, and their particular quietness when directly asked about what happened.

And in the ground, near a hog farm outside Montreal, beneath soil that has not been systematically excavated, the rest of the evidence waits.

No one has told it to come out yet.

There is a clinical detail that deserves more space than it usually receives in accounts of the Duplessis Orphans case, and it is this: some of the children who were reclassified as mentally deficient eventually did develop genuine mental illness. This is not a coincidence. It is a documented consequence of early institutional trauma.

The developing brain, subjected from infancy or early childhood to the chronic stress of an environment it cannot escape and cannot control, undergoes measurable physiological changes. The hypothalamic-pituitary-adrenal (HPA) axis, the body's primary stress response system, becomes dysregulated under sustained, uncontrollable threat. Cortisol floods the developing brain repeatedly. The hippocampus, a structure critical for memory consolidation and fear modulation, is particularly sensitive to this chronic cortisol exposure and can be measurably reduced in volume. The amygdala, the brain's alarm system, can become hyperactivated, primed to detect threat in environments that are objectively safe. The prefrontal cortex, which in ordinary development learns to exert regulatory control over the amygdala's fear responses, develops more slowly or less completely in children who spend their critical developmental years in states of chronic stress.

What this means, in practice, is that children who entered Quebec's institutions healthy and left them damaged were not simply carrying psychological scars. Their brains had been architecturally altered by the experience. They were more likely to develop depression, anxiety disorders, PTSD, and, in some cases, the very psychotic disorders they had been falsely diagnosed with as children. The false diagnosis, through the mechanism of the harm done in its name, became a self-fulfilling prophecy. The system that labelled children mentally deficient to profit from them, then, through the treatments applied under that label, produced the conditions under which genuine mental illness was more likely to develop.

This is perhaps the most precise description of what was done. The institutions did not merely warehouse children under false pretences. They damaged those children neurologically, in ways that made them more vulnerable to the mental health difficulties that the institutions had claimed they already possessed. They created the thing they had falsely diagnosed. And when the children emerged, carrying the neurological consequences of a decade or more of institutionalisation, the world looked at them and saw, as it was meant to see, people who could not cope, not people who had been deliberately made unable to cope by the actions of the state, the Church, and the medical establishment acting in concert.

That is the full shape of what was done. The children were stolen from ordinary development by a financial arrangement. They were held inside institutions that abused them. The abuse neurologically altered them in ways consistent with psychiatric vulnerability. Those vulnerabilities, in adulthood, produced difficulties that, from the outside, appeared to confirm the original label. And no one, in any institution of power, has faced criminal accountability for any of it.

Nestor, speaking into a microphone in a tucked-away office at Montreal's Concordia University, connecting by video to survivors in Dublin who had experienced a different version of the same institutional logic, found the right word for what had been done. He said, "When you are a bastard, you will be the dirt of society."

He said it in French. The Irish survivors, listening across the ocean, didn't need a translation.

They knew exactly what he meant.

The timeline of the Duplessis Orphans' campaign for justice illustrates, with particular clarity, how long an institution can hold its position against the people it has harmed when it controls the records, the legal mechanisms, and the political relationships that would otherwise produce accountability.

The first survivors spoke publicly in 1989. By 1991, books had been published, and a committee had formed. By 1992, legal action had begun. By 1997, the provincial ombudsman had formally recommended compensation. By 1999, ten years after survivors first spoke publicly and 30 years after the institutions had closed, the government offered $1,000 per orphan and called it a resolution. The Catholic Church established a separate fund and called it 'compassion'. Both offers came with implicit conditions: accept this, and stop asking for more.

Many survivors accepted because they had no realistic alternative.

They were old. They were unwell. They had spent decades bearing the institutional damage without the professional support that might have mitigated it. A thousand dollars was not justice. It was also nothing, and for people who had very little, nothing was the realistic alternative to accepting it.

The 2018 class action seeking $875,000 per survivor from eight religious orders, a sum calibrated to represent something approaching the actual cost of a stolen childhood, was rejected. The courts ruled the claims time-barred. The law's limitation periods, designed to prevent the prosecution of grievances so old that evidence has decayed and witnesses have died, operated here to protect the institutions that had ensured, through the management of records and the strategic absence of criminal charges in the 1960s and 1970s, that the clock ran out before the full case could be made.

The ground-penetrating radar surveys are still the most recent development. They have found anomalies. The anomalies have not been investigated further. The call for exhumation continues. The institutions, and the government that continues to balance its relationship with them, have not authorised it.

What would the exhumations prove? They would prove that children died in quantities that institutional records do not account for. They would allow forensic examination of remains that might reveal causes of death inconsistent with natural causes. They would give the dead their names back, or at a minimum, establish how many of them there are. They would make visible, in the most physical and irreducible way possible, the scale of what was done.

Whether or not the exhumations happen, the Duplessis Orphans case stands as the book's most systematic example of institutional possession not the dramatic, singular possession of a single person by a named evil, but the sustained, administrative possession of thousands of children by a system of intersecting powers that removed from them the most fundamental thing a child can have: the right to be treated as a person.

Every child who entered those institutions as a healthy child and left carrying damage created by the institution was possessed in that sense: their inner life, their development, their capacity for adult functioning were taken over and reshaped by something external that did not have their interests at its centre. The possessing force was not demonic in the theological sense. It wore the faces of nuns and politicians and physicians and signed its work in administrative triplicate.

It called itself charitable. It called itself medical. It called itself the will of God.

The children knew what it was. They just didn't have anyone willing to believe them until they were old enough to say it themselves, in public, into microphones, to anyone who would listen.

Nestor said: We did nothing wrong to God.

He meant: what was done to us was wrong, and it was done in the name of God, and that is the full obscenity of it.

He was right. And the ground near the hog farm in East End Montreal still holds whatever the institutions put there, unnamed and unexamined, waiting.

CHAPTER XVIII

The Man Who Wrote His Own Diagnosis

YATTON, SOMERSET, SUMMER 1788

George Lukins was possessed by seven demons, he said, and only seven clergymen praying over him simultaneously could drive them out.

Seven. That is a very specific number. Most people in extremity ask for a doctor, or a priest, or someone they love. George Lukins asked for a theologically precise configuration of ministers, in line with a New Testament precedent. Mary Magdalene had been possessed by seven demons, according to the Gospel of Luke, and seven was therefore the number required to oppose them. He had thought this through. He arrived, in other words, with a complete diagnosis and a detailed treatment plan. He had been waiting eighteen years for someone to administer it.

That is the thing about this case that both believers and sceptics tend to rush past in their hurry to argue about whether he was genuinely possessed or a shameless fraud. He was not new to this. He had not suddenly collapsed one afternoon in 1788 and been carried to a vestry. He had been having fits since 1770, had seen every doctor in Somerset he could find or afford, had spent twenty weeks as an inpatient at St George's Hospital in London, one of the foremost medical institutions in England and had been discharged incurable. Eighteen years of fits, strange voices, barking, blasphemy and singing hymns backwards. The medical profession had nothing for him. So he turned to the Church instead and told them exactly what he needed.

Whether that makes him a fraud or a desperate man is not, I think, as straightforward as it sounds.

Yatton is a village in the Somerset Levels, a few miles south of Bristol. In 1770, when Lukins's troubles began, Somerset was caught between worlds. The Industrial Revolution was beginning to rewrite what England was. The Enlightenment was rewriting what educated people believed. Methodist revivalism, which John Wesley had spent decades constructing, was rewriting what ordinary working people believed about God and the devil and their own souls. All three of these forces were running simultaneously through the same landscape, through the same communities, through the same people, and they did not fit together neatly.

George Lukins was a tailor by trade, a common carrier, and a performer of Christmas mummeries, the folk theatrical tradition that went from house to house during the festive season. By every account, he was a man of excellent character, well-liked by his neighbours, a regular churchgoer who received the sacraments and caused no trouble. He was cheerful his whole life, people said, right up until something knocked him down during a mummers' play in 1769, and everything changed.

His account of the inciting incident is worth recording precisely. He was performing one evening at the house of a Mr Love. He had been drinking rather more than was advisable, given that two neighbours, a man named Avery and a man named Read, were needed to escort him home. On the way, or possibly at his door, he collapsed. He said he had felt a supernatural slap. A blow from nowhere that felled him and left him, he believed, in the possession of evil spirits.

His contemporaries noted, apparently without irony, that all of this had occurred whilst he was drunk, in the dark, in the middle of winter.

What followed over the next eighteen years was a condition that defeated every doctor who examined it. The Gentleman's Magazine, reporting on the case years later, attributed his symptoms to epilepsy and St Vitus's dance. St Vitus's dance is what we now call Sydenham's chorea, an involuntary movement disorder that typically follows streptococcal infection and produces jerking, writhing, uncontrolled movements of the limbs and face. Combined with epilepsy, it would produce exactly the kind of frightening, inexplicable fits that witnesses described: violent convulsions, vocalisation, altered states, periods of apparent amnesia. Lukins was seen by an eminent local surgeon named Dr Smith of Wrington. He was examined by other physicians. He spent that twenty-week inpatient stay at St George's Hospital. Nobody could help him. He was discharged incurable, although one attending physician noted in the records that at least some of his symptoms appeared to be performed rather than involuntary, and that the lameness he presented alongside the fits was similarly suspicious.

That note was written by a man who had seen Lukins for a matter of weeks. Samuel Norman, a surgeon in Yatton, had known him for the better part of twenty years. And Norman's conclusions, published in two pamphlets in 1788, were rather more pointed.

In the spring of 1788, Lukins was forty-four years old and had apparently resolved on a course of action. A woman named Sarah Barber, a parishioner of Temple Church in Bristol who had previously lived in Yatton and knew of his condition, encountered him and was sufficiently alarmed to contact her vicar. That vicar was the Reverend Joseph Easterbrook, an Anglican clergyman with strong Methodist sympathies — the kind of man who found the evangelical revival thoroughly congenial and was not, therefore, inclined to dismiss the idea that demons were real.

Mrs Barber's description was vivid. When in his fits, she said, Lukins sang and screamed in sounds that did not resemble the human voice. He cursed and swore in ways that seemed beyond his normal character. He declared that no doctor could help him. And he said he was possessed by seven devils, who could only be expelled by seven clergymen praying in faith.

Seven clergymen. Specific. Matching a New Testament precedent. Not a coincidence, and not a detail that Lukins had arrived at in the forty-eight hours since Mrs Barber had noticed him.

Easterbrook visited Lukins in person. Whatever he witnessed convinced him. He began assembling the required seven ministers, contacting Methodist colleagues, and securing the Temple Church vestry in Bristol as a venue. He also attempted, with an optimism that events would quickly disprove, to keep the whole business quiet.

He failed at that almost immediately. Someone sent a letter to the Bristol Gazette describing Lukins's case in language calculated to produce maximum attention: "the most singular case of perverted reason and bodily suffering that I ever heard of." The letter ran in early June 1788, before the exorcism had taken place. By the time the seven ministers gathered on the morning of 13th June, it was no longer the private spiritual event Easterbrook had envisioned. It was news.

The seven clergymen who assembled that morning were an unusually mixed theological company for 1788. Easterbrook was Anglican. The other six, John Broadbent, John Valton, Benjamin Rhodes, Jeremiah Brettell, Thomas McGeary, and William Hunt, were Methodist. John Wesley, the founder of Methodism and the most prominent religious figure in England, had been invited. He was sixty-five, in declining health, and did not attend. But he sent a private warning to Easterbrook that was quietly prescient: publishing an account of these proceedings, Wesley advised, would invite ridicule and potentially harm the Church's credibility. He prayed for the man. He did not want his name publicly attached.

Wesley was right. He usually was.

The exorcism was dramatic. Lukins was brought into the vestry in the state witnesses described as possession: fits, strange voices, violent behaviour. The seven ministers prayed and sang hymns. Lukins claimed to be the devil. He growled and barked. He sang the Te Deum in inversion, which the observers found particularly significant, since it implied supernatural knowledge of the liturgy's correct order. He was violent. He was frightening. The clergymen persisted, commanding the demons to depart in the Trinitarian formula used for such occasions. After some time, Lukins cried out, "Blessed Jesus!", praised God, recited the Lord's Prayer, and thanked the ministers who had prayed over him.

He was, according to everyone present, immediately calm. Lucid. Grateful.

The account of the exorcism was promptly published in the Bristol Gazette and printed as a pamphlet, A Narrative of the Extraordinary Case of George Lukins, of Yatton, Somersetshire, Who Was Possessed of Evil Spirits for Near Eighteen Years, signed by all seven ministers and prefaced by Easterbrook. It is a careful document, dignified in tone, making no outlandish claims beyond the events themselves. Easterbrook clearly knew, from Wesley's warning, that he was writing for a sceptical age and was trying to pre-empt the objections. He pointed to scripture and to Church precedent. He described what he and the other ministers had witnessed. He did not editorialise excessively.

It made no difference. The sceptics arrived anyway.

The response in the Bristol Gazette was extensive, passionate, and pseudonymous, the way letters-page debates always are when something has genuinely got under people's skin. Multiple writers attacked the ministers. Multiple writers defended them. The argument, stripped of 18th-century circumlocution, was essentially this: was what happened to George Lukins a spiritual event or a medical one? Was he possessed, or was he a man with a condition nobody understood? And if nobody understood it, and the exorcism worked, what on earth does that prove?

Into this correspondence, with considerable force and considerable clarity, stepped Samuel Norman.

Norman had been the surgeon in Yatton for years. He had known Lukins personally and had observed his fits many times. He published two pamphlets in quick succession. The first was Authentic Anecdotes of George Lukins, the Yatton Daemoniac. The second, and you can feel Norman's temperature rising from the title alone, was The Great Apostle Unmasked. His position was clear: Lukins was an impostor.

This deserves careful treatment. Norman was not simply a sceptic reaching for a convenient explanation. He had specific evidence. He documented the St George's Hospital discharge, in which an attending physician had noted that some symptoms appeared to be feigned, and that the lameness accompanying the fits was similarly suspect. He observed that Lukins had specified the terms of his cure: seven demons, seven clergymen, a New Testament precedent not at the time of the exorcism but long before, as though he had been rehearsing it. He pointed out that this specification did not emerge organically from a suffering man's distress. It was something Lukins had clearly thought through and articulated deliberately, and had been telling people for some time.

Norman's implication was plain: George Lukins had, over years of genuine suffering with a condition nobody could treat, evolved a solution. Not medicine, which had failed him. Not ordinary prayer, which had resolved nothing. A very particular spiritual intervention, prescribed with exact numbers and delivered with precise theological authority. He had waited, apparently with considerable patience, until he found clergymen willing to provide it.

Whether that makes him a fraud in any meaningful sense is a question I have been turning over since I first encountered this case, and I do not think the answer is simple.

Consider what Lukins's position actually was by 1788. He was forty-four years old. He had been having uncontrolled fits for eighteen years. He had sought medical help from every available source, including one of London's premier hospitals, and had been sent home. His fits were frightening to those around him and presumably terrifying to experience from the inside. He lived in a community that understood his behaviour through a religious lens, because that was the primary lens available. He was a devout churchgoer who understood his own behaviour through a religious lens, because that was the primary lens available to him. And within that framework, the explanation that made sense of the voices, the violence, the altered states, the barking and the blasphemy was demonic possession. Not because he had calculated it cynically, but because that was the only coherent account his vocabulary offered.

The specification of seven clergymen may have arrived through genuine theological reasoning rather than theatrical calculation. He had read the Gospel of Luke. He knew Mary Magdalene's possession had involved seven demons. He believed seven demons were inside him. He therefore concluded that seven ministers would be needed to address them. This is not obvious fraud. This is a man applying the available frameworks with more than average theological care.

What it is, however, is a case in which the person presenting symptoms has substantially shaped the diagnosis he receives and the treatment he is given. And that is psychologically significant regardless of whether the possession itself was real.

Here is what we actually know about what happened in the Temple Church vestry on 13th June 1788: George Lukins's fits stopped. Or appeared to stop. For a period. The length of that period is not entirely clear in the historical record. Nichols and Taylor, writing a century later, reported that the fits left him from that hour and that he led a sober Christian life thereafter, becoming a member of the Wesleyan society in Bristol in 1798. Reverend Valton noted that he had been briefly employed as a bill poster by Mr R. Edwards, a not particularly glamorous role, but one that provided stability he had not previously achieved.

The parish records tell a more complicated story. In 1788, the same year as the exorcism, Yatton paid Lukins ten shillings and sixpence in temporary relief, the designation for charity payments to the destitute, and noted that further payment had been offered on condition that he go to work for a Mr Say. He refused. He said he would go to Bristol and not return until the parish forced him to. This is not the portrait of a man cured and reintegrated. It suggests someone who, freed from the fits that had defined him for eighteen years, found himself without income, without occupation, and without any clear path forward.

He died in February 1805, according to the Bristol Mirror. He had been living in extreme poverty, supplementing what little he earned by begging and selling small books. He was described as a chronic invalid with numerous complaints, though the dramatic fits did not appear to have returned in their former shape. He died having never really recovered from his recovery.

There is something in that which feels true to me, though I recognise that it is a subjective response. The fits had given Lukins an identity. A role. He was the Yatton daemoniac. People knew him. Prominent ministers had come from Bristol to pray over him. His case had been published in national papers. And then the fits stopped, and he was just an indigent former tailor in Yatton with no work and no prospects, refusing parish employment and insisting on going to Bristol where the exorcism had briefly made him interesting.

I do not think he was primarily a fraud. I think he was a man with a genuine, untreatable condition, in an era that offered him nothing medically, who did what people do: he reached for the explanatory framework his culture provided, found a solution within it, and promoted it until someone was willing to try. The fact that the solution appeared to work, and his fits reduced after the exorcism, does not prove possession was real. It may simply demonstrate that suggestion, expectation, and the experience of a focused ritual performed by seven ministers in sincere response to a belief you have held for years can produce measurable changes in how a condition presents.

Psychologists describe this as the placebo effect operating through conviction. When you believe something will happen, it very often does. Lukins believed seven ministers would drive out seven demons. Seven ministers prayed over him with complete sincerity. His brain, which had been generating fits for eighteen years, appears to have accepted the ritual as valid. The symptoms changed. Whether that is grace, a neurological response, or some inseparable combination of the two is a question 18th-century medicine could not answer. The 21st century has not entirely resolved it either.

What makes the Lukins case historically significant beyond one Somerset tailor's affliction is its timing. It landed in 1788 at the precise intersection of the Enlightenment and the evangelical revival, and the argument it generated was the argument of this book, conducted in real time on the letters pages of the Bristol Gazette, with the stakes entirely visible.

Enlightenment scepticism had been building for decades. Educated men in 1788 were increasingly inclined to attribute unusual behaviour to natural causes rather than supernatural ones. The language of enthusiasm, meaning excessive religious fervour, was used dismissively by the kind of people who read the Gentleman's Magazine. When that publication attributed Lukins's fits to epilepsy and St Vitus's dance, it was not merely offering a diagnosis. It was making a statement about which explanations were respectable.

At the same time, Methodist revivalism had given tens of thousands of ordinary English people a renewed and vivid conviction that spiritual warfare was real. Wesley himself believed in demons. He believed possession occurred. His theology was experiential; it concerned what God actually did in people's bodies, emotions, and everyday lives, and was therefore naturally sympathetic to a man who said he had spent

18 years fighting evil spirits and needed 7 ministers to help him finish the job. The six Methodist ministers in that vestry were not naïve. They were acting in accordance with a theological framework developed with considerable rigour. They simply believed something different from what Samuel Norman believed.

Wesley's private warning to Easterbrook that publishing this would invite ridicule demonstrates that he understood the cultural moment exactly. He knew the Enlightenment had shifted the terms of credibility, and that a story about a Somerset tailor exorcised by seven ministers would be read very differently in 1788 than it would have been in 1688. He was right. Satirical verse appeared in Bristol almost immediately. "Lo, Lukins comes, and with him comes a train / Of Parsons famous for a lack of brain," one local poet wrote, which gives you a fair sense of the temperature. Norman's pamphlets followed. The Gentleman's Magazine offered its secular diagnosis. The consensus among educated commentators was consistent: this is not what enlightened people do.

And yet the seven ministers were not stupid men. Easterbrook's 1788 pamphlet An Appeal to the Public Respecting George Lukins is a substantial and careful document. He acknowledged the sceptics directly. He addressed the fraud argument. He pointed to the signed testimony of six other ministers who had all been present and described the same events. He observed that if Lukins had been performing, maintaining that performance for eighteen years in the presence of sceptical doctors, including the physicians at St George's Hospital who had found no natural explanation, would have required extraordinary discipline. And he asked a question that Norman and his allies notably declined to answer: what would you have had us do? Leave this man to another eighteen years of suffering because the medical profession could not help him?

It is a reasonable question. It does not settle the debate. But it is reasonable.

The aftermath of the Lukins case nudged English Protestantism toward greater caution regarding possession belief. The Methodist movement continued to take spiritual warfare seriously, but the public embarrassment of the affair, the satirical verse, the pamphlet debate, and Wesley's well-publicised private misgivings encouraged ministers involved in such matters to be considerably less public about them. Easterbrook appears to have suffered no lasting damage to his own reputation, but he did not make exorcism a regular feature of his ministry. The case remained famous in Bristol for decades, chiefly as a subject of controversy.

Interestingly, the records suggest that several lower-profile exorcisms were quietly conducted by Methodist ministers in the Bristol area in the months following the Lukins affair, apparently inspired by the precedent. Whether the Lukins case had opened a door that could not easily be closed, or whether such practices were already occurring and simply became temporarily more visible, is difficult to say with certainty.

The question that I keep returning to is simpler than any of this. What was George Lukins actually suffering from?

Epilepsy combined with Sydenham's chorea is the most plausible medical answer, and it fits the documented symptoms reasonably well. Epileptic fits can involve vocalisation, altered states, and periods of amnesia. Chorea produces exactly the uncontrolled writhing movements that witnesses described. In someone with no access to effective treatment in the 1770s, the combination could easily produce a presentation that looked like possession to an 18th-century observer and, perhaps, from the inside, to the person experiencing it.

But Lukins was not simply experiencing involuntary symptoms. He was constructing a narrative around them. He attributed them to specific demons, specified the number of those demons, and identified the exact theological intervention required. That level of elaboration suggests something beyond basic epilepsy and chorea. He may have had what modern psychiatry would recognise as a conversion disorder layered onto genuine neurological symptoms, a condition in which psychological distress produces physical symptoms that follow the contours of what the person believes illness looks like, rather than any anatomical logic.

Conversion disorder is not deliberate performance. People with conversion disorders experience their symptoms as entirely real and are not consciously generating them. But the symptoms are shaped by the person's understanding of what illness looks like, which in Lukins's case meant they were shaped by the framework of demonic possession. The barking, the blasphemy, the inverted hymns, the specific claim of seven demons: these are not the random products of a seizing brain. They are culturally informed. They reflect what Lukins believed was happening to him, and what he had perhaps learned to perform over years of having his behaviour interpreted through a religious lens.

There is also a dimension the surviving records do not adequately explore: the role of his audience. Lukins performed Christmas mummeries. He was a performer, in a modest but genuine sense, a man accustomed to playing roles in front of people and receiving responses. Eighteen years of being the Yatton daemoniac had given him, if nothing else, a kind of notoriety. Neighbours were frightened of him. Ministers came to pray over him. Doctors examined him. His case interested educated people. That is nothing, for a man who would otherwise have been an unremarkable tailor in a Somerset village, largely invisible to the world. When the fits apparently stopped after the exorcism, the notoriety went with them. The parish records show him refusing to return to ordinary working life, insisting instead on Bristol, where the exorcism had briefly made him matter.

None of this makes him a villain. It makes him human. A man with a genuine condition and no real options who found, within the available frameworks, a solution that worked, imperfectly and temporarily, and was left with less than he had started with when it resolved.

Samuel Norman's scepticism was not wrong. His prediction that posterity would find the Lukins affair an object of astonishment and contempt was simply premature. The astonishment he anticipated has not arrived. Not in 1788, not in 1888, not now. The argument between Norman's pamphlets and Easterbrook's defence, conducted in the Bristol Gazette, is still being waged, in different languages and venues, whenever a case like those in this book arises. The Enlightenment did not end belief in possession. It complicated it, drove it into communities where Enlightenment critique had less reach, and produced precisely the uncomfortable cultural split that the Lukins case embodied so clearly: medicine saying this is epilepsy and chorea, we understand it, there is nothing spiritual here; and seven ministers saying we do not much care what you call it, the man is suffering and we can help.

Both of those positions were honestly held. One of them was scientifically correct. The other apparently helped.

Sit with that for a moment. Because it is uncomfortable in ways that have not gone away.

The medical framework identified what was almost certainly happening in George Lukins's brain. The spiritual framework provided the only intervention that produced any visible change in his condition. Neither framework, on its own, was adequate to the human being before it. The doctors discharged him. The ministers took him from there. And between the two of them, over eighteen years and one June morning in a Bristol vestry, they managed something that was partial, impermanent, and possibly more than anyone had a right to expect.

The cases that follow Lukins, historically the ones in the chapters that precede and follow this one, tell a different story. In those cases, the spiritual framework does not step in after medicine has given up. It displaces available medicine, preventing treatment that could have saved lives. That is the difference between Lukins and Anneliese Michel, between 1788 and 1976, between a man discharged incurable and a woman starved to death whilst her doctors waited outside. The possession framework is not always fatal. It becomes fatal when it replaces care that exists, rather than filling the space left by care that has been exhausted.

George Lukins died in poverty in February 1805. His fits had apparently gone. His life had not recovered. The Bristol Gazette moved on to other controversies. The Temple Church vestry is still standing, though the church itself was gutted in the Second World War bombing. Yatton is still there, still quiet, still the kind of village that looks timeless in photographs and isn't.

Nobody visits. Nobody needs to. George Lukins was not a saint or a martyr. He was a man with uncontrolled fits in a world that couldn't explain them, who found within the frameworks available to him a solution that worked well enough, for a while, and then died alone in the county where he had always lived.

He suffered for eighteen years. Then he suffered differently. Then he died.

Whether the seven demons were real, whether Norman was right about the imposture, whether the exorcism cured him or simply gave his brain permission to stop none of that changes the basic shape of it. What it meant, we are still arguing about.

There is one further dimension worth examining, because the Lukins case introduced something into English possession history that would not be resolved cleanly for centuries: the problem of the patient who co-authors his own condition.

When we read the Loudun possessions, we are looking at a situation where the diagnosis of possession was imposed from outside. Sister Jeanne des Anges did not arrive at the Ursuline convent, announcing that she was possessed by seven demons and needed seven exorcists. The framework was applied to her, shaped by Canon Mignon, directed toward a predetermined political target. The nuns were subjects of a process they did not fully control, even when they appeared to be driving it.

Lukins is different. He had constructed his possession over eighteen years, in the absence of any institutional pressure to do so, in a context where the medical profession was actively trying to provide an alternative explanation and failing. The seven-demons framework was not given to him. He arrived at it, or arrived at something that crystallised into it. He brought it to the exorcists rather than having it imposed upon him. This makes him, at minimum, an active agent in his own story rather than a passive subject of other people's beliefs.

That distinction matters clinically. Modern psychiatry recognises a category of illness behaviour in which patients develop elaborate and self-consistent accounts of their conditions, accounts that may be psychologically functional, providing explanation, identity, and community even when they are medically inaccurate. These accounts are not straightforwardly delusional in the clinical sense; Lukins does not appear to have believed he was the only person in England possessed by demons, or that his possession was of cosmic significance. His framework was modest and specific. Seven demons. Seven ministers. One man in Somerset. He was not grandiose. He was practical.

What he resembles, from the vantage point of the 21st century, is someone who had found, within the framework of possession, a way of living with something that medicine had pronounced unlivable. The fits were real. The suffering was real. The medical profession's helplessness was real. What Lukins did was construct an account of that suffering that made it legible and, eventually, addressable. Whether the address was effective in any permanent sense is another matter. But the construction of the account appears to have been psychologically essential to him. It was, in a very literal sense, the thing that kept him going.

The ministers who prayed over him understood this, perhaps better than they knew. Easterbrook's appeal to the public carefully notes that the ministers did not set out to confirm possession in the abstract. They set out to help a man who had been suffering for eighteen years and had come to them asking for something specific. The theological correctness of what he asked for was, in some sense, secondary to the pastoral reality. Here was a man. He was suffering. He had asked for help in the terms available to him. They provided it.

Samuel Norman found this inexcusable. From his perspective, providing a supernatural explanation for a natural condition was neither helpful nor helpful: it confirmed Lukins in a false belief, encouraged others to seek religious solutions for medical problems, and made the work of rational medicine harder. His fury, expressed through the rather wonderful title The Great Apostle Unmasked, was the fury of a man who could see exactly what was wrong and could not understand why anyone with eyes and a functioning brain would choose not to see it.

He was right about the diagnosis. He was wrong about the simplicity of the choice.

Because the choice was not, for a man in Yatton in 1788, between a true medical explanation and a false spiritual one. The choice was between a true medical explanation that produced no treatment and a false spiritual one that appeared to produce some relief. Norman knew what epilepsy and chorea were. He did not know how to treat them. He could write devastating pamphlets about what Lukins was not suffering from, but he could not tell Lukins what to do on the mornings when the fits came.

The seven ministers in the Temple Church vestry had no better diagnostic framework than Norman. But they had a ritual, performed with sincerity, in response to a specific belief held with great intensity by a person in considerable distress. And something changed. Not permanently, not completely, not in any way that medicine would now regard as a cure. But something shifted. The fits, by all accounts, diminished after 1788. Lukins spent seventeen more years in poverty and ill health, but not in the kind of dramatic public suffering that had defined his previous decades.

That is the uncomfortable heart of the Lukins case, the part that neither side in the Bristol Gazette correspondence quite managed to say directly: the wrong explanation may sometimes produce the right outcome, and the right explanation may sometimes produce nothing at all.

CHAPTER XIX

The Walls That Break Minds

SHERMAN, TEXAS. WINTER 2004.

Andre Thomas, twenty-one years old, sat alone in a padded cell at Grayson County Jail. Five days earlier, he'd murdered his estranged wife, Laura Boren, their four-year-old son Andre Jr., and her thirteen-month-old daughter Leyha Hughes. He'd stabbed all three to death, cut open their chests, and removed their hearts, thinking he was setting them free from evil. Then he'd stabbed himself three times in the chest, expecting to die. When he realised he wasn't dying, he walked to the police station and confessed. God had told him to do it, he said. They were demons. Jezebel, the Antichrist, is an evil spirit. He had to kill them.

Now, in isolation, waiting for trial, Andre Thomas raised his right hand to his face and dug his fingers into his eye socket. He pulled. Hard. His eyeball came out, optic nerve torn, blood streaming down his face. When the guards found him, he was holding his eye in his hand, calm, explaining that the Bible says, "If your right eye causes you to sin, pluck it out and cast it from thee." So, he had.

They rushed him to the hospital, tried to save what vision they could, and returned him to custody. Psychiatrists evaluated him, diagnosed paranoid schizophrenia, and prescribed antipsychotic medication. But the trial proceeded anyway. In February 2005, an all-white jury in Grayson County rejected his insanity defence and convicted him of capital murder. The judge sentenced him to death. He was transferred to death row at the Polunsky Unit in Livingston, Texas.

On 27th January 2009, four years into his death sentence, Andre Thomas pulled out his left eye. This time, he ate it. When guards discovered him, both eye sockets were empty, bloody. He told them he'd needed to destroy the eye to prevent the government from using it to spy on him. Eating it was the only way to be certain. He'd been hearing voices for days, God speaking, demons tormenting, commands coming from everywhere and nowhere.

The Texas Department of Criminal Justice declared him incompetent to be executed. Under current US Supreme Court precedent, you cannot execute someone who's insane, and a blind man who's pulled out and eaten both his own eyes clearly qualifies. Andre Thomas remains on death row today, twenty years later, blind, psychotic, medicated enough to be manageable but not enough to be well, waiting for an execution that legally cannot proceed but hasn't been officially cancelled.

His lawyers argue he was psychotic when he committed the murders, that he genuinely believed his wife and children were possessed by demons, that killing them was the only way to save their souls. They have psychiatric reports documenting years of untreated schizophrenia beginning in childhood, auditory hallucinations from age nine, first suicide attempt at ten, escalating delusions about spiritual warfare, and apocalyptic obsessions with the Book of Revelation. The prosecution argued he knew right from wrong, that psychosis doesn't equal legal insanity under Texas law, and that he deserves to die for murdering three people, including two young children.

Neither side disputes that Andre Thomas hears voices. Neither side disputes that he genuinely believed demons were involved. The question isn't whether he's mentally ill; he demonstrably is. The question is whether that illness absolves him of responsibility for three murders, and whether a society that claims to be civilised should execute someone so profoundly broken that he's mutilated himself repeatedly whilst in custody.

But before examining the legal and ethical tangles of executing the mentally ill, before discussing what possession means when the person claiming it is locked in a cage with no escape from whatever's happening inside their head, we need to understand what isolation does to the human mind. Because Andre Thomas isn't unique. He's just the most extreme example of something that happens constantly in prisons and gaols across the world. People who were barely managing on the outside broke completely once locked up. And people who had no mental illness before custody develop it there, start hearing voices and seeing things that aren't present because the conditions they're kept in are specifically designed to break human psychology.

The research on isolation-induced psychosis is extensive and disturbing. Pelican Bay State Prison in California opened in 1989, built specifically to house the state's most dangerous inmates. The Security Housing Unit, known as the SHU, was designed for long-term solitary confinement. Inmates spend twenty-two and a half to twenty-four hours daily in windowless concrete cells. No human contact except guards passing food trays. No programmes, no work, no meaningful activity. Just walls, silence and time.

By the mid-1990s, psychiatrists and human rights investigators started documenting what happened to people kept in those conditions. Inmates with no previous mental health history were developing symptoms of auditory hallucinations, visual hallucinations, and paranoid delusions. Some thought guards were poisoning their food. Others believed they were being experimented on, that walls were watching them, that demons came through the concrete at night.

The medical term is SHU syndrome, though researchers also use "isolation psychosis" or "sensory deprivation psychosis." The symptoms are consistent across different populations and facilities. After weeks or months in isolation, people lose their grip on what's real. They hear voices. They see shadows moving in empty cells. They develop elaborate delusional systems to explain their experiences.

The worst cases develop what psychiatrists call "perceptual distortions": walls seem to move, breathe, and close in. Time stops making sense. Some inmates report losing the ability to distinguish between thoughts and external sounds, between memories and present events. One man told investigators he heard demons whispering through the ventilation system, giving him commands, telling him what guards were planning. Another saw messages written in blood on the walls that disappeared when the guards arrived.

None of these people was psychotic before solitary confinement. They developed symptoms in response to the conditions, and in many cases, symptoms resolved or improved significantly when they returned to the general population. This suggests the psychosis was environmentally induced, a direct response to sensory deprivation and social isolation rather than underlying psychiatric illness.

But some inmates interpreted their symptoms through religious or supernatural lenses. They weren't hallucinating; they were being visited by demons. They weren't experiencing psychosis; they were under spiritual attack. And once that interpretation took hold, it shaped everything else. The voices became more specific, more consistent with demonic possession as they understood it. Visual distortions became demonic entities. Paranoid thoughts became part of a cosmic battle between good and evil, with them at the centre.

This isn't unique to prisons. Psychosis always gets interpreted through available cultural frameworks. Someone in a strictly religious environment might hear God or demons. Someone in a culture that believes in ancestral spirits might be visited by dead relatives. Someone exposed to conspiracy theories might develop delusions about government mind control. The underlying neurological experience is similar to the brain misfiring, creating perceptions without external stimuli, developing beliefs not grounded in reality, but the content varies based on what cultural material the person has available to make sense of what's happening.

In prison, especially in isolation, that cultural material is often limited. No internet, limited reading materials, and no conversation beyond brief exchanges with guards. Many inmates only have religious texts available. So, when they start hearing voices and reality fragments around them, they interpret them through the lens of the Bible, the Quran, or whatever spiritual worldview they can access. And once they interpret it that way, it becomes real in that framework. They're not mentally ill, they're possessed. They're not having a psychiatric emergency; they're experiencing spiritual warfare.

Samuel Richard Shockley arrived at Alcatraz Federal Penitentiary on 23rd September 1938. He was serving life for bank robbery and kidnapping, transferred from Leavenworth after medical evaluations there showed an IQ of 68, a mental age of ten years, ten months, with emotional instability and episodes of hallucinations. Rather than sending him to the Medical Centre for Federal Prisoners in Springfield, Missouri, officials sent him to Alcatraz, believing the strict routine would better manage him.

They placed him in D-Block, the isolation unit, for three years. Most of that time was spent in "the Hole" or "Dungeon", darkened, stripped cells on the ground level where inmates experienced near-total sensory deprivation. Darkness. Silence. No human contact. No stimulation. For months at a time.

The isolation destroyed what remained of Shockley's fragile mental health. By 1942, the prison physician described him as emotionally very unstable with episodes of hallucinations. His IQ had dropped to 54, a mental age of eight years, nine months, indicating significant cognitive deterioration. Psychiatrists documented auditory hallucinations (hearing voices), visual disturbances (flashes of light), paranoia about contaminated food, and unfounded fears of cancer. Classic signs of schizophrenia, all exacerbated by prolonged solitary confinement.

Shockley told other inmates that people talked to him through the walls, that he heard conversations happening in cells far from his own, and that spirits of dead inmates gave him messages. He believed he was a "human radio receiver." He covered his mouth with duct tape and refused to speak to his family. His behaviour became increasingly erratic, confused, and childlike.

On 2nd May 1946, during what became known as the Battle of Alcatraz, inmates Bernard Coy, Joseph Cretzer and Marvin Hubbard overpowered guards, seized weapons, and released prisoners from D-Block, including Shockley and Miran Thompson. The escape attempt failed; they couldn't find the key to the recreation yard. Instead of surrendering, Shockley and Thompson urged Cretzer, who had a gun, to kill the hostage guards. Cretzer opened fire, wounding five officers. One, William Miller, died from his wounds.

The two-day siege ended with Coy, Cretzer and Hubbard dead. Shockley, Thompson and nineteen-year-old Clarence Carnes were charged with murder. At trial in November 1946, Shockley's defence attorney, William Sullivan, centred his case on insanity. The evidence was overwhelming: Shockley had been documented as mentally impaired for years, his IQ had dropped significantly during isolation, he experienced hallucinations and delusions, and he'd spent prolonged periods in conditions that would break anyone's mind.

Dr John Alden, a psychiatrist who examined Shockley, documented all these symptoms in a report to Sullivan. But then testified in court on 11th November 1946 that Shockley was "legally sane", able to understand the nature and consequences of his actions. The distinction between psychiatric illness and legal sanity proved decisive.

On 21st December 1946, the jury convicted Shockley of first-degree murder. On 3rd December 1948, he was executed in the gas chamber at San Quentin alongside Miran Thompson. His last words were rambling, confused, about voices, spirits, and people talking to him. Whether those voices were auditory hallucinations from isolation-induced psychosis or whether Shockley genuinely believed he was hearing supernatural entities, the outcome was the same. The isolation broke him, and then the state killed him for what he did while broken.

These aren't isolated cases. Human Rights Watch has documented hundreds of examples across American prisons over three decades. Their reports include testimony from inmates in isolation units nationwide, and the patterns are remarkably consistent. People with no mental health history who develop symptoms after months or years in solitary confinement. Auditory hallucinations interpreted through religious frameworks. Visual hallucinations of demons, angels, spirits. Paranoid delusions incorporating both prison staff and supernatural entities.

What's striking in the Human Rights Watch documentation is how culturally specific the hallucinations become. Muslim inmates hear Quranic verses being recited, see djinn moving through cells. Christian inmates hear biblical commands, see demons matching descriptions from Revelation or medieval demonology. Inmates from indigenous backgrounds report visits from ancestral spirits or nature beings. The content varies, but the underlying experience of hearing voices, seeing entities, and believing in external forces controlling or communicating with them remains constant.

This isn't because the supernatural manifests differently across cultural contexts. It's because psychosis uses material available in a person's mind to construct its delusions. If your cultural framework includes demons and spiritual warfare, that's how your brain interprets the misfiring neurons creating hallucinations. If your framework includes ancestors and spirits, that's the shape your psychosis takes. The brain doesn't create hallucinations from nothing. It pulls from memory, from belief systems, from stories heard and images seen.

Which means that in prison, where religious materials are often the only reading available, where chaplains may be the only non-staff visitors some inmates see, where spiritual language is one of the few acceptable ways to express suffering, psychosis naturally takes religious or supernatural forms. An inmate who starts hearing voices has limited frameworks for understanding that experience. "I'm mentally ill and need treatment" requires acknowledging illness, which in prison culture is often seen as weakness. "I'm being attacked by demons" fits within acceptable religious language, might even generate sympathy or spiritual support from other inmates or chaplains.

But there's a darker pattern. Sometimes, claiming possession is the only way to get help. Prison medical care for mental health is notoriously inadequate. Getting access to medical treatment, especially in isolation units, can be nearly impossible. But claiming religious experiences, saying you're hearing God or being attacked by demons, sometimes gets attention. Chaplains get called. Guards pay more attention. Maybe you get moved out of isolation for a psychological evaluation. Maybe you access a psychiatrist who wouldn't have seen you otherwise.

This creates a perverse incentive structure. Genuine mental health symptoms get packaged in religious language because that's the only way the system responds. This makes it harder to distinguish between genuine psychosis, religious experience and strategic performance. And critically, it means inmates genuinely suffering from environmental psychosis, the kind caused by isolation that would improve with different conditions, don't get appropriate treatment because their symptoms are interpreted as spiritual rather than medical.

The research on psychosis in prisons is extensive and deeply troubling. People in custody experience psychotic disorders at rates three to five times higher than the general population. Part of that's selection bias; people with untreated mental illness are more likely to end up incarcerated. But studies controlling for pre-existing conditions still find elevated rates of new-onset psychosis among inmates, especially those in isolation or other high-stress environments.

Groups at ultra-high risk include young men experiencing their first arrest, especially with a family history of mental illness. People with trauma histories who are re-traumatised by prison conditions. Inmates are in solitary confinement for extended periods. People with substance abuse histories are going through withdrawal. Immigrants are held in detention without clear information about their legal status or timeline. All show significantly elevated rates of developing psychotic symptoms whilst in custody.

The neurological mechanisms underlying this are well-documented. Prolonged sensory deprivation disrupts normal brain function in measurable ways. The human brain requires external stimulation to maintain stable perception and cognition. Visual, auditory and social input calibrate our sense of reality. When that input is dramatically reduced or eliminated, the brain begins generating its own stimulus hallucinations that feel as real as genuine sensory experiences.

Neuroimaging studies of people in isolation show changes in brain activity patterns. The default mode network, which is active when we're not engaged in external tasks, becomes hyperactive. This network includes regions associated with self-referential thinking, memory and imagination. When it dominates without external input to balance it, the boundary between internal mental states and external reality becomes porous. Thoughts feel like they're coming from outside. Memories get confused with present perceptions. Imaginings become indistinguishable from actual events.

The auditory cortex shows vulnerability. Studies using sensory deprivation chambers demonstrate that healthy volunteers begin experiencing auditory hallucinations within hours. The brain's auditory processing centres, deprived of input, begin misfiring, creating auditory perceptions without acoustic stimuli. For inmates in prolonged isolation, this process intensifies and persists. The voices don't stop when external sound is reintroduced. The brain has adapted to creating its own auditory reality.

Sleep disruption compounds the problem. Isolation units typically have lights on twenty-four hours or irregular lighting that disrupts circadian rhythms. Sleep deprivation produces symptoms virtually identical to psychosis, hallucinations, paranoia, and disorganised thinking. Chronic sleep disruption creates a state of perpetual semi-psychosis even in previously healthy people. For someone already experiencing schizophrenia, isolation and sleep disruption accelerate psychotic symptoms catastrophically.

And there's a feedback loop making everything worse. Untreated psychosis leads to violence, both against others and oneself. It leads to disciplinary infractions, which lead to more isolation, which worsens psychosis. It leads to an inability to follow prison rules, which can result in longer sentences or prevent parole. It dramatically increases recidivism rates because people are released still psychotic, unable to function, without adequate follow-up care.

The literature on this is extensive and consistent. Early screening works. Treating psychosis reduces violence, reduces self-harm, improves behaviour, and decreases recidivism. Keeping people with serious mental illness out of isolation improves outcomes across every measured variable. Providing continuity of care between prison and the community significantly reduces reoffending rates.

But most prison systems don't do these things adequately. Screening is minimal or non-existent. Treatment is inadequate. Isolation is still used as a disciplinary response even for inmates with diagnosed mental illness. Discharge planning for mentally ill inmates is almost non-existent; they're released with perhaps a two-week supply of medication and no plan for follow-up care.

People like Andre Thomas slip through every crack. He had symptoms before he killed his family, symptoms that should have been recognised and treated. He was psychotic at the time of the murders, should have been found not guilty by reason of insanity and sent to a psychiatric facility. He's remained psychotic throughout incarceration, has mutilated himself twice, and is still on death row waiting for an execution that legally cannot proceed because he's insane but hasn't been officially cancelled.

The system failed him at every point. Failed to treat his illness before he became violent. Failed to recognise the illness as a legal defence. Failed to provide adequate psychiatric care in custody. Failed to prevent him from mutilating himself twice. And now fails to resolve his legal status appropriately because that would require admitting all the previous failures.

Andre Thomas began experiencing symptoms in childhood. Auditory hallucinations started around age nine. He attempted suicide at ten. His family was "beset by a long history of mental illness, addiction and poverty", the kind of multigenerational damage that creates fertile ground for psychiatric illness. Despite these circumstances, Thomas showed early promise. He was placed in gifted-and-talented programmes as a young boy, demonstrating intellectual capacity that belied his chaotic home environment. He struggled against overwhelming odds and, for a short time, succeeded.

But mental illness doesn't care about potential. Through adolescence and early adulthood, his symptoms intensified, including obsessions with apocalyptic concepts from Revelation, difficulty keeping jobs, and increasingly bizarre beliefs. He met Laura Boren (born 7th November 1983) when they were teenagers. Several years into their relationship, she became pregnant. Thomas dropped out of school in ninth grade, earned a high school equivalency diploma, and worked multiple jobs trying to support Laura and the baby. Andre Jr. was born in August 1999. Thomas married Laura on his eighteenth birthday in 2001; she was seventeen.

They moved into Thomas's mother's house. Two weeks after the marriage, his mother forced them out. Laura and Andre Jr. moved in with her parents. Thomas moved in with one of his brothers. The separation came four months into the marriage. Laura began a new relationship, moved in with her boyfriend, and gave birth to Leyha in February 2003. For Thomas, the dissolution of his marriage marked the beginning of more intense delusions and suicidal thoughts.

He began believing Laura was Jezebel, the wicked queen from the Old Testament, synonymous with evil and corruption. He believed Andre Jr. was the Antichrist. These weren't vague associations or metaphorical thinking. They were concrete, psychotic beliefs that shaped his perception of reality. He thought the meaning of life was encoded in the images on a US dollar bill. He experienced persistent, overwhelming déjà vu. He sometimes covered his mouth with duct tape and refused to speak to his family, possibly believing that speaking aloud would allow demonic forces to hear his thoughts.

He struggled with longstanding alcohol abuse, a common form of self-medication for people with untreated schizophrenia. In spring 2004, he began recreationally using Coricidin cold medication. Coricidin contains dextromethorphan, which in high doses produces dissociative effects, a particularly dangerous choice for someone already experiencing psychotic symptoms. The combination of untreated schizophrenia, alcohol abuse and dextromethorphan intoxication created a neurochemical catastrophe.

Thomas's brother was stabbed during a fight with Andre, though

Andre wasn't indicted. The brother was committed for psychiatric treatment, another indicator of the family's pervasive mental health problems. Andre had been accused of stabbing his own sibling, yet no intervention occurred. Living on his own, Thomas had difficulty paying his utilities. Laura began limiting his visitation with Andre Jr., a reasonable response to his deteriorating behaviour, but one that intensified his paranoid beliefs about being persecuted.

In March 2004, two days after going to the emergency room (presumably seeking help for his deteriorating mental state, though what he told doctors there, whether he described his symptoms, whether anyone recognised the severity of his illness, remains undocumented), Thomas went to Laura's third-floor apartment and kicked the door open. Her boyfriend was at work. Laura was home with Andre Jr., now four, and her thirteen-month-old daughter Leyha from her new relationship.

Thomas fatally stabbed all three. He cut open their chests. He attempted to remove their hearts, succeeding with the two children but only managing to extract part of Laura's lung, which he mistook for her heart in his psychotic confusion. This detail is particularly revealing: his actions followed an internal logic driven by delusion. He wasn't simply killing in rage or revenge. He believed he was performing a spiritual operation, literally removing the evil from their bodies to "set them free." The bizarre post-mortem mutilation wasn't sadism; it was a psychotic mission.

After killing them, he stabbed himself three times in the chest, expecting to die. The plan, such as psychotic thinking, allowed for plans, was apparently that he would die alongside them, perhaps believing this would complete the spiritual ritual. When he realised, he wasn't dying when the physical reality of his surviving contradicted his delusional expectations, he placed the organs in his pockets, walked home, threw them in the rubbish, then walked to the police station and confessed.

He told police God had instructed him to commit the killings. He believed all three were demons. Laura was Jezebel, Andre Jr. was the Antichrist, and Leyha was an evil spirit. This wasn't a defence strategy concocted afterwards. This was his immediate explanation, given whilst still covered in blood, still in the grip of active psychosis.

Psychologists who interviewed Thomas after his arrest diagnosed him with paranoid schizophrenia. He was declared incompetent to stand trial and sent to North Texas State Hospital in mid-June 2004. After forty-seven days, psychiatrist Dr Joseph Black wrote to the court that Thomas had "drug-induced psychosis," that he was competent, and that he might attempt to exaggerate his mental illness through self-harm or other aberrant behaviour.

This last prediction proved tragically accurate. Five days after returning to Grayson County Jail, Thomas pulled out his right eye. But Dr Black's suggestion that this might be manipulation to exaggerate illness fundamentally misunderstood the nature of psychosis. When someone experiencing religious delusions about sin and eyes offending literally interprets Matthew 5:29 and mutilates themselves accordingly, that's not malingering. That's active psychosis requiring immediate, intensive intervention.

Thomas's trial began on 15th February 2005. He was tried only for Leyha's death, as capital murder of a child under six carries an automatic death penalty. The jury was all-white. Thomas, who is Black and had been in an interracial relationship with Laura, faced jurors, three of whom had indicated on questionnaires that they opposed interracial marriage. His defence attorney, R.J. Hagood, was ill with pancreatitis during the trial and later said he regretted not objecting to certain testimony and evidence.

The jury rejected the insanity defence. They convicted Thomas of capital murder and sentenced him to death. Under Texas law, which uses modified M'Naghten Rules, the question wasn't whether Thomas was mentally ill clearly; he was. The question was whether his mental illness prevented him from knowing his conduct was wrong. The jury concluded it hadn't. Thomas understood killing was illegal and morally condemned. Therefore, he could be held responsible and executed.

But this legal standard often fails to capture the reality of psychotic experience. Thomas knew killing was against the law. He also believed he was following God's commands to destroy demons. When someone genuinely believes they're acting under divine instruction to save souls from evil, do they really "know" their conduct is wrong in the moral sense the law requires? Or are they operating in a different reality where earthly laws are superseded by spiritual imperatives they believe to be real?

Four years into his death sentence, still psychotic despite medication, Thomas became convinced the government was reading his thoughts through his remaining eye. On 27th January 2009, he pulled it out and ate it to destroy the evidence. This second act of self-mutilation finally resulted in him being declared incompetent for execution. But it didn't result in his sentence being commuted or his case being reconsidered. He simply remains on death row, blind, psychotic, in legal limbo.

His lawyers have filed clemency petitions supported by dozens of Texas doctors and therapists and more than a hundred faith leaders. They argue that executing someone this mentally ill would be "a senseless act of vengeance," that Thomas is "one of the most mentally ill prisoners in Texas history," and that only someone profoundly psychotic could undertake such acts of permanent self-mutilation. The Grayson County District Attorney's Office responds that "a jury has spoken about what justice should be in this case" and that Thomas's victims and their families should not be forgotten.

Both positions have validity. Laura Boren, Andre Jr., and Leyha Hughes were real people whose lives were brutally ended. Their family members live with unbearable grief. The horror of what Thomas did, stabbing a four-year-old and a thirteen-month-old to death, removing their hearts, is almost incomprehensible. The impulse to hold him accountable, to execute him for these murders, comes from a place of legitimate moral conviction about justice and consequences.

But Andre Thomas also deserves consideration as a human being whose brain has been profoundly, catastrophically broken by mental illness since childhood. A person who experienced auditory hallucinations from age nine, whose family was "beset by a long history of mental illness, addiction and poverty," who sought treatment repeatedly and was not adequately helped, whose psychosis erupted in horrific violence that he genuinely believed was commanded by God. And who, even after conviction, has been held in conditions that allowed him to mutilate himself twice, suggesting that the state's interest in punishment has consistently trumped any interest in treatment or prevention of further harm.

The question becomes: what purpose does executing Andre Thomas serve? It cannot bring the dead back. It cannot undo the horror. Texas houses him in a psychiatric facility rather than standard death row, medicates him daily with powerful antipsychotic drugs, acknowledges he's too mentally ill to be executed under current law, but pursues his execution anyway. This isn't justice. It's vengeance against someone whose capacity for moral agency at the time of his crimes, and continuing capacity now, is profoundly compromised by severe mental illness.

The broader pattern these cases reveal is more troubling than any individual tragedy. Modern prison systems, particularly in America, routinely create conditions that cause or exacerbate mental illness. Isolation units designed for punishment function as engines of psychological destruction. Inmates with no previous mental health history develop psychotic symptoms. Those with existing mental illness deteriorate catastrophically. And when symptoms manifest, especially when interpreted through religious or supernatural lenses, the system responds with more punishment rather than treatment.

The walls don't talk. But isolation makes people hear them talking. Sensory deprivation creates perceptions without external input. Chronic stress and trauma rewire the brain in ways that produce symptoms. And in custody settings where none of this gets treated appropriately, where punishment compounds medical crisis, where possession might be the only available language for describing psychiatric breakdown, people lose their minds, and we call it evil rather than illness.

Sam Shockley's IQ dropped from 68 to 54 during his time in Alcatraz isolation. That's measurable cognitive deterioration directly attributable to the conditions he was kept in. He developed hallucinations and delusions documented by prison physicians. He participated in a violent escape attempt whilst psychotic. He was executed despite obvious, documented mental illness. And his case from 1946 isn't a historical aberration; it's a template for how prison systems continue to operate.

Andre Thomas has been blind and psychotic on death row for fifteen years. He receives powerful antipsychotic medications that "only manage to mitigate his auditory and visual hallucinations", meaning he's still experiencing symptoms despite maximum treatment. He lives in the psychiatric facility where Texas houses "the most mentally ill prisoners." And yet his execution date gets set, gets postponed, remains legally possible despite being practically impossible under Supreme Court precedent prohibiting the execution of the insane.

This legal and ethical incoherence reflects broader societal ambivalence about mental illness, responsibility and punishment. We want to believe that people who commit horrific crimes must be held accountable. We want to believe that mental illness doesn't excuse violence. We want to believe that the death penalty serves justice. But when cases like Andre Thomas's expose the uncomfortable reality that severe mental illness can produce violence that the ill person genuinely believes is righteous, that prison conditions worsen mental illness rather than managing it, that executing someone this profoundly broken serves no legitimate purpose, we face a choice. We can acknowledge these failures and change how we respond to mental illness in criminal justice settings. Or we can continue pursuing executions that satisfy our desire for vengeance whilst violating our stated principles about humane treatment and moral responsibility.

The possession narratives in these cases, Andre Thomas believing his family were demons, Sam Shockley hearing spirits of dead inmates, and countless isolation inmates experiencing spiritual warfare, are symptoms of psychiatric illness shaped by cultural context. They're not evidence of supernatural reality. They're evidence of brains breaking under intolerable conditions, constructing explanations from available cultural material to make sense of experiences that feel overwhelmingly real but aren't grounded in external reality.

The tragedy is that we know how to prevent this. Early screening for mental illness. Appropriate psychiatric treatment. Avoiding isolation for people with serious mental illness. Providing continuity of care. Creating conditions that don't destroy human psychology. None of this is complicated or mysterious. The research is detailed and consistent. We simply choose not to implement it because prisons exist primarily to punish, not to care, and because there's limited political will to spend resources on people who've committed crimes.

The walls keep breaking minds. The isolation keeps producing psychosis. The religious frameworks keep shaping how that psychosis manifests. And people like Andre Thomas and Sam Shockley keep falling through every crack in a system fundamentally not designed to help them. The demons aren't real. The failure to treat treatable illness, to prevent preventable deterioration, to acknowledge when punishment has become mere cruelty, that failure is entirely real and entirely our responsibility.

CHAPTER XX

The Faith That Kills

"You believe that there is one God. Good! Even the demons believe that and shudder." James 2:19

THE THEOLOGICAL CONCEPT APPEARS STRAIGHTFORward enough. Intellectual acknowledgement of God's existence doesn't equal saving faith. Demons know God is real. They know who Jesus is. They recognise divine authority and tremble before it. But that knowledge doesn't redeem them. It's what Christian theologians call "dead faith": belief without transformation, acknowledgement without submission, cognition without salvation. The demons believe, and they're still damned.

It's meant as a warning to believers. Don't mistake mental agreement for genuine faith. Don't think that knowing theological facts saves you. Even demons have corrected theology. What matters is whether belief changes how you live, whether faith produces works, whether acknowledgement of God translates into obedience and transformation.

However, there's another way faith can become fatal. Not the metaphorical death of a faith that doesn't save, but actual physical death. When religious frameworks convince people that psychiatric symptoms are demonic activity, when theological certainty overrides medical reality, when the language of spiritual warfare prevents someone from getting the help that would save their life, faith doesn't just become dead. It becomes deadly.

The irony is cruel. The very communities warning against "demon faith," against belief that's all knowledge and no transformation, often demonstrate the deadliest form of faith imaginable when confronted with mental illness. They know their theology. They can quote scripture. They believe passionately in spiritual realities. But that knowledge, that belief, that passion, applied to someone experiencing trauma or neurological differences or psychiatric crisis, becomes the thing that kills them.

Victoria Climbié was eight years old when her great-aunt Marie-Thérèse Kouao decided she was possessed. The possession belief didn't emerge from nowhere. It developed gradually as Kouao's abuse escalated and she needed a framework to explain her own cruelty. The more she hurt Victoria, the more she needed demons to justify it. By the time Victoria died on 25th February 2000, with 128 injuries on her body and a core temperature too low to measure, Kouao had been telling social workers, doctors, and church leaders for months that her niece was demonically controlled. Every person who heard that explanation and accepted it, or failed to look past it, shares responsibility for Victoria's death.

Terrance Cottrell Jr. was eight years old, too. He had autism, which his community in Milwaukee didn't fully understand and which his church interpreted as demonic interference. For three weeks in August 2003, his mother brought him to Faith Temple Church of the Apostolic Faith, where Pastor Ray Hemphill held him down during exorcism sessions. On 22nd August, a 170-pound man pressed onto a seventy-pound child for two hours whilst the congregation prayed. Terrance died of mechanical asphyxia. The autopsy found no demons. It found a dead child.

Both Victoria and Terrance knew something was wrong. They felt it in their bodies, in their fear, in the way nobody was actually listening. Neither could articulate the difference between genuine care and its deadly imitation. But their suffering was the testimony. And the people around them, armed with conviction and scripture, couldn't hear it.

What connects them, including Joanna Demafelis, Kiran Bala, and Odette Newmark, isn't the presence of evil. It's the absence of the right question: what if this isn't possession? Joanna could have been provided with mental health care and protection by her employers. Kiran could have been treated for postpartum psychosis. Odette could have received medication for her schizophrenia.

None of them died because demons were powerful.

The pattern across all these cases is worth naming precisely. It isn't that religion caused harm. It's that a specific application of religion, one where spiritual interpretation overrides medical reality and the authority of a pastor is considered more reliable than a doctor's assessment, that created the conditions where harm became inevitable.

Joanna Demafelis had travelled from the Philippines to Kuwait to work as a domestic worker. She was found in a freezer in 2018, having been dead for over a year. Her employers, Nader Essam Assaf and his wife Mona, had accused her of being possessed by djinn. They'd beaten her. They'd subjected her to rituals. They'd locked her away. And when she died, whether from the abuse, the neglect, or both, they wrapped her in plastic bags and put her in the freezer rather than call anyone. The possession belief had done its work: it explained Joanna's behaviour in ways that justified everything done to her, and it explained her death as spiritual failure rather than murder. Nader Assaf was sentenced to death in Kuwait. His wife received a similar sentence. But Joanna, who had come so far trying to build a better life, never came home.

Kiran Bala was a young woman in India whose in-laws decided, shortly after she gave birth, that she was possessed. What they were almost certainly witnessing was postpartum psychosis: a genuine medical emergency affecting roughly one in a thousand new mothers, characterised by confusion, hallucinations, paranoia, and sometimes violent behaviour. It is treatable. With the right intervention, most women recover fully. Without it, they deteriorate. Kiran's in-laws had no mental health framework available to them. They had the framework that their community had always used. They beat her. She died from her injuries. The tragedy isn't that they were evil people. The tragedy is that a treatable medical condition killed her because the only interpretive tool available to her family was spiritual.

Odette Newmark's story is different but follows the same lethal logic. She had schizophrenia, which in its worst expressions can include profound religious content: direct communications from God, divine missions, the certainty that death is commanded from above. She died by suicide during a psychotic episode, having concluded that God required her death. Her faith made psychiatric treatment feel like betrayal. Her delusions and her theology had become indistinguishable. The medication that could have quieted those voices sat untaken because taking it meant doubting God. She was, by every clinical measure, a person in psychiatric crisis. By her own measure, she was being obedient.

What these four cases share, Victoria, Terrance, Joanna, Kiran, and Odette among them, isn't demonic involvement. It's a specific and fatal failure of interpretation.

The pattern across all these cases is worth naming precisely. It isn't that religion caused harm. It's that a specific application of religion, one where spiritual interpretation overrides medical reality and the authority of a pastor is considered more reliable than a doctor's assessment, that created the conditions where harm became inevitable.

Joanna Demafelis had travelled from the Philippines to Kuwait to work as a domestic worker. She was found in a freezer in 2018, having been dead for over a year. Her employers, Nader Essam Assaf and his wife Mona, had accused her of being possessed by djinn. They'd beaten her. They'd subjected her to rituals. They'd locked her away. And when she died, whether from the abuse, the neglect, or both, they wrapped her in plastic bags and put her in the freezer rather than call anyone. The possession belief had done its work: it explained Joanna's behaviour in ways that justified everything done to her, and it explained her death as spiritual failure rather than murder. Nader Assaf was sentenced to death in Kuwait. His wife received a similar sentence. But Joanna, who had come so far trying to build a better life, never came home.

Kiran Bala was a young woman in India whose in-laws decided, shortly after she gave birth, that she was possessed. What they were almost certainly witnessing was postpartum psychosis: a genuine medical emergency affecting roughly one in a thousand new mothers, characterised by confusion, hallucinations, paranoia, and sometimes violent behaviour. It is treatable. With the right intervention, most women recover fully. Without it, they deteriorate. Kiran's in-laws had no mental health framework available to them. They had the framework that their community had always used. They beat her. She died from her injuries. The tragedy isn't that they were evil people. The tragedy is that a treatable medical condition killed her because the only interpretive tool available to her family was spiritual.

Odette Newmark's story is different but follows the same lethal logic. She had schizophrenia, which in its worst expressions can include profound religious content: direct communications from God, divine missions, the certainty that death is commanded from above. She died by suicide during a psychotic episode, having concluded that God required her death. Her faith made psychiatric treatment feel like betrayal. Her delusions and her theology had become indistinguishable. The medication that could have quieted those voices sat untaken because taking it meant doubting God. She was, by every clinical measure, a person in psychiatric crisis. By her own measure, she was being obedient.

What these four cases share, Victoria, Terrance, Joanna, Kiran, and Odette among them, isn't demonic involvement. It's a specific and fatal failure of interpretation.

They died because religious belief, no matter how sincere, no matter how well-intentioned, prevented the appropriate response to medical emergencies. The faith that should have provided comfort and support instead provided the framework that made harm possible or inevitable.

That's the uncomfortable truth these cases force us to confront. Religion can heal, but it can also kill. Faith can sustain people through terrible suffering, but it can also become the reason they suffer unnecessarily or die preventably. Spiritual belief can coexist with good medical care, but it can also override medical reality in ways that cost lives.

Understanding this isn't about attacking religion. It's about recognising that when spiritual frameworks become the only lens for interpreting mental health symptoms, when religious authority trumps medical expertise, when faith requires refusing treatment, people die. And those deaths aren't mysterious acts of God or victories of demons. They're predictable outcomes of interpretive frameworks that prioritise belief over evidence, spiritual authority over medical knowledge, faith over the simple physical reality that brains malfunction and need treatment like any other organ.

The theological problem central to these cases is what we might call the asymmetry of certainty. When a pastor tells a mother her child is possessed, that claim carries enormous authority. It comes with scriptural backing, community validation, and the weight of tradition. The competing claim, that her child has a neurological or psychiatric condition requiring medical care, carries different authority. It requires trusting systems and institutions that may feel alien or actively hostile.

For many of the families in this book, medicine wasn't a neutral alternative. It was a foreign language, a white institution, an expensive system, a Western framework that pathologised what their culture understood as spiritual. Choosing the doctor over the pastor wasn't simply a matter of weighing evidence. It was a choice about identity, community, and what kind of person you were. People who took their child to an exorcist rather than a psychiatrist weren't making an irrational choice by their own lights. They were making the most reasonable choice available to them within their community and worldview.

That's not a defence of the outcomes. Victoria is still dead. Terrance is still dead. But it matters for understanding why these things keep happening. Telling religious communities that possession beliefs are dangerous doesn't help if we don't also reckon with why those beliefs are compelling, why medical frameworks sometimes feel threatening, and why the gap between spiritual and medical interpretations persists.

The most effective faith communities, the ones that don't produce these tragedies, tend to be ones that have found ways to hold both. They affirm spiritual realities whilst also insisting that God works through medicine, that psychological distress deserves treatment, and that seeking psychiatric care isn't abandoning faith. They've integrated the two frameworks rather than treating them as mutually exclusive. Their pastors refer rather than perform. Their congregations support people in crisis by helping them access professional care, not by escalating spiritual interventions.

That integration is possible. It happens. The Reverend who prays with you before surgery rather than instead of surgery. The church community that funds therapy alongside providing pastoral support. The pastor who tells a grieving family, " This looks like depression, let's get you to a doctor, and I'll still be here.

Those pastors exist. Those communities exist. The cases in this book are those in which that integration failed, in which the spiritual framework colonised the medical space entirely, and in which certainty about demons prevented the question that could have saved a life: what if we're wrong about what we're seeing?

That question, simple and humble and honest about medicine, is the difference between the faith that heals and the faith that kills.

Consider the prison system, where I've seen this dynamic play out firsthand. When someone in solitary confinement starts hearing voices and believing they're receiving divine messages, the institution faces the same interpretive choice. Chaplains sometimes encourage spiritual interpretations of what are clearly stress-induced psychotic symptoms. When they're available, mental health staff often push for medical explanations. The two groups sometimes work in opposition, each convinced that its framework is the right one.

What I've seen work is when they work together. When a chaplain says: I'm going to sit with you, and I'm also going to make sure the mental health team sees you, and these two things are not in conflict. When the psychiatric unit says: We'll treat your symptoms, and we understand your faith is part of who you are, and we're not asking you to choose.

That integration is harder when the stakes are higher. When a family is watching someone they love suffer, when the community around them has a clear explanation and a clear response, the pressure to choose the spiritual path and stay there is immense. Medical care can feel like doubt made visible. Seeking a psychiatrist can feel like admitting the demons aren't real, which can feel like admitting the whole foundation isn't real.

This is why the problem isn't simply education. Telling people that psychiatric illness exists doesn't automatically override possession frameworks, because the issue isn't ignorance. It's that the two frameworks make fundamentally different claims about reality, and choosing between them isn't just a matter of choosing a treatment plan. It's choosing a worldview.

What changes outcomes isn't education alone. It's authority. When trusted religious leaders say, "This looks like illness, and we should treat it as illness, and that is the faithful response," people listen. When denominations build medical evaluation into their response protocols for apparent possession, outcomes change. When faith communities normalise the combination of prayer and psychiatry, lives are saved.

The cases where possession beliefs led to death almost always share a common factor: the absence of any voice within the religious community willing to say, wait, let's make sure. A pastor who hesitates. An elder who first suggests a medical opinion. A church member who knows someone who went through something similar and got help from a doctor. That single voice, carrying the authority of shared faith rather than external challenge, can interrupt the momentum toward harm.

Its absence is what made these deaths possible. Not the evil of the perpetrators. Not the absence of love. The absence of one person, trusted within the community, willing to ask: What if we're seeing this wrong?

The theological irony is worth sitting with. The warnings in scripture about deception: about false prophets, the need to test the spirits, the danger of being led astray. These warnings were meant to create exactly this kind of epistemic humility. The tradition itself contains the tools for its own correction. The question is whether communities are willing to use them, whether they can hear the voice that says, " We should be careful here, we should be certain, we should know what we're doing before we act.

Victoria, Terrance, Joanna, Kiran and Odette didn't need miracles. They needed one person in their situation with enough doubt to ask a doctor first.

Let's be concrete about what those safeguards look like. Because this isn't abstract theology. It's a practical policy, and the difference between communities that have it and communities that don't is measurable in the cases that do and don't end in tragedy.

The Catholic Church, for all its institutional failures in other domains, has maintained since the 1999 revision of its exorcism rite that formal exorcism requires prior medical and psychiatric evaluation. Before a Catholic priest can perform a formal exorcism, they must be convinced through consultation with medical professionals that the symptoms don't have a natural explanation. This isn't a perfect safeguard. It gets circumvented. Informal exorcisms happen outside the protocol. But as a structural requirement, it embodies the kind of interpretive humility that reduces the likelihood of catastrophic harm. It builds the question into the process: have we ruled out the medical explanation?

Many evangelical and charismatic communities lack equivalent protocols. The decision to identify possession and respond with spiritual intervention can be made by a single pastor, a family, or a prayer group, with no requirement for external evaluation. The authority is self-certifying. The framework provides its own evidence. And the cases in this book cluster in exactly these settings, not because evangelical or charismatic Christianity is uniquely harmful, but because the absence of structural safeguards creates vulnerability that bad outcomes can exploit.

What would adequate safeguards look like? At a minimum, a mandatory medical evaluation is required before any spiritual intervention that involves physical restraint or isolation. A clear protocol for stopping interventions when someone is in physical distress. Accountability structures that extend beyond the immediate community: a responsible denominational body, a pastoral oversight board, something with the authority to say, " This has gone too far. The critical thing: training pastors and church leaders to recognise psychiatric emergencies and make appropriate referrals.

None of this requires abandoning belief in possession or spiritual warfare. It requires building epistemic humility into institutional practice. The Catholic requirement isn't that priests must disbelieve in demons. They must first rule out a medical explanation. That's a modest and eminently reasonable requirement, and the argument against adopting it universally is difficult to make without sounding like you're prioritising spiritual authority over human safety.

The communities that resist these safeguards often do so on the grounds that medical evaluation undermines faith or provides grounds for a materialist worldview. But this argument proves too much. Nobody argues that praying before surgery undermines faith in medicine. Nobody claims that seeing a doctor for a broken leg betrays God. The asymmetry is this: psychiatric medicine is treated as spiritually threatening in ways that other medicine isn't. That reflects cultural anxiety rather than theological necessity. There's no scriptural reason why epilepsy should be treated differently from appendicitis. Both are medical conditions. Both respond to medical treatment. Both can be accompanied by prayer.

The resistance to psychiatric medicine in certain religious communities is, at its root, a resistance to the implications: that the experiences the community has been interpreting as spiritual warfare might be brain chemistry, that the voices people hear might be symptoms rather than communications, that the help needed isn't the help the community can provide. These are genuinely destabilising implications. Sitting with them requires a kind of theological maturity that not every community has developed.

But developing it is the only alternative to producing more Victorias, more Terrances, more Arelys. The cases in this book will keep happening until communities build the capacity to say, sincerely and without shame: we might be wrong about what we're seeing, and we're going to find out before we act.

The people who died in these cases deserved better. They deserved communities that could hold both faith and medical reality. They deserved religious leaders who knew their limitations and referred them to appropriate care. They deserved families who didn't have to choose between belief and survival. They deserved to live, and their deaths should force religious communities everywhere to ask hard questions about when and how their worldviews fail the vulnerable people who need help most.

CHAPTER XXI

When Movies Teach You How To Be Possessed

THE FIRST TIME MOST PEOPLE SEE DEMONIC POSSES-sion, it's not in a church, hospital, or someone's home. It's on a screen. A young girl's head spins backwards. A voice like gravel and broken glass promises obscene things. Crucifixes become weapons. Priests sweat and shout Latin whilst furniture flies. Bodies contort in ways that seem to break bones. And somewhere in your mind, probably without fully realising it, a template gets laid down for what possession looks like, sounds like, behaves like.

That template matters more than you might think. Because when people later experience or witness something that might be a psychiatric crisis, when they're searching for frameworks to explain behaviour that frightens them, that cinematic image of possession is often the first reference point their mind reaches for. Not medical textbooks about psychosis. Not case studies of dissociative disorders. *The*

Exorcist. The Conjuring. The Rite. Decades of horror films have taught audiences exactly what possession is supposed to look like.

And here's the uncomfortable truth: people often perform the possession they've been taught to perform. Not consciously, not as deliberate deception, but because when your mind is breaking, when you're in crisis and grasping for ways to express or understand what's happening to you, you reach for the cultural scripts available to you. And modern culture has provided incredibly detailed scripts for how possessed people are supposed to behave.

I've seen this pattern. The young person in psychiatric crisis starts speaking in the growling, distorted voice they've heard in horror films. The individual experiencing dissociation suddenly exhibits the specific physical contortions they've seen in *The Exorcist*. The way symptoms escalate when someone's been told they might be possessed suddenly conforms more closely to cinematic possession than to typical presentations of mental illness. The script is there, internalised from years of media consumption, and when a crisis hits, the brain follows it.

This doesn't mean the crisis isn't real. The suffering is genuine. The psychological distress is authentic. But the form that distress takes, the specific ways it manifests, those get shaped by cultural expectations about what possession looks like. And those expectations are increasingly set not by religious tradition or historical accounts but by Hollywood, by streaming services, by YouTube videos claiming to show "real exorcisms," by true crime podcasts that sensationalise possession cases whilst stripping out the psychological context that would make them comprehensible as mental health crises.

December 1973. *The Exorcist* opened in twenty-six cinemas across America. Within six months, it had grossed over $165 million and become a cultural phenomenon unlike anything cinema had seen before.

People queued for hours. Some fainted during screenings. Emergency personnel were stationed at theatres. The film was marketed as being based on a true story, which it loosely was, but the true story was Roland Doe's 1949 case, which itself was far more ambiguous and less dramatic than the film's portrayal.

What *The Exorcist* gave audiences was a visual and auditory vocabulary for possession. The contortions, the voice changes, the profanity, the violence, the way the possessed person seemed to have access to secret knowledge, the way multiple people had to hold her down, the dramatic confrontation between good and evil. None of this was invented by the film. Most of it has historical precedent in possession accounts going back centuries. But the film crystallised it, made it iconic, created a template that subsequent possession narratives, both fictional and supposedly real, would follow.

The film's impact was immediate and documented. Reports of possession cases increased. Requests for exorcisms to Catholic dioceses rose dramatically. People who'd been experiencing mental illness symptoms started interpreting them through the possession lens the film had made culturally available. And critically, people who performed exorcisms, both authorised Catholic priests and unauthorised practitioners, started seeing symptoms in their subjects that matched the film rather than historical possession accounts. Hollywood had rewritten the cultural script.

Before *The Exorcist*, possession was a relatively obscure concept in mainstream American culture. Catholics knew about exorcism, certain religious communities practised deliverance ministry, but for most people, it wasn't a worldview they'd seriously consider for explaining unusual behaviour. The film made possession visceral, terrifying, and somehow plausible. It transformed an ambiguous case of possible adolescent psychiatric disturbance into an epic battle between good and evil, with a girl's soul as the prize. That transformation, that dramatisation for entertainment, has shaped possession beliefs for 50 years.

This pattern continues with every possession film marketed as "based on true events." *The Conjuring* says it's based on the Warrens' files. *The Exorcism of Emily Rose* claims to draw on the case of Anneliese Michel. *A Haunting in Connecticut* presents another Warren investigation. The marketing tells audiences these stories are fundamentally true, even as the films take massive liberties with the facts, invent dramatic scenes, and present supernatural explanations as validated, when the real cases were far more ambiguous and often had clear psychiatric or medical explanations that the films minimise or ignore.

The Conjuring franchise has created a modern vocabulary of possession. Released in 2013, the first film grossed over $319 million worldwide and spawned a cinematic universe that emphasises jump scares, sudden violence, and the idea that demons attach to objects which can then spread possession to new victims. The films present possession as sudden, violent, and requiring immediate dramatic intervention. They show possessed people demonstrating impossible physical feats. They emphasise the contagious nature of demonic influence, the idea that investigating or even being near possessed people puts you at risk.

Whether Ed and Lorraine Warren's cases were legitimate or whether they were skilled self-promoters who exploited vulnerable people whilst building a lucrative career is debatable. What's not debatable is that their cases, as filtered through Hollywood's interpretation, have shaped how contemporary audiences understand possession.

These narrative patterns matter because they set expectations. When someone experiences or witnesses a potential possession, their baseline understanding comes from media, not from medical knowledge or even religious tradition. They expect the possessed person to behave in specific ways. When those expectations aren't met, when someone's psychiatric crisis doesn't look enough like a movie possession, they might not recognise it as something requiring help. Conversely, when symptoms do match the cinematic template, even if they have clear medical explanations, the possession interpretation seems validated because it aligns with what everyone knows possession looks like.

The "based on a true story" marketing is particularly insidious. It gives the films an authority they don't deserve, suggesting that the events depicted, no matter how exaggerated for dramatic effect, happened that way. Audiences leave cinemas believing they've learned something true about possession when what they've absorbed is Hollywood's interpretation filtered through multiple layers of dramatisation and invention. Those audiences then carry that false knowledge into real-world situations where it shapes their interpretations and decisions.

Social media has amplified these effects exponentially. YouTube hosts thousands of videos claiming to show real possession and exorcism. Many are obvious fakes, staged performances designed to generate views and ad revenue. But many others show genuine psychiatric distress being misinterpreted as possession, with comment sections full of people affirming the supernatural explanation and condemning anyone who suggests mental illness or medical evaluation.

The algorithm rewards sensational content, so possession videos get promoted, recommended, and pushed to new audiences. Someone experiencing a psychological crisis who searches online for understanding might find hundreds of videos showing behaviour similar to theirs labelled as possession, with comments insisting demons are real and medication is what the devil wants you to take to suppress your spiritual gift.

TikTok has created new possession panics, particularly among young people. Videos showing alleged possession symptoms go viral, accumulate millions of views, and spawn imitation videos where other users perform similar symptoms. Whether the original videos show genuine distress, deliberate performance, or something in between becomes irrelevant once the cultural contagion takes hold. Young people, especially those experiencing mental health crises or seeking attention and validation, adopt the behaviour patterns that generate engagement.

The platform's emphasis on short, dramatic content pushes users toward increasingly extreme presentations, and possession provides ready-made dramatic content requiring no special effects budget. The monetisation creates perverse incentives. Content creators make money from views, from engagement, from keeping audiences hooked. Debunking possession claims, showing clearly that medical explanations account for all the symptoms, makes for less engaging content and thus less revenue. So there's financial motivation to preserve ambiguity, to suggest medical explanations can't account for everything, to leave room for supernatural possibilities even when the evidence doesn't support them.

This has real consequences. Families dealing with a member in psychiatric crisis increasingly turn to online content for information and find themselves in ecosystems that promote possession interpretations. Someone searches "why is my son talking to himself and acting strange," and the algorithm serves them possession videos alongside or instead of content about schizophrenia. The possession content is watched more, commented on more, and is more likely to be recommended. The family encounters possession frameworks before or instead of medical frameworks, which shape how they interpret what they're seeing and the interventions they pursue.

San Jose, California. September 2021. Claudia Hernandez had been speaking to God daily for three weeks. During her prayers for her three-year-old daughter, Arely Naomi Proctor, God gave her a specific message: He would take Arely. Not someday in the distant future. On 24th September 2021. God told Claudia this was happening because she was never meant to be a mother.

Claudia didn't tell anyone about her conversations with God or her visions. On the night of 23rd September, she woke her twenty-year-old brother Aaron after midnight in their Mountain View flat. They were taking Arely to their church, Iglesia Evangelica Apostoles y Profetas, to cast out a demon. Their father, 60-year-old Rene Trigueros Hernandez, was the pastor of the small Pentecostal church located in a back room of a multi-family home on 2nd Street in downtown San Jose.

The previous night, Arely had been screaming and crying in her sleep, saying "no, no, no" whilst moving her arms. When Claudia looked at her daughter's eyes, they appeared different. Empty. It wasn't her, Claudia explained later. The child was possessed.

What happened over the next twenty hours at that church would leave Arely Naomi Proctor dead on the altar, her thirty-eight-pound body riddled with injuries. Brain swelling. Blood in the lungs. Marks on her neck. Injuries inside her mouth. A tear in her aorta on the right side of her heart. Bruising throughout her body. The medical examiner would determine the cause of death as mechanical asphyxia and smothering. She would testify there was no realistic scenario in which the child could have died innocently. "This was a child that died at the hands of another," Dr Michelle Jorden stated in court. "I can't think of a situation where smothering could be considered accidental."

The exorcism lasted through the night and into the next day. Claudia, Aaron, and Pastor Rene squeezed Arely, trying to induce vomiting to expel the demon. They grabbed her by the neck forcibly. Arely struggled. She fought for her life. She tried to escape from the three adults. She repeatedly said "No!" Court documents would later reveal that Arely told her mother, "I love you," during the ordeal.

Aaron, who attended church four days a week, believed God had given him multiple gifts: the ability to speak in tongues, the gift to heal, the gift to interpret tongues, the gift of seeing visions, and the gift of reprimanding. During the exorcism, he witnessed what he interpreted as a spiritual battle. Arely's grandfather told police later that the child struggled throughout the ritual, which he interpreted as "power" that he could not "destroy."

At some point, they realised Arely had died. Her body appeared pale, lifeless, "as if someone had passed." Authorities would later allege the defendants did not attempt to call for help for hours after the child became unresponsive. When Claudia finally dialled 911 on the afternoon of 24th September, firefighters found Arely deceased on the church altar.

When Officer Reyes arrived at the scene and asked Claudia what happened, she explained why she believed her daughter was possessed. She described how Arely looked different, how her eyes looked empty.

Pastor Rene told investigators that one of the catalysts for Arely's purported demonic possession was that the child had been allowed to use her mother's mobile phone and might have viewed something sinister.

Claudia wasn't arrested until 31st January 2022. Aaron and Pastor Rene were arrested on 11th May 2022. All three were charged with felony assault on a child, causing death. The case would have remained hidden, but Arely's death drew no public attention for nearly eight months, except that the police investigating an unrelated kidnapping searched the church and discovered what had happened there.

In October 2021, before her arrest, Claudia called San Jose Police Lieutenant J.J. Vallejo to make another statement. She sat down with him and explained about her conversations with God, about how He had told her that Arely would die on 24th September. When the lieutenant asked how she felt about "God's plan," Claudia replied, "I've learned to accept what it is."

When questioned by the police, Aaron appeared emotionally upset, whilst Claudia did most of the talking. Over the course of several police interviews, Aaron and his father changed their stories about how Arely died during the exorcism and whether any efforts were made to revive her. Aaron told police that Claudia most likely delivered the fatal blow by grabbing Arely's neck. Like his mother and grandfather, Aaron believed the girl was possessed. Arely's death made him question his gift to heal.

Pastor Rene admitted to this newspaper that he performed the exorcism before his arrest. The exorcism wasn't his first experience with such things. As a pastor preaching in his native El Salvador and in San Jose, he'd witnessed instances of possession, including a woman who had gone to the United States, had a spell cast on her, and came back possessed. He believed in deliverance. He believed demons were real. He believed God had given his son the gift of healing.

Defence attorneys would later argue the case resulted from police detectives' scepticism of the defendants' Pentecostal faith, claiming it prejudiced them against considering non-criminal scenarios. They insisted there was no intent to kill when the three took part in the exorcism. They characterised Arely's death as the result of a genuine, if misguided, attempt to purge her of a demon.

Judge Hanley Chew ruled prosecutors had enough evidence for the trio to stand trial. Santa Clara County District Attorney's Office is seeking a punishment of twenty-five years to life in prison. Defence attorneys call the charges unprecedented in California for any case stemming from "a genuine effort at faith healing, with no ulterior criminal motive."

As of this writing, Claudia Hernandez, Aaron Hernandez Santos, and Pastor Rene Trigueros Hernandez remain in Santa Clara County Jail without bail, awaiting trial for the death of three-year-old Arely Naomi Proctor, who died whilst saying "No" and "I love you" as the people she trusted most suffocated her whilst trying to cast out a demon that wasn't there.

The question that haunts the Arely Proctor case is the same that haunts every modern possession tragedy: where did the framework come from? Claudia believed she was speaking to God daily. Aaron believed he had the gift of healing. Pastor Rene believed he'd witnessed genuine possession in El Salvador. But the specific form their beliefs took, the particular ways they interpreted Arely's behaviour, the methods they used to try expelling the demon, all of this was shaped by cultural input, including media representations of what possession looks like and how exorcism works.

When a family sees behaviour that matches media depictions of possession, everyone is working from scripts written by the entertainment media. The family then seeks help based on that shared misunderstanding, potentially delaying or preventing appropriate treatment. In Arely's case, Claudia saw her daughter's eyes looking "different" and "empty." This matches countless cinematic portrayals of possession, where the possessed person's eyes change, appearing vacant or inhuman. But it's also entirely consistent with a distressed child, perhaps ill, perhaps experiencing night terrors, perhaps simply exhausted.

The screaming and crying, the saying "no" in her sleep whilst moving her arms, these are symptoms any parent might recognise as nightmares or sleep disturbances requiring comfort, not exorcism. But filtered through a possession framework reinforced by media consumption and religious belief, they became evidence of demonic presence requiring immediate spiritual warfare.

True crime podcasts have found possession cases to be reliable content. The format is perfect for sensationalising supernatural elements whilst maintaining a veneer of investigative journalism. Podcasters can present cases like Anneliese Michel or the Arne Johnson murder, emphasise the most disturbing details, play up the question of "was it really demons," and attract massive audiences without having to commit to any clear explanation.

The ambiguity becomes a feature rather than a bug. The podcast can present medical explanations whilst simultaneously treating possession as a viable alternative, leaving listeners to decide, but structuring the content to make the supernatural interpretation seem more compelling and mysterious than the medical one.

This approach fundamentally misunderstands how belief formation works. When you present two explanations as equally valid, when you give equal time to "she had schizophrenia" and "she was possessed by demons," audiences don't weigh the evidence neutrally. They're drawn to the more dramatic explanation, the one that makes a better narrative, that offers transcendent meaning rather than mundane medical reality. Psychiatric illness is scary but comprehensible. Demonic possession is terrifying and inexplicable, which makes it more compelling story material. So even when podcasts present medical evidence, even when they interview psychiatrists, the possession narrative tends to dominate listener takeaway because it's simply better entertainment.

The commercialisation of paranormal investigation has compounded these problems. Following *The Conjuring*'s success, there's been an explosion of paranormal investigation content, ghost-hunting shows, and demon-hunting programmes, all presenting supernatural explanations as reasonable responses to phenomena that usually have mundane causes. These shows teach audiences that unusual experiences, electronic voice phenomena, temperature changes, strange sounds, and feelings of being watched are evidence of a supernatural presence rather than explainable by psychology, environment, or normal human perception.

When someone in a psychiatric crisis reports experiences that could be hallucinations, delusions, or sensory distortions from stress and sleep deprivation, family members who've consumed paranormal media might interpret those reports as evidence of haunting or possession rather than recognising them as psychiatric symptoms. The media has taught them to reach for supernatural explanations before considering medical ones, or to see supernatural and medical explanations as equally valid when they're not.

The way exorcism is portrayed in the media also shapes expectations in ways that make genuine possession claims harder to evaluate. Films show possessed people accessing secret knowledge, speaking languages they've never learned, and displaying impossible physical strength. These are the classic signs of possession in religious tradition. But they're also incredibly difficult to verify and often don't hold up under scrutiny.

When someone claims the possessed person spoke Latin, an investigation usually reveals that they spoke gibberish that sounded like Latin, or a few phrases that could have been learned from cultural exposure, including, ironically, from watching possession films. But because the media has established that these are what possession looks like, witnesses are primed to perceive them even when they don't occur.

Someone in a psychotic crisis speaks in word salad, the combination of random sounds that happens when language processing breaks down neurologically. Witnesses hear that as speaking in tongues or speaking an unknown language because that's what they expect possessed people to do. Someone experiencing an adrenaline surge during a psychiatric episode displays the temporary strength increase that comes with fight-or-flight activation. Witnesses interpret that as supernatural strength because possession media has taught them that's a sign of demons.

The expectation creates the perception, and the perception reinforces the belief. This is confirmation bias running on cultural scripts provided by entertainment media. And it makes it nearly impossible to definitively disprove possession claims because any evidence can be reinterpreted to fit the template everyone's internalised from decades of horror films and sensationalised documentaries.

There's also a documented phenomenon where people model

their experiences on media representations without fully conscious awareness that they're doing so. Someone who's internalised *The Exorcist*'s depiction of possession, who's seen that film and a dozen others like it, might start exhibiting those specific symptoms during a psychological crisis, not because they're deliberately imitating but because their mind is using the available cultural script to express and understand distress that otherwise feels incomprehensible.

This is particularly common in dissociative disorders where identity fragmentation creates alternative self-states. Those self-states often incorporate cultural material, and in cultures saturated with possession media, possession becomes a ready framework for understanding and expressing dissociation. An alternate identity might present as a demon because the person has seen possessed people act that way. That's what the culture has taught them: alternate identities in the context of spiritual experience look like.

This doesn't mean the dissociation isn't real or that the person is faking. The psychiatric condition is genuine. But the form it takes, the specific way it manifests, gets shaped by cultural input, including media representations. Understanding this doesn't require dismissing the person's experience. It requires recognising that even genuine psychiatric conditions express themselves through cultural frameworks, and modern culture's primary framework for understanding altered mental states with spiritual dimensions comes from entertainment media.

The challenge is that pointing this out is often heard as dismissing possession entirely, as if saying anyone who claims possession is copying movies. That's not the argument. The argument is that media shapes how people experience and express psychological crises, that possession films and viral content provide templates that both witnesses and people in crisis use to make sense of confusing symptoms, and that those media-derived templates often prevent recognition that psychiatric intervention is what's actually needed.

When a family sees their teenager exhibiting symptoms that perfectly match *The Conjuring*'s depiction of possession, saying "they probably watched the movie and are reproducing what they saw" sounds like you're calling the teen a liar or attention-seeker. But the more nuanced truth is that the teen might be experiencing genuine dissociation, genuine psychosis, genuine crisis, and the form that crisis takes has been shaped by media consumption in ways that make it look like possession without any demons being involved.

Social media has also created new forms of possession panic through viral misinformation. A post claiming certain symptoms indicate possession, shared widely enough, can trigger mass anxiety and symptom reporting. People who experience common psychological phenomena, such as sleep paralysis, intrusive thoughts, and dissociative episodes, see posts describing those experiences as demonic attacks and reinterpret their own experiences accordingly. Then they share their own stories, confirming the original post's claims, creating a feedback loop in which common experiences are collectively reframed as supernatural.

This happens most powerfully in religious communities that already have some baseline belief in possession. A viral post about a demonic attack gets shared in Christian Facebook groups, Islamic online communities, and Hindu spiritual forums. Community members who've experienced anything ambiguous or unsettling start commenting about their own possible encounters with evil forces. Others affirm those interpretations, share prayers or rituals for protection, and warn about the dangers of scepticism. Within days, what started as one person's misinterpretation of a nightmare or anxiety attack has become a community-wide belief in an active demonic threat.

The algorithm sees engagement and promotes the content further. More people see it, more people interpret their experiences through the lens of possession, and more comments and shares signal to the platform that this is popular content worth spreading. The panic becomes self-sustaining because the mechanism for spreading social media engagement is designed to amplify emotional and controversial content, regardless of whether it is accurate or harmful.

Some content creators deliberately exploit this dynamic. They post videos claiming to show possession, knowing it will generate massive engagement, even if it's obviously fake or shows psychiatric distress being misrepresented. They use clickbait titles, manipulative editing, sinister music, all the tools of viral content creation to make their videos spread. Whether the creator believes in possession or is cynically exploiting others' beliefs for profit doesn't matter. The effect is the same. Audiences absorb possession narratives presented with production values and algorithmic endorsement that make them seem more credible than they are.

We need better media literacy around content ownership. Audiences need to understand that entertainment media, even when marketed as based on true events, are not documentary evidence. They need to know that possession films systematically exaggerate and invent for dramatic effect. They need to recognise that YouTube videos claiming to show real possession are often either staged or show psychiatric distress being misrepresented. They need to understand that viral social media content about demons often spreads because it's engaging, not because it's accurate.

But asking people to develop that literacy requires competing with the algorithmic amplification of sensational content, with the financial incentives that make possession of content profitable, with the psychological appeal of supernatural explanations that make suffering seem meaningful rather than random. It requires teaching critical thinking skills in an information environment designed to bypass critical thinking and appeal directly to emotion and fear.

The media's influence on possession beliefs isn't going away. If anything, it's accelerating as content creation becomes more decentralised and algorithms become more sophisticated at identifying and promoting emotionally engaging content. More people will encounter possession frameworks through media than through religious education or medical information. More families will interpret psychiatric crises through the lens of entertainment. More individuals in distress will model their symptoms on what they've seen in viral videos.

Understanding this doesn't solve the problem, but it's essential context for understanding modern possession cases. When we ask, "Why did they think it was possession?" the answer often includes "because the media taught them that's what this looks like." When we ask, "Why didn't they seek psychiatric help?" part of the answer is "because the media presented possession as a viable alternative explanation deserving equal consideration." When we ask, "Why did the symptoms match possession stereotypes so precisely?" media influence is frequently part of the answer.

The Exorcist didn't create the belief in possession, but it standardised what possession looks like for modern audiences. *The Conjuring* franchise didn't invent exorcism, but it shaped contemporary understanding of how demons operate and how they're defeated. YouTube didn't originate possession content, but it created distribution networks that make possession interpretations more accessible than medical information. TikTok didn't invent psychological contagion, but its algorithm is remarkably effective at spreading possession-related content and triggering imitative behaviour.

These media influences don't make possession cases less real or less tragic. If anything, they make it more complicated by adding layers of cultural performance and media-derived expectations on top of genuine suffering. The person experiencing a crisis is still suffering. The family seeking help is still desperate. The harm caused by pursuing exorcism instead of psychiatric care is still devastating.

But the route that led everyone to possession interpretation often runs through media consumption that none of them fully recognises as having shaped their beliefs and perceptions. Three-year-old Arely Naomi Proctor said "No" and "I love you" whilst the people who believed God had told them she was possessed held her down and suffocated her for over twenty hours. The demons weren't real. But the media ecosystem that teaches people to see demons, that rewards content creators for producing possession narratives, that algorithmically promotes supernatural explanations over medical ones, that's absolutely real. And it's claiming victims as surely as any possession belief system ever has.

The tragedy is that the people most vulnerable to psychiatric crises are often the same people most exposed to possession media content. Young people experiencing early symptoms of schizophrenia spend hours on social media platforms that algorithmically serve them content about spiritual warfare and demonic attack. Families in religious communities dealing with a member's psychiatric crisis turn to YouTube for guidance and find channels promoting exorcism over therapy. Individuals experiencing dissociation or stress symptoms search for understanding online and encounter personal explanations that seem to fit their experiences better than clinical descriptions of PTSD or dissociative disorders.

The medical and mental health professions have been slow to recognise and address this dynamic. Psychiatrists and psychologists understand that cultural factors shape symptom presentation, but many haven't fully grasped how powerfully modern media functions as a cultural force that provides ready-made frameworks for interpreting psychological distress. When a patient presents with symptoms that match cinematic possession, doctors and therapists might recognise the psychiatric condition but miss that the specific form it's taking has been shaped by media consumption.

This matters clinically because understanding the media's influence can inform treatment. If someone's dissociative symptoms are presenting as demonic alternate identities because that's the cultural script available to them, therapy needs to address not just the dissociation but also the possession framework through which they're understanding and expressing it. If a family is interpreting their teenager's psychotic break as demonic possession because that's what they learned from *The Conjuring*, intervention needs to include education about how media shapes belief and why psychiatric treatment is appropriate despite the possession-like symptoms.

The challenge is doing this without dismissing or invalidating the person's experience or the family's concerns. Telling someone "You're not possessed, you've just watched too many horror movies" is both reductive and therapeutically useless. The more effective approach acknowledges that their symptoms are real, that their suffering is genuine, and that the form their experience is taking makes sense given the cultural inputs they've had, whilst also offering a medical framework that explains why treatment will be more helpful than exorcism.

Filmmakers and content creators bear responsibility for the influence their work has, though market forces make it unlikely they'll voluntarily reduce the sensationalism that makes possession content profitable. Platforms could adjust their algorithms to deprioritise possession content in favour of mental health resources, though their business models make that unlikely too. Religious communities with formal protocols for evaluating possession claims should be enforcing them, not bypassing them when a family arrives convinced by what they saw on TikTok.

In the absence of systemic solutions, individuals and families have to develop their own critical instincts. When symptoms match movie possession precisely, that's a reason for scepticism, not confirmation. When YouTube seems to validate a possession interpretation, that's a sign to seek multiple perspectives, including medical evaluation.

It means asking hard questions: Why does this crisis look exactly like what we've seen in films? Where did our understanding of what possession looks like come from? Have we sought medical evaluation before concluding this is supernatural? Are we certain enough of our interpretation to risk the consequences if we're wrong and this is a treatable psychiatric condition?

Those questions might have saved Arely Naomi Proctor's life. They might have led her mother to seek a medical assessment for herself when she started hearing daily messages from God predicting her daughter's death. They might have prompted her grandfather to recognise that a three-year-old screaming "No" during what her family interpreted as an exorcism wasn't demonic resistance but a child begging for mercy. They might have helped her uncle question whether his claimed gifts of healing were genuine or whether he'd been raised in an insular religious community that reinforced delusional beliefs.

But without those questions, without the critical thinking tools to evaluate possession claims against media-influenced expectations, the family proceeded with deadly certainty. They believed the script media and religious culture had written for them. They performed the exorcism they'd learned was necessary for such situations. And Arely died whilst saying "I love you" to people who loved her but whose love had been poisoned by a framework that made torturing her to death seem like an act of faith.

That's what media-influenced possession belief does. It doesn't just misinform. It transforms love into violence, care into cruelty, and help-seeking into harm-causing. It takes the people most desperately wanting to save their loved ones and gives them methods that kill. And all of it happens whilst feeling righteous, feeling necessary, feeling like spiritual warfare against genuine evil rather than what it is: mentally ill or misinformed people attacking vulnerable individuals based on fictional templates they've mistaken for reality.

CHAPTER XXII

Life After Possession

MOST OF THE STORIES IN THIS BOOK END BADLY. People die. Children are tortured. Families are destroyed. Mental illness goes untreated until it's too late. That's the honest reality of what happens when possession beliefs override medical care, when spiritual frameworks prevent appropriate intervention, when vulnerable people are subjected to exorcisms instead of getting the help they need.

But not everyone dies. Some people survive.

They survive the exorcisms performed on them. They survive the abuse framed as deliverance. They survive families who chose the supernatural explanation over the human one. And then they have to figure out how to live with what happened — how to make sense of experiences that violated their bodies and their minds, whilst the people responsible still believe they were saving their souls.

Recovery from that isn't straightforward. It's not six months of therapy and then fine. The damage runs deep because it isn't just physical harm or psychological trauma in isolation. It's a violation wrapped in religious language. Abuse justified by spiritual authority. Suffering that the people who caused it still maintain was necessary and right.

How does someone heal from something when the people who hurt them insist they were helping?

The first barrier to recovery is often that survivors don't identify what happened as abuse at all.

For someone raised in a religious environment where possession is real, and exorcism is appropriate spiritual care — where everyone they trusted told them the suffering was necessary to save their soul — they might spend years or decades believing that themselves. The cognitive dissonance between "these people loved me" and "these people hurt me" is difficult to hold. In some ways, it's easier to maintain the framework. What happened was a necessary spiritual intervention. Not abuse. Deliverance.

This is why many survivors don't seek help until much later in life, if ever. They don't recognise they have damage that needs treating because the framework they were raised in doesn't categorise exorcism as trauma. The suffering was evidence that the exorcism was working. There is no evidence of harm.

Breaking out of that framework usually requires exposure to alternative perspectives. Sometimes it's going to university and encountering people who respond with horror when someone mentions casually that they were exorcised as a child. Sometimes it's reading about psychology and recognising that symptoms had natural explanations, that what they experienced could have been treated medically. Sometimes it's having children and realising the impossibility of doing to them what was done to you, which forces a confrontation with the reality that it was wrong.

But even after recognising what happened as abuse, even after accepting that help is needed, finding appropriate treatment is complicated. Most therapists aren't trained in religious trauma specifically. They understand PTSD, they understand childhood abuse, but the particular dynamics of abuse justified by possession beliefs — the way spiritual language was used to frame violation as care — requires a specialised understanding that most clinicians simply don't have.

The therapy that helps most, based on the limited research and documented case studies available, works through several things.

First: validation. Survivors of exorcism often doubt whether their memories are accurate, whether it was really as bad as they remember, and whether they're overreacting by calling it abuse. Having a therapist clearly state that what was done was wrong, that it caused harm, that the suffering is real and valid, that provides the foundation for everything else.

Second: separating identity from the possession narrative that was imposed on them. Someone who spent their childhood being told they were possessed, that demons were controlling them, that they couldn't trust their own thoughts because evil might be influencing them, they don't have a clear sense of who they are outside that narrative. Therapy has to help reconstruct identity. Help them figure out where they end, and the imposed beliefs begin. Help build trust in their own mind and body after years of being told something inside them was corrupt.

Third: processing the betrayal. Children depend on parents, relatives, and religious leaders to protect them. When those people hurt them whilst telling them it's love, the betrayal damages the capacity to trust anyone. Working through that understanding it without excusing it, learning to form healthy attachments despite that foundational wound, is slow and difficult work that doesn't always fully succeed.

Fourth: addressing the psychiatric conditions that co-occur. Many survivors develop dissociative disorders, PTSD, depression, and anxiety. Some of those conditions might have existed before the exorcism, might even have been the symptoms that got misinterpreted as possession. Others develop in response to the trauma of exorcism itself. Either way, they need treatment.

Ronald Hunkeler, the boy whose 1949 exorcism inspired *The Exorcist,* survived. But he never recovered.

He lived seventy-one years, terrified someone would discover his identity. Every Halloween, he fled his house. He told almost no one what had happened to him. "He had a terrible life from worry, worry, worry," his companion said after his death. He built a successful career, contributed to the space programme, and functioned in the world. But he carried the trauma and the shame and the fear from age thirteen until he died at eighty-five.

That's survival without recovery. He lived, but he never healed. The wound stayed open for seven decades.

It's not uncommon. Many survivors carry what happened to them their entire lives, learn to function around it rather than resolve it, build walls between themselves and the past rather than processing what's behind them. That's not failure. That's survival using whatever tools are available. But it isn't the hopeful recovery narrative people want to hear.

The survivors who do best manage to separate their spirituality if they maintain any from the specific religious framework that enabled their abuse. Believing in God whilst rejecting the theology that says children need exorcism is possible. Maintaining faith whilst recognising that the people who caused harm were wrong about possession is achievable. That separation allows keeping whatever was meaningful about a religious upbringing whilst discarding the parts that caused damage.

Many survivors can't make that separation. For them, any religious context becomes triggering because it's too entangled with their trauma. The smell of incense. The sound of prayers. Someone raising their hands in worship. All of it can trigger flashbacks to being held down during an exorcism. They have to rebuild their entire worldview without the spiritual framework they were raised in, which is grief on top of trauma. It's not just dealing with what was done. It's mourning the loss of belief that once gave life meaning.

There's also the reality that some survivors never want to frame what happened as abuse at all. They maintain the religious interpretation, believe the exorcism was necessary even if it was painful, and see their suffering as having spiritual meaning. From a mental health perspective, that's concerning; it means the damage isn't being addressed, and they remain vulnerable to future abuse because they haven't recognised the patterns that enabled the first. But their framework might also be what allows them to function. Accepting it as abuse might destabilise a worldview they can't afford to lose.

That's not a judgement. It's a reality that anyone working with exorcism survivors has to reckon with.

The people least likely to recover are those who are most vulnerable in every other way, too: already dealing with serious mental illness, without financial resources or stable housing, isolated from supportive relationships, still trapped in the community that enabled the abuse. For them, recovery isn't a long-term project. Survival is day to day.

Some don't survive at all, not as themselves. The psychiatric damage from exorcism, combined with untreated underlying conditions, leads to chronic illness, hospitalisation, and sometimes suicide. They exist, but they're not living in any meaningful sense. The exorcism that was supposed to save them destroyed them instead.

What would help survivors most is religious communities acknowledging that exorcism causes harm that even when well-intentioned, it creates trauma, and that people subjected to it need support and treatment, not silence and shame. Most communities that practice exorcism don't see it that way. They don't track outcomes. They don't follow up with people who've been exorcised to see how they're doing years later. They don't create space for someone to say "that harmed me" without being told they're lacking faith or inviting demons back in.

Until that changes, survivors are largely on their own. Finding their own path to recovery without support from the communities that hurt them. Navigating trauma that many therapists don't fully understand. Rebuilding identity, trust, and a sense of safety without any map for how to do it.

Some manage. They get good therapy, develop healthy coping strategies, and eventually reach a place where the trauma is integrated rather than controlling their lives. They carry scars, but they're not defined by their wounds.

Others never get there. They survive but don't thrive. They accommodate the damage rather than processing it. That's also real. That's also valid. Survival itself is an achievement when someone's been through what they've been through.

There are no guarantees and no clear roadmap. Recovery is possible. It's also incomplete, difficult, and often partial. Many survivors never fully heal. Some build good lives anyway.

The harm done through exorcism is real. But it doesn't have to be the final word.

For anyone considering pursuing an exorcism for themselves or someone in their care, understanding what recovery requires should weigh heavily in that decision. The potential for lasting harm isn't hypothetical. The trauma isn't just possible, it's likely. And recovery, if it happens at all, takes years, leaves marks, and is never entirely finished.

Is that risk worth taking based on a belief in possession that might be wrong?

Those are questions each person must answer. But they should be answered with a clear understanding of the stakes, which include not just whether exorcism works, but whether the person subjected to it can survive what comes after.

Most of the cases in this book ended in tragedy. The few that didn't still left survivors carrying damage they may never fully escape.

That's the reality. It's worth sitting with before anyone decides to act on it.

CHAPTER XXIII

Conclusion: The Mirror

I'VE SPENT THIS BOOK SHOWING YOU POSSESSION through one lens: medical explanations, psychological mechanisms, stress responses, and psychiatric illness. I've taken cases where people claimed demons were real and shown you how every symptom, every behaviour, every supposedly supernatural sign can be explained through neuroscience and psychology. How isolation produces hallucinations. How grief triggers psychosis. How epilepsy creates religious visions. How suggestion shapes symptoms. How group dynamics spread beliefs. How trauma fractures identity in ways that look exactly like possession to people who don't understand dissociation.

And I've shown you the cost of getting the interpretation wrong.

Victoria Climbié, eight years old, 128 injuries, tortured to death because her great-aunt looked for evil where there was only a suffering child. Terrance Cottrell, an autistic boy, suffocated during an exorcism because adults interpreted neurodevelopmental differences as demons. Anneliese Michel died at twenty-three from starvation, whilst priests performed sixty-seven exorcisms instead of providing the psychiatric care that would have saved her life. Ronald Hunkeler lived seventy-one years in fear because an exorcism at thirteen marked him forever. Women were killed for Sanguma in Papua New Guinea. Prisoners heard voices in solitary confinement. Children couldn't escape families convinced they were possessed. Three-year-old Arely Naomi Proctor said "No" and "I love you" whilst her mother, uncle, and grandfather suffocated her over twenty hours because they believed God had told them she was possessed.

The pattern is clear. Possession beliefs prevent appropriate help. They are applied to vulnerable people experiencing explainable crises. They enable abuse whilst making it seem righteous. They traumatise or kill whilst claiming to save souls. They persist because the frameworks are self-sealing: every piece of evidence gets interpreted to confirm possession, and nothing can contradict a belief system that has an answer for every question.

My position is clear. Demons aren't real. Possession is misinterpreted as mental illness, trauma, and medical conditions. Exorcism causes harm, whilst religious frameworks make that harm seem necessary. People die unnecessarily because spiritual interpretations override medical reality. We need better mental health access, stronger legal protections, more education about psychiatric conditions, and systems that intervene before beliefs become deadly.

But here's what I haven't said: I can't prove demons aren't real.

I can show you that every possession symptom has natural explanations. I can show you that psychiatric treatment works when exorcism doesn't. I can show you that the patterns make perfect sense without supernatural involvement. But showing that supernatural explanations are unnecessary isn't the same as proving they're wrong.

It's possible, however unlikely I think it is, that demons exist and sometimes possess people, and the symptoms happen to overlap perfectly with psychiatric conditions whilst still being genuinely supernatural. I don't believe that. But I can't prove it's false any more than believers can prove it's true.

What I can prove is that when people interpret suffering as possession, when they pursue exorcism instead of medical care, people die who shouldn't have died. That's not a matter of belief. That's a documented fact. Victoria, Terrance, Anneliese, Kristy, and Arely are dead. The exorcisms didn't save them. The possession frameworks prevented the help that might have worked.

The question I want to leave you with isn't whether demons are real.

The question is what you're willing to risk on that belief.

If you believe possession is possible, if you think spiritual warfare is real, if your faith includes demons as active forces in the world, what does that belief cost? How do you ensure it doesn't prevent you from recognising when someone needs psychiatric help rather than an exorcism? How do you create space for being wrong about possession without abandoning your entire spiritual framework?

Because the people in this book who caused the most harm weren't evil. They were certain.

They knew what they were seeing. They had frameworks that explained everything, religious authorities who validated their interpretations, and communities that shared their beliefs. They loved the people they hurt. They were convinced they were doing God's work, thought they were fighting evil, and believed suffering was necessary to save souls.

And they were wrong.

Whether or not demons exist in general, in these specific cases, they were wrong. Victoria wasn't possessed; she was being abused. Terrance wasn't possessed; he was autistic. Anneliese wasn't possessed; she had epilepsy and psychosis. Arely wasn't possessed; she was a three-year-old child having nightmares. Their certainty, their absolute conviction that possession explained what they were seeing, killed people.

If you believe in possession, if your faith includes that possibility, how do you avoid their mistake? What is the difference between genuine demonic influence and psychiatric illness that looks similar? What evidence would make you question whether possession is the right interpretation? At what point do you seek medical evaluation even though you believe it might be spiritual? How much risk are you willing to take that you're wrong before pursuing interventions that might cause harm?

Here's what makes it hard: possession beliefs and psychiatric care often require mutually exclusive actions. If someone is possessed by demons, exorcism is appropriate, and medication might be seen as interfering with spiritual battle. If someone is experiencing psychosis, medication is necessary, and exorcism is at best useless, at worst, traumatising and dangerous. You can't fully do both. You have to choose. And that choice, made in crisis without time for careful evaluation, determines whether someone gets help or gets harmed.

The evidence throughout this book points in one direction. Psychiatric explanations account for all the symptoms. Medical and psychological interventions work when spiritual ones don't. The people who got appropriate treatment recovered or stabilised. The people who got exorcisms died, were traumatised, or survived despite the intervention rather than because of it.

That's not subtle. That's a clear pattern across centuries, cultures, and cases.

But evidence doesn't necessarily change belief. People don't abandon spiritual frameworks because medical explanations exist. Faith operates on a different epistemology than science, values different forms of knowledge, and finds truth in ways that aren't empirically testable. I understand that. I'm not asking believers to abandon their faith, deny their spiritual experiences, or pretend demons aren't real if that's genuinely what they believe.

What I'm asking for is humility.

Recognition that you might be wrong about specific cases, even if you're right about demons existing in general. Willingness to seek medical evaluation before pursuing spiritual intervention. Creating safeguards that prevent harm when possession interpretations are incorrect. Accepting that if you're wrong, if what you think is possession is actually a psychiatric illness, the cost of that mistake is someone's life or well-being.

And I'm asking you to sit with the discomfort of the cases in this book.

To really think about Victoria Climbié's 128 injuries. About Terrance Cottrell suffocating under a sheet. About Anneliese Michel's body shutting down from starvation. About Kristy Bamu, who drowned in a bath on Christmas Day after four days of torture. About three-year-old Arely Proctor fighting for her life for twenty hours, saying "No" and "I love you" whilst three adults she trusted held her down.

Ask yourself whether possession beliefs enabled those deaths. Whether spiritual frameworks prevented appropriate help. Whether certainty about demons overrode clear evidence of a psychiatric and medical crisis.

If looking at those cases makes you uncomfortable, if something in you wants to say "that's different from real possession" or "they did exorcism wrong" or "those were clearly mental illness, not demons", sit with that discomfort. Because that's cognitive dissonance, the recognition that your beliefs might have costs you haven't fully confronted, that possession frameworks might enable harm in ways you haven't wanted to acknowledge.

You don't have to resolve that dissonance by abandoning belief. But you do have to do something with it. You have to find ways to hold your faith whilst also recognising the potential for harm. You have to create protocols for yourself and your community about when to pursue medical evaluation, what signs indicate a psychiatric crisis rather than a spiritual attack, and how to balance religious beliefs with responsibility to protect vulnerable people.

Because the next Victoria or Terrance or Anneliese or Arely might be someone you know.

It might be your child. Your sibling. Your friend. Someone in your congregation. And when that moment comes, when someone starts exhibiting behaviour that could be possession or could be psychiatric illness, what framework will you reach for? What will you do first? Whom will you call?

And how will you know if you're wrong before it's too late?

I've given you the medical and psychological frameworks throughout this book. I've shown you what psychiatric conditions look like, how trauma manifests, and what environmental factors produce possession-like symptoms. I've explained the mechanisms in detail because

I want you to have alternative explanations available, frameworks for understanding suffering that don't require demons.

But I can't make you use those frameworks. I can't force you to seek a psychiatric evaluation before pursuing an exorcism. I can't prevent you from interpreting symptoms through possession lenses if that's where your beliefs lead you.

All I can do is show you what happens when people get it wrong. What is the cost of certainty when that certainty is misplaced? What gets lost when spiritual interpretations prevent medical help?

The people whose stories fill this book are gone. They can't benefit from better mental health access, from legal reforms that might have protected them, from education that might have helped their families recognise psychiatric illness. But future people in similar situations might benefit if this book changes how readers think about possession, how they respond when they encounter someone who might be experiencing it, and what they're willing to risk in favour of spiritual interpretations versus medical ones.

That's my hope. That someone reads about Victoria and recognises similar patterns in a child they know and calls child protection instead of assuming it's spiritual. That someone reads about Terrance and realises the "possessed" child in their church is actually autistic and needs understanding, not exorcism. That someone reads about Anneliese and recognises epilepsy or psychosis in a family member and pursues medical evaluation before spiritual intervention.

But I also know that for many readers, this book won't change core beliefs about possession. You'll finish it still believing demons are real, still thinking exorcism is sometimes necessary, still convinced that spiritual warfare happens and requires spiritual responses.

I can't change that. I'm not trying to.

What I hope changes is how certain you are in specific cases. How quickly you reach for possession as an explanation. How much evidence do you need before you're willing to say "this is demons, not illness"?

Because certainty is what killed the people in this book. Not belief in demons necessarily, but certainty about possession in cases where that certainty was wrong.

If the adults around Victoria had been less certain she was possessed, if they'd been willing to consider that her behaviour might have natural explanations, she might have been saved. If Terrance's family had been less certain about demons and more open to autism as an explanation, he'd be alive. If Anneliese's family and the priests had been less certain, more willing to try psychiatric treatment alongside or instead of exorcism, she might have recovered. If Claudia Hernandez had been less certain that God was speaking to her and telling her Arely would die, if she'd sought help when she started hearing those voices, her daughter might still be alive.

Certainty closes doors. It makes you stop looking for alternative explanations because you've already decided what's true. It makes you ignore evidence that contradicts your interpretation because you know what you're seeing. It makes you pursue interventions that confirm your beliefs even when they're not working, even when they're causing harm, because doubt feels like a lack of faith.

Humility opens doors. It makes you consider multiple explanations. It makes you test interpretations against evidence. It makes you willing to change course when interventions aren't working. It makes you seek help from multiple sources rather than trusting one framework to have all the answers.

I'm not asking you to abandon certainty about your core faith.

But I am asking you to abandon certainty about specific possession cases. To hold your interpretations loosely enough that evidence can change them. To be willing to say, "I thought this was possession, but maybe I was wrong", before that mistake costs someone their life.

The mirror I'm holding up isn't to your beliefs about whether demons exist. It's to your beliefs about your own ability to correctly identify possession, to distinguish it from psychiatric illness, to know with certainty that exorcism is appropriate and medical care isn't needed.

The people in this book who caused harm all believed they could accurately make those distinctions. They all thought they knew what they were seeing. Marie-Thérèse Kouao was certain Victoria was possessed. Patricia Cooper was certain Terrance had demons. The priests were certain Anneliese needed exorcism, not psychiatry. Eric Bikubi was certain Kristy was practising Kindoki. Claudia Hernandez was certain God was speaking to her about Arely.

They were all certain. And they were all wrong.

So look in that mirror. Ask yourself honestly whether you have better judgment than they did, better ability to distinguish possession from illness, better certainty that you won't make the same mistakes. Ask yourself what evidence would make you question your interpretation. Ask yourself how many of Victoria's 128 injuries you'd be willing to risk, how many minutes of Terrance's suffocation you'd accept, how many pounds Anneliese lost before you'd accept the interpretation could be mistaken, how many times you'd let a three-year-old say "No" and "I love you" before you'd stop.

Those are hard questions. They should be. Because the stakes are life and death, the margin for error is small, and the cost of getting it wrong is measured in bodies and broken minds and trauma that never heals.

There's a pattern I've noticed throughout these cases that I want you to see clearly. The people who were most certain about possession, who moved most quickly to exorcism, who were least willing to consider alternative explanations, those were the people whose interventions caused the most harm.

The ones who hesitated, who sought multiple opinions, who tried medical approaches first or alongside spiritual ones, those people had better outcomes. Not perfect outcomes always, but better. Fewer deaths. Less trauma. More recovery.

That pattern should tell you something.

It suggests that the safest approach, even for believers, is to default to medical evaluation. To seek psychiatric care first. To rule out natural explanations before concluding something is supernatural. Not because demons aren't real, but because the cost of being wrong in the other direction is too high.

If you believe someone is possessed and you're wrong, if you pursue exorcism when they actually need psychiatric care, they might die. They might be traumatised. They might suffer unnecessarily. The harm is direct and severe.

If you believe someone needs psychiatric care and you're wrong, if you pursue medical treatment when they're possessed, what's the worst that happens? They get medication that might not help, but probably won't hurt. They get therapy that, at a minimum, provides support. They get an evaluation by professionals trained to recognise serious conditions. And if it genuinely is possession, if demons are real and involved, presumably those demons can wait a few weeks whilst medical options are explored. Presumably God, or whatever spiritual forces exist, can work through psychiatric treatment or alongside it.

The asymmetry of risk should be obvious. Defaulting to medical care first causes less harm if you're wrong than defaulting to spiritual intervention first. That's true whether demons exist or not.

What stays with me are the children. Victoria, Terrance, Kristy, and Arely. They haunt me in ways the adult cases don't, though those are tragic too. But children are so completely dependent on adults to correctly interpret their reality. They can't advocate for themselves. They can't seek help independently. They can't escape when adults decide they're possessed. They're trapped by adult certainty.

And the adults who killed them loved them. That's what makes it so heartbreaking. These weren't monsters. They were parents, aunts, siblings, and pastors who genuinely cared about these children and genuinely believed they were helping. Their love wasn't in question. Their certainty was the problem.

Kouao believed she was saving Victoria's soul. Patricia Cooper believed she was freeing Terrance from demons. Eric Bikubi believed he was protecting his household from Kindoki. Claudia Hernandez believed God was speaking to her about Arely. Their beliefs were sincere. Their love was real. And their certainty killed children who trusted them.

If people who loved these children could be that wrong, could be that certain whilst being that wrong, what makes you confident you'd be different? What makes you think your judgment is better, your ability to distinguish possession from illness more accurate, your certainty more justified?

That's not a rhetorical attack. It's a genuine question that demands an honest answer. Because if you can't articulate what makes you different from the people who caused harm in this book, if you can't identify specific safeguards and protocols you'd follow to avoid their mistakes, then you're vulnerable to making the same errors they did.

Let me be clear about something. I'm not arguing that faith is harmful or that religious belief inevitably leads to tragedy. Most believers never hurt anyone. Most people with possession beliefs never perform an exorcism. Most religious communities have mechanisms that prevent the kind of harm documented in this book.

What I'm arguing is that possession beliefs without appropriate safeguards create vulnerability to catastrophic error. And that the burden of proof should be extraordinarily high before pursuing exorcism, especially on children or other vulnerable people who can't consent or advocate for themselves.

The safeguards matter. Requiring a psychiatric evaluation before exorcism. Having protocols for recognising when spiritual interventions aren't working. Being willing to change interpretations based on evidence. Consulting medical professionals even whilst pursuing spiritual approaches. Having accountability structures that catch dangerous certainty before it destroys someone.

In practice, that means: get a psychiatric evaluation before anything else. Treat any identified medical conditions first and give treatment time to work. If symptoms persist after appropriate medical care, then consider spiritual factors. Monitor outcomes honestly. If someone is getting worse during spiritual intervention, stop. Have accountability structures so no single person makes these decisions alone.

The Catholic Church, whatever its other failings, has rigorous protocols along exactly these lines. They require a medical evaluation first, the involvement of trained professionals, and a willingness to stop if the exorcism isn't helping. They built those protocols because they learned from history. They've seen what happens when certainty overrides caution.

Many communities don't have those structures. Many believers with possession beliefs have no protocols for testing their interpretations, no mechanisms for recognising when they're wrong before someone dies. If you believe in possession, you need them. Not just for others' protection, but for your own. Because the next crisis could involve you, it could depend on your judgement, and could end with you having caused harm whilst trying to help.

Here's what I want you to take from this book, whether you believe in demons or not.

Every symptom attributed to possession has natural explanations that fully account for it. Hallucinations, voice-hearing, personality changes, violent episodes, unusual strength, convulsions, all of it documented, understood, and treatable without requiring any supernatural involvement. Chapter One explains the mechanisms. The rest of the book shows what happens when those mechanisms go unrecognised.

The patterns in possession cases match psychiatric conditions so precisely that distinguishing them without medical evaluation is essentially impossible. You can't tell the difference just by observation, no matter how certain you feel. That conviction, the sense that you're seeing something supernatural, isn't special discernment. It's pattern recognition shaped by your existing beliefs. Every exorcist who claimed they could reliably identify possession got it wrong sometimes. Provably wrong. What makes you confident you'd be different?

Psychiatric and medical treatment works. When people get appropriate care, they improve. Symptoms resolve or become manageable.

People recover. The success rate vastly exceeds that of exorcism. That evidence base is extensive and clear.

Exorcism causes harm. Even when it doesn't kill directly, it traumatises. It delays treatment. It enables abuse. People who've survived exorcisms describe it as among the most traumatic experiences of their lives, violated by people they trusted, marked by experiences that changed how they understand themselves. That matters even when it doesn't kill.

And certainty correlates with harm. The more certain people are that demons are involved, the less likely they are to seek alternative explanations, the more harm they cause. Humility protects people. Uncertainty saves lives. Certainty kills.

Those are facts. Documented patterns across hundreds of cases, supported by medical research, psychiatric literature, historical documentation, and court records. They're true whether demons exist or not.

What you do with those facts is the question. Do you dismiss them because they challenge your beliefs? Do you acknowledge them but insist your situation would be different? Do you recognise the pattern and decide to prioritise caution over certainty?

Because those are your choices. You can't unhear what this book has shown you. You can't unknow the harm that possession beliefs enable. You can't pretend you weren't warned about the costs of getting the interpretation wrong.

You know now. The question is what you'll do with that knowledge.

I'll close with this.

The demons might be real. I don't believe they are, but I can't prove they aren't. What I can prove is that mistaking psychiatric illness for possession kills people. And that's true whether demons exist or not.

Question your beliefs. Not whether demons are possible in general, but whether you can reliably identify them in specific cases. Not whether exorcism has spiritual value, but whether it has practical safety when applied to people who might be mentally ill. Not whether your faith is true, but whether your certainty might be dangerous.

Because the people in this book, the ones who caused harm, were people of faith too. They believed deeply. They were certain. They thought they were fighting evil.

And they were wrong in ways that destroyed lives.

You might be right about demons. But you might also be the certainty that kills, the belief that enables harm whilst claiming to save souls. And you won't know which until you're willing to question, to doubt, to hold your interpretations lightly enough that evidence can change them.

That's the mirror. That's the reflection I'm asking you to look at. Not your beliefs about the supernatural, but your beliefs about yourself. Your judgement. Your ability to know with certainty what's happening when someone's mind is breaking.

The question isn't whether demons are real.

The question is whether you're willing to risk being wrong.

And if the answer is yes, if you're willing to risk pursuing exorcism when the person in front of you actually needs psychiatric care, then ask yourself one more thing:

Whose life are you willing to bet on that certainty?

Because it might not be your own. It might be a child who can't escape. A vulnerable person who can't advocate for themselves.

Someone who trusts you to interpret their suffering correctly and get them appropriate help.

It might be someone who says "No" and "I love you" whilst you hold them down, certain you're helping, certain you're fighting demons, certain you're saving their soul.

And you might be killing them instead.

That's the cost of being wrong. That's what certainty looks like when certainty kills.

Are you willing to risk that?

Because the people whose stories fill this book weren't.

They were certain they were right.

ABOUT THE AUTHOR

Josiah Cornell is an author whose work bridges lived experience and rigorous scholarship. With over a decade of experience working in prisons, probation services, domestic violence intervention, and local government, he has spent his career at the intersection of society's most pressing challenges. His writing draws on this direct engagement with individuals often overlooked by mainstream discourse people navigating trauma, addiction, systemic failure, and resilience.

Cornell holds qualifications in Criminology and Psychology from South Essex College and the University of East London. His understanding of human behaviour is informed not only by academic training but by personal experience with trauma and recovery. This combination of professional expertise and lived insight gives his work an authenticity that resonates deeply with readers who describe his books as "a lifeline" or "the book I didn't know I needed."

His nonfiction addresses the aspects of personal experience that are frequently marginalised in public conversation: domestic violence, addiction, male sexuality, shadow psychology, and the mechanisms by which people are broken and, sometimes, made whole. His approach is unflinching but compassionate, offering readers frameworks for understanding their own lives without reducing complexity to platitudes.

Cornell's fiction explores similar themes through mythology and storytelling. His narratives are structured to provoke reflection, using fantasy as a lens through which to examine questions of identity, power, and transformation.

He also works as a musician, bringing the same honesty and emotional clarity to his performances as to his writing. His music is available on major streaming platforms.

Josiah Cornell's work challenges readers to confront uncomfortable truths. It does not offer easy answers, but it does offer clarity, recognition, and the possibility of meaningful change. For those seeking writing that takes its subject seriously and its audience seriously, his books provide exactly that.

OTHER BOOKS

- The Neuroscience Of The Shadow - Mapping The Obscure Psyche

- Who Am I Without The Trauma - A Journey Back To Yourself

- The Masculine Crisis - How To Rewrite Manhood In An Age Of Social Struggle

- Breaking The Silence - The Truth About Domestic Violence

- The Rise & Fall Of Starmer and The Labour Party

- The Emerald Guardian - Hougun Manor